ADDITIONAL PRAISE FOR
THE BOGLEHEADS' GUIDE TO INVESTING

"This book is written with great charm, wit, and humility by a troika of retired, self-educated investors who themselves have become experts in financial planning and investing. Here they share what they have learned at the school of hard knocks. It is to trust the wisdom of their chosen mentor, John Bogle, who advocates investing in low cost, tax efficient mutual funds and using common sense in all financial decisions. Furthermore, the authors have mastered the complexities of their subject to the point where they can explain financial concepts simply and clearly. Readers and clients often ask me to recommend a book on financial planning investing. I will recommend this one."

> —*Kay H. Kamin, president of Sutton Place Financial Inc.*
> *and financial columnist for* Today's Chicago Woman

"The Bogleheads' Guide offers up the distilled wisdom from thousands of posts on the web's most distinguished investment board. The authors mix a heady brew of down-home common sense and advanced financial economics, while providing a clear, concise, and easily followed action plan that is highly effective, low cost, low risk, and low maintenance. Read and profit!"

> —*Frank Armstrong, III, CFP, president, Investor Solutions, Inc.*

"From beginning investors to those in retirement, *The Bogleheads' Guide to Investing* is packed with simple and sophisticated investment advice, offering an abundance of resources for a winning investment strategy. It is written with wit, clarity, and wisdom, and is sure to become a treasured resource for long-term investors."

> —*Bill Schultheis, author,* The Coffeehouse Investor

The Bogleheads'

Guide to Investing

The Bogleheads'

Guide to Investing

Second Edition

Mel Lindauer
Taylor Larimore
Michael LeBoeuf

Foreword by John C. Bogle

WILEY

Cover image: © iStock.com / ImpaKPro
Cover design: Wiley

Published by John Wiley & Sons, Inc., Hoboken, New Jersey.

The First Edition was published by John Wiley & Sons, Inc. in 2006. It was then
published as a paperback edition in 2007.

Published simultaneously in Canada.

For general information on our other products and services or for technical support,
please contact our Customer Care Department within the United States
at (800) 762-2974, outside the United States at (317) 572-3993 or fax (317) 572-4002.

Wiley publishes in a variety of print and electronic formats and by print-on-demand.
Some material included with standard print versions of this book may not be included
in e-books or in print-on-demand. If this book refers to media such as a CD or DVD
that is not included in the version you purchased, you may download this material at
http://booksupport.wiley.com. For more information about Wiley products, visit
www.wiley.com.

Library of Congress Cataloging-in-Publication Data:

ISBN 978-1-118-92128-9 (Hardcover)
ISBN 978-1-118-92235-4 (ePDF)
ISBN 978-1-118-92236-1 (ePub)

Printed in the United States of America

10 9 8 7 6 5 4 3 2 1

To John C. Bogle, founder of
The Vanguard Group

A man whom we knew from afar for many years but
have since come to know and cherish as a friend.
While some mutual fund founders chose to make
billions, he chose to make a difference.

Contents

PART II
FOLLOW-THROUGH STRATEGIES TO
KEEP YOU ON TARGET

Acknowledgments

Anyone who writes a book knows that many more people than the authors are responsible for turning an idea into the finished product. In bringing this particular book to fruition, we wish to acknowledge and give special thanks to the following people:

Bill Falloon, our editor at John Wiley & Sons, who proposed the idea of a Bogleheads' book to Taylor and wouldn't take no for an answer.

Alexis Hurley, for being an excellent and supportive agent.

Rick Ferri, for the countless hours and invaluable assistance he provided critiquing the chapters and checking figures to make this a better, more accurate book. He is a quality person and a true friend.

Boglehead Bob Beeman, for his original work on the after-tax, real returns of I Bonds.

Excel wizard Alec Stanley, for his work in expanding on Bob Beeman's original work and for providing other valuable spreadsheet assistance to us whenever we asked for it (and that was often).

Morningstar for creating the Vanguard Diehards Forum, and Alex Frakt and Larry Auton for creating the bogleheads.org website. Also, special thanks to Ralph Arveson for our Bogleheads contest and Bogleheads Local Chapter websites.

All those who showed so much enthusiasm for the book and offered encouragement, which made all of our hard work seem worthwhile. (You know who you are.)

Last, and certainly not least, we want to thank our wives, Pat Larimore (deceased), Marlene Lindauer, and Elke LeBoeuf for their patience and understanding during the long hours we spent working on our computers preparing this labor of love.

Foreword

Nothing is more deserving of your attention than the intellectual and moral associations of Americans. Americans of all ages, all conditions, and all dispositions constantly form associations [of a] thousand kinds . . . religious, moral, serious, futile, general or restricted, enormous or diminutive. I have often admired the extreme skill with which the inhabitants of the United States succeed in proposing a common object for the exertions of a great many men and inducing them voluntarily to pursue it.

As soon as several of the inhabitants of the United States have taken up an opinion or a feeling which they wish to promote, they look out for mutual assistance, and as soon as they have found one another out, they combine. From that moment they are no longer isolated men, but a power seen from afar, whose actions serve for an example and whose language is listened to.

Only by the reciprocal influence of men upon one another are feelings and opinions recruited, is the heart enlarged, and is the human mind developed. . . . This can only be accomplished by associations. What political power could ever carry on the vast multitude of lesser undertakings which the American citizens perform every day, with the assistance of the principle of association?
—Alexis de Tocqueville
Democracy in America, 1840

The Bogleheads of the Internet, it seems to me, are the paradigm of the American association described with such perceptive power by Alexis de Tocqueville in his seminal work. This association of intelligent, integrity-laden, and like-minded investors has provided not only a sound *intellectual* rationale for the successful accumulation of wealth but, just as de Tocqueville suggested, a sound *moral* rationale as well. No wonder *Democracy in America*—from a Frenchman who visited America for just nine months when he was but 25 years old!—has stood the test as the defining text of the American way for nearly 170 years.

During its decade-plus of existence, the Bogleheads have moved from a loose association of dedicated investors to a formal website, Bogleheads.org. (The Bogleheads previously gathered online at the Vanguard Diehards message board on Morningstar.com.) The Bogleheads website now attracts an incredible 50,000 visits and as many as 1,500 individual posts each day. *The Bogleheads' Guide to Investing* marks a major milestone for this extraordinary association.

Two especially notable characteristics mark the Boglehead culture. One is *rationality*. These individual investors are awash in common sense, intolerant of illogic, and permeated with a preference for facts over hyperbole. Today's popular investment misconceptions—short-term focus and fast-paced trading, the conviction that exceptional past fund performance will recur, the ignorance of the importance of fund operating expenses, sales commissions, hidden portfolio turnover costs, and state and federal taxes—are anathema to them. Bogleheads have come to accept as the core of successful investing what I have called "the majesty of simplicity in an empire of parsimony."

The second characteristic is, of all things, caring. Bogleheads care about one another. They are eager to help all investors—regular visitors to the website and new ones, informed and naïve, experienced and novice alike—who have questions on almost any investment subject, and willing to discuss the investment issues of the day, sometimes even the national and global issues, with no holds barred (except for rudeness or coarseness). Fund selection, fund performance, types of investments, retirement planning, savings programs, tax management—none are beyond the scope of this remarkable association of investors who, without compensation or bias, strive to help their fellow investors. If there is a website that bespeaks the Golden Rule, surely the Boglehead site is its paradigm.

BOGLE AND THE BOGLEHEADS

The Bogleheads had been associating for at least three years before they came to my attention. I had heard them discussed by Vanguard's public relations staff, and early on got the idea that they were not only firm advocates of my approach to investing—expressed in the investment strategies and human values that represented Vanguard's rock foundation when I created this upstart firm in 1974—but were also a pretty special group of people.

However, it was not until February 3, 1999, that I met my first Bogle-head. The occasion was "The Money Show" in Orlando, Florida, where I gave a contentious speech about investment principles ("The Clash of the Cultures in Investing: Complexity vs. Simplicity") that at once seemed to confound the hosts who invited me to address the show, to infuriate the sponsor firms (all offering their own routes to easy riches), and to amaze and delight the audience of several thousand individual investors.

Shortly before my talk, Taylor Larimore (there with his wife Pat) introduced himself to me. Taylor, then and now considered the unofficial leader of the Bogleheads, proved to be as fine a human being as I've ever met—warm, thoughtful, intelligent, investment-savvy, and eager to help others. A combat veteran of World War II and an exceptional sailor are only a few aspects of Taylor's background. I mention them because the first demands courage and discipline; the second, careful planning and staying the course one has set, all the while adjusting to the winds and tides. These traits, as it happens, are the principal traits of the suc-cessful investor.

In March 2000, when I spoke again in Florida, Taylor invited me to meet with the Bogleheads at his Miami condominium located at virtually the same location where Taylor was born—he honors me by calling it "the house that Jack built"—and I enthusiastically agreed. When I came down into the hotel lobby, there to meet me was Mel Lindauer, unofficial asso-ciate leader of the group, next to a sign that read "Bogleheads Meet Here."[1] We all went to Taylor's lovely home, and Pat's hospitality at din-ner made what came to be known as Diehards I an evening of extraordi-nary warmth, energy, and delightful conversation, and some 20 investors who had never met one another before quickly became friends.

The following year, at Diehards II, the group met in Valley Forge, Pennsylvania. The festivities began on June 8, 2001, with a dinner addressed by *Money* journalist Jason Zweig, now with 40 Bogleheads in attendance. He would later write an article extolling the group: "By singing in harmony from the same page of the same investing hymnal, the Diehards drown out market noise." The next day included an extended visit to Vanguard's head office in Valley Forge, where I acted as host, tour guide, and keynote speaker. The questions and answer session that fol-lowed was broad-ranging, and ended with the Reverend Bob Stowe,

---

[1]It is no coincidence that Taylor and Mel, among the most active participants on the web-site, teamed up to write this book. They were joined by Michael LeBoeuf, whom I have also come to know, another major contributor to the Boglehead website, and an author in his own right.

a Massachusetts Boglehead, presenting me, on behalf of the association, with a handsome regimental bugle of World War II vintage, symbolizing my "clarion call to build an industry that protects and serves the average investor." (I couldn't help but respond with this quotation from St. Paul: "If the trumpet shall give an uncertain sound, who shall prepare himself to the battle?")

Diehards III, kindly hosted by website provider Morningstar, took place in Chicago on June 26, 2002, as some 50 Bogleheads from all over the country participated in the firm's annual investment conference, taking in my speech ("The Tell-Tale Chart"), and having an active series of gatherings. In Chicago, this association of good human beings who happen to be intelligent investors and who seek to spread the gospel grew ever more familiar and friendly.

The next gathering (Diehards IV) took place on May 10, 2004, when some 60 Bogleheads gathered in Denver, Colorado, guests of the annual conference of the Association for Investment Management and Research, the professional organization that represents securities analysts and money managers. (AIMR has now taken the name The CFA Institute, with the acronym standing for Chartered Financial Analyst.) The Bogleheads were given seats in a special section for my speech ("Creating Sound Governance: The Shareholder's Perspective"), which was followed by an extensive question and answer session. The final question put to me by the moderator was "What is a Boglehead?" What a treat it was to have the opportunity to tell the 1,000-person audience of investment professionals about the wonderful people who constitute this dedicated association of individual investors and the sound investment strategies that they both employ and propagate.

The annual Bogleheads gatherings have continued to attract passionate investors to reconnect with friends old and new, to hear speeches from investment professionals, and, of course, to meet with their namesake. The conferences have been held all over the country—in Las Vegas, Washington, DC, San Diego, and Dallas/Ft. Worth. In recent years, the Bogleheads have held their annual conference in Valley Forge, Pennsylvania, where Vanguard's headquarters is located.

THE BOGLEHEADS MESSAGE

The Bogleheads' Guide to Investing is a wonderful, witty, and wise book. As an investor for my entire adult lifetime, I found most rewarding the sage understanding of Messrs. Larimore, Lindauer, and LeBoeuf that the practice of investing is, as they put it, "so different from most of life." Why?

Largely because our financial markets are essentially closed systems in which an advantage garnered by a given investor comes at the disadvantage of the other investors in the same market. The authors recognize this eternal truth: As a group, we investors are inevitably average, so beating the market is a zero-sum game. (After our investment costs are deducted, of course, it becomes a loser's game.) Importantly, they note that relying on the typical common sense approaches that apply to most of life's challenges is "destined to leave you poorer." For example, they warn against following life principles like these:

- If you don't know how to do something . . . hire an expert.
- You get what you pay for.
- If there's a crisis, take action!
- The best predictor of future performance is past performance.

In short, the principles that work in most aspects of our daily lives simply lead to failure in investing. Understanding that contrarian wisdom is the first step toward investment success.

But if that warning is both precisely accurate and grandly counterintuitive, the basic thrust of *The Bogleheads' Guide to Investing* is both precisely accurate and grandly intuitive. "Choose a sound financial lifestyle. Start early and invest regularly. Know what you're buying. Preserve your buying power. Keep costs and taxes low. Diversify your stock portfolio [and diversify your stock risk with a bond portfolio]." Investors who follow these simple tenets will earn their fair share of whatever returns the financial markets are kind enough to deliver in the years ahead.

THE BOGLEHEADS AND BENJAMIN FRANKLIN

When I completed my perusal of *The Bogleheads' Guide to Investing*, I had a certain sense of déjà vu. For I suddenly realized that I'd only recently seen a similar collection of sound, simple, and successful ways to save and invest that were written 250 years earlier, suggesting that these precepts may be not only effective, but eternal. They were expressed, as it happens, by Benjamin Franklin in 1757, in his widely circulated pamphlet *The Way to Wealth* (also entitled *The Art of Making Money Plenty*, or *Father Abraham Speaks*), republished in 2002 by the American Philosophical Society:

- If you would be wealthy, think of Saving as well as Getting.
- He that lives upon Hope will die fasting.
- There are no Gains, without Pains.

- He that hath a Trade hath an Estate.
- Taxes are indeed very heavy (but) we are taxed twice as much by our Idleness, three times as much by our Pride, and four times as much by our Folly.
- Beware of little Expences; a small Leak will sink a great Ship.
- Learning is to the Studious, and Riches to the Careful.
- If you would have a faithful Servant, serve yourself.
- Always taking out of the Meal-tub, and never putting in, soon comes to the bottom.
- Great Estates may venture more, but little Boats should keep near shore.
- For Age and Want, save while you may; no Morning Sun lasts a whole Day.

In all, Franklin's legacy matches the legacy of the Bogleheads, "a doctrine, my friends, of Reason and Wisdom . . . and Frugality and Prudence, though excellent Things. Ask God's blessing humbly and be not uncharitable to those who seem to want it, but comfort and help them . . . What is the noblest question in the world? 'What good may I do in it?'" Again using the words Franklin chose, the members of this investment association have "dedicated themselves to assuming the obligations of virtue and of serving others."

WHAT'S A BOGLE TO THINK ABOUT THE BOGLEHEADS?

Put yourself, for a moment, dear readers, in my position. How would *you* feel if an association of American citizens named themselves "(insert your last name here) -heads"? It would all depend—wouldn't it?—on their character, their values, and the extent to which their intellectual and moral principles coincided with your own. Here, the Bogleheads gain high scores, espousing the investment strategies and human values to which I've dedicated my entire career. More than that, just as Alexis de Tocqueville suggested, they have "taken up an opinion . . . they wish to promote, they look for mutual assistance, and as soon as they have found one another out they combine . . . influencing one another with opinions recruited, the heart enlarged, the human mind developed."

So, of course I'm honored and of course I'm pleased, not only with the endorsement and friendship of this stellar group of followers who have named themselves after me and adopted my principles. The final objective of my career—in investing, in management, in entrepreneurship, and in public service—is to depart this world with my reputation intact. (But not too soon!) And so I confess that, yes, I'm filled with pride at how my life's mission has found burgeoning acceptance, not only among the Bogleheads but among millions of honest-to-God, down-to-earth human beings who deserve a fair shake in their efforts to achieve financial security for their families.

Pride, of course, is hardly an unmixed blessing, and I realize that it is a trait of character to be handled with care. Here is how Benjamin Franklin wisely expressed it:

> *In reality, there is, perhaps, no one of our natural passions so hard to subdue as* pride. *Disguise it, struggle with it, beat it down, stifle it, mortify it as much as one pleases, it is still alive, and will every now and then peep out and show itself; you will see it perhaps often in my history; for even if I could conceive that I had completely overcome it, I should probably be proud of my humility.*

If, in the history I have recounted today, I have allowed my own pride to peep out and show itself, I assure you that it is with great humility that I accept the honor that this association of Bogleheads has paid to this particular Bogle by their choice of name, by their enthusiastic endorsement of my principles and values, and by their dedication in this wonderful book. Take heed of its guidance, and you will enjoy investment success.

John C. Bogle
Valley Forge, Pennsylvania
June 2014

Introduction

*Do not value money for any more nor any less than its worth; it
is a good servant but a bad master.*
             —Alexander Dumas fils, *Camille*, 1852

Contrary to what you may believe, a Boglehead is not one of those funny
little dolls you occasionally see bouncing in the back window of a car in
front of you. That's a bobblehead.

Bogleheads are an entirely different animal. While less visible than
bobbleheads, our legions number in the millions. We are investors who
follow the philosophy and strategy of investing advocated by John C.
"Jack" Bogle, founder of The Vanguard Group.

MEET OUR LEADER

What Jack Bogle has made possible for the individual investor is truly
extraordinary. Thanks to his creation of no-load, low-cost, tax-efficient
mutual funds, millions of investors enjoy significantly greater returns on
their investment dollars than they otherwise would have. His introduction of the first index fund for retail investors was labeled *Bogle's Folly* by
its detractors. Today, that same fund, Vanguard's 500 Index fund, is the
largest mutual fund in the world. Thanks to Jack Bogle, more of each
investor's money is put to work for them instead of going into the pockets of brokers, fund managers, or the taxman. For the everyday investor
this translates into items such as nicer homes for families, college educa-
tions for children, more enjoyable retirements for seniors, and more
money to be passed on to loved ones and causes they care about.
Although a few other investment fund families have joined the low-cost
revolution, it was Jack Bogle who sounded the bugle and led the charge,
and it's Vanguard that continues to lead the way.

You may think that such an enormous lifetime contribution is
enough for one man, but Jack Bogle is no ordinary man. Since stepping

down as chairman of The Vanguard Group for a heart transplant in 1996, Jack Bogle has devoted his life to educating investors on how to get a greater return on their investment dollars. Moreover, his teachings simplify investing, making it very easy for the average person with no financial background to understand. His books, *Bogle on Mutual Funds*, *Common Sense on Mutual Funds*, and many others are classics.

In addition to creating a great family of mutual funds and teaching others how to invest efficiently and effectively, Jack Bogle is a tireless advocate for the individual investor. It's common to see him speaking to professional groups, at commencements, or being interviewed on radio and television. His editorials frequently appear in the *Wall Street Journal*. His messages to the investment community are always consistent: Give investors a "fair shake" for their money, tell them the truth, and remember that character counts. He has fittingly been labeled "the conscience of the industry." His honors are too numerous to mention, but they include being selected as one of *Time* magazine's "100 Heroes and Icons Who Shape Our Lives" in 2004. When Thomas Jefferson remarked, "One man with courage is a majority," he could have been speaking about Jack Bogle.

MEET THE BOGLEHEADS

Thanks to Morningstar, an investment research firm in Chicago, a meeting place was created in 1998 where Bogleheads throughout the world can meet, discuss investment ideas, and help each other. As you might suspect, we meet in cyberspace. This Bogleheads Forum can be accessed via www.bogleheads.org. Thanks to the work of Bogleheads Alex Frakt and Larry Auton, the bogleheads.org website is a place where you can see a list linking to the most recent conversations, learn more about the Bogleheads, and find answers to frequently asked questions. Participation is open to the public. You can read conversations and post on the Bogleheads Investment Forum at no cost.

At the risk of appearing immodest, we believe the Bogleheads Forum is the best investment forum in cyberspace. The site gets more than a million hits per day. Our members include some of the best investment planners, authors, and minds in the business. Post a question and you will likely get an answer from one or more of them. Better yet, you will get an honest, unbiased answer from someone with no hidden sales agenda. Our forum frowns heavily on persons who attempt to troll for business, and commercial posts are quickly deleted. Our members range in age from 12 and up, and we range in wealth and experience from beginning investors just starting out to experienced investors with multimillion-dollar portfolios.

Boglehead meetings don't begin and end in cyberspace. Starting in 2000, there have been annual reunions where all Bogleheads are invited to meet and greet each other in person. Jack Bogle attended every reunion with the exception of one (he was in the hospital). He generously shares his time with us, gets to know us as individuals, and answers our investing questions. All of these national events were smash hits, and we continue to hold an annual get-together.

In addition, local Boglehead chapters are popping up in cities and regions throughout the country as well as in Europe and Asia. Local chapters provide an opportunity for Bogleheads to meet face-to-face, enjoy a meal together, and discuss investing. The national Bogleheads Conferences and Local Chapter meetings are a microcosm of the USA—a very diverse but very nice group of people who come to learn, share what they know, and help others.

ABOUT THE BOGLEHEADS' GUIDE

We wrote this guide to give you a taste of the Boglehead approach to investing. We know it will enable you to become a better investor and manager of your own financial resources. We assume no financial knowledge on your part. In fact, knowing nothing about investing might be a benefit. You won't have to unlearn many popular beliefs propagated by Wall Street and the media that aren't true.

The three of us combined have well over a century of investing experience. Through trial and error, we each independently adopted the Boglehead approach to investing for one simple reason: It has given each of us the best, after-tax return with the least risk on our investment dollars. It's that simple.

Several key topics are covered in this book:

- How to get on a sound financial footing before you start investing
- What the various types of investments actually are
- How to protect your investments against the ravages of inflation
- How to determine how much you need to save
- Steps to building a simple but effective investment portfolio
- Excellent ways to save for college
- How to not let a windfall slip through your fingers
- How to decide if you need a financial advisor, and how to choose one if you do

- How to determine when to rebalance your portfolio, and how to do it
- How to identify and tune out the noise from Wall Street and the media that's designed to benefit them and not you
- How investors' emotions can be their own worst enemy, and how to keep them from ruining your nest egg
- Steps to take to prevent financial catastrophes
- How to live a comfortable retirement without running out of money
- How to pass assets on efficiently to your heirs
- How to keep your investing style simple, giving you more time to live your life to the fullest

We have no hidden agendas. We aren't financial planners or money managers looking for clients. We don't have a high-powered, get-rich-quick weekend seminar to sell you. We are all well over 70 years of age, financially secure, and haven't missed a meal yet. If you want to read the book at the bookstore, the library, or borrow it from a friend, that's fine with us. Our primary mission is simply to support Jack Bogle's mission by teaching others how to get the best long-term return on their investment dollars.

We also have a secondary mission. We hope this book will encourage you to join the legions of Boglehead investors online. Drop-in and say hi at www.bogleheads.org. Post any questions you may have, and share with us what you've learned about investing. We are all there to learn, to help, and to enjoy the friendship of the Bogleheads. Welcome!

Taylor Larimore
Mel Lindauer
Michael LeBoeuf

PART I

---◆---

ESSENTIALS OF
SUCCESSFUL INVESTING

CHAPTER ONE

Choose a Sound Financial Lifestyle

Drive-in banks were established so most of the cars today could see their real owners.

—E. Joseph Grossman

It's an old statistic that has held very consistent over time. Take 100 young Americans starting out at age 25. By age 65, one will be rich and four will be financially independent. The remaining 95 will reach the traditional retirement age unable to self-sustain the lifestyle to which they have become accustomed.

Without assistance from government programs such as Social Security, Medicare, and Medicaid, many would literally starve. And if you are harboring dreams of the government providing you with a full and prosperous retirement, it's time to wake up. Although the government won't let you starve, it's not committed to making your golden years golden. That's up to you. A lifestyle totally based on government handouts has always been uncomfortable at best.

With 76 million baby boomers in or nearing retirement, it could get a whole lot worse.

We live in the richest country in world history. Our wealth is enormous and growing. Yet only 5 percent of us manage to become financially independent by age 65. Why is this? More often than not, the answer lies in what we choose to do with the money that comes into our lives.

WHAT'S YOUR FINANCIAL LIFESTYLE?

Although you might not be aware of it, you have chosen the financial lifestyle that you currently live. For purposes of simplicity, let's look at three common financial lifestyles lived by three different couples. As you read about each lifestyle, you will likely be reminded of people you know. But the most important question is, "Which financial lifestyle is closest to yours?"

The Borrowers

"Forget about tomorrow, let's live for today." That's the creed of Bill and Betty Borrower. It's a financial lifestyle literally built on a house of cards—credit cards. To the Borrowers, paying cash for almost anything is unheard of. They drive the newest and best cars, wear the latest high-fashion jewelry and clothing, and live in a great big house, all financed by enormous debts. The big house was purchased with little or no money down and the balance is financed with an interest-only, variable-rate mortgage. Similarly, the cars are leased or financed to the max with hefty car loans. And anything that can be charged to credit cards is charged to credit cards. To the Borrowers, credit cards are one terrific deal—almost like free money. Just pay the credit card companies only 2 percent of the balance due each month—forever. It's one of the first lessons they learned in college.

Bill and Betty are dying to take that luxury cruise that their friends the Braggarts took and rave about. Unfortunately, the price is light-years past their credit card limits. However, there is a ready source of financing nearby. As fate would have it, Bill and Betty's home has appreciated substantially. So they simply take out a home-equity loan and go cruising. Better yet, since the interest on the loan is tax deductible, part of the money spent to take the cruise is courtesy of Uncle Sam. Isn't America great?

Unless the Borrowers make drastic changes, their financial future is headed over a cliff. Not only are they failing to build wealth, they're building negative wealth, better known as debt. A job loss here, an accident or illness there, and the Borrowers' high living is history. Cars are repossessed. The mortgage is foreclosed, and they are forced out of their home.

They declare bankruptcy, and many of their prized possessions are auctioned off to pay creditors. Friends and neighbors are totally shocked, and remark, "They appeared to be doing so well." (In Texas, this syndrome is known as "big hat, no cattle.") Bill and Betty declare themselves victims of bad luck. The reality is that they robbed tomorrow to pay for today.

The Consumers

Fortunately, most Americans are more responsible than the Borrowers. Instead, their financial lifestyle more closely parallels that of Chad and Cathy Consumer. While the Borrowers spend with a credit card mentality, the Consumers spend with a paycheck mentality. Instead of borrowing to the max, Chad and Cathy spend to the max based on their combined net incomes. They look at their take-home pay, see how much it is, and then go out and buy as much stuff as they can afford. After all, isn't that why they work?

Like most Americans, Chad and Cathy can't afford to pay cash for major purchases such as a home, a new car, or that big-screen HDTV like the one their neighbors have. When it comes to making a major purchase, the buying decision usually boils down to finding the answer to the magic question:

Can we afford the monthly payments?

They never stop to consider how much they're adding to the cost of the purchase or how long they will be paying for it. Details like that just don't interest them. If they can swing the payments, they're buying the goods. Their financial lifestyle is all about earning to spend.

Chad and Cathy have heard about Roth IRAs, where they can accumulate money tax-free for retirement. And both of their employers have 401(k) plans in which the employer provides a company match of any money that they are willing to save and invest on a tax-deferred basis. However, they pass up the offers of free money and the opportunity to build wealth tax-free. Of course, they would like to save. Unfortunately, there are too many things they need right now: a new car, that big-screen TV, an iPod, a new cell phone with a digital camera, a trip to Disney World, and scores of other life necessities. Their soul may belong to God, but Madison Avenue is in control of their wallet.

About the only good thing you can say for the Consumers' financial lifestyle is that it's better than the Borrowers'. Although Chad and Cathy believe they own their lifestyle, the truth is that they are just renting it. Like the Borrowers, a job loss, accident, or illness could hold dire financial consequences. Without a cash cushion and a long-term plan for achieving financial independence, they will continue to live a rented lifestyle until they choose to retire, or can no longer work. From then on, they will live a very spartan financial lifestyle dictated to them by a government bureaucracy.

The Keepers

While most Americans go through life with a credit card or paycheck mentality, a third, very wise group has a different financial mind-set. As Ken and Kim Keeper put it, "Debt is deadly, and earning to spend gets you nowhere. The people who reach financial freedom focus on accumulating wealth over time." While others pay attention to their net income, the Keepers are far more interested in their net worth.

The Keepers have no higher income than the Borrowers or Consumers. In fact, they may earn less. But over the course of a lifetime, they will likely have far more money to spend and more work-free years to enjoy it than the other two couples.

What's the difference? It begins with what the Keepers do with money as soon as they earn it. The first thing they do with every paycheck is to make a payment toward their future financial freedom. A minimum of 10 percent of their take-home pay is taken off the top to be saved and invested. They eagerly participate in any employee saving and/or matching programs at work. They contribute the maximum legal amount to their Roth IRA accounts every year.

Do they have debts and credit cards like the Borrowers and Consumers? Yes, they do. However, their debts are likely to be in the form of a home mortgage with a payment they can well afford, or a student loan to pay for an education that boosted their earning potential significantly. If they have car loans, they are likely to be for two- or three-year-old cars they purchased and plan to keep for a long time. They know that depreciation in the first few years of a car's life is the greatest cost of owning one. They look for a car that's a good buy, in good condition, and let the original owner take the depreciation hit. As for credit cards, they use them for convenience and pay the full balance each month without fail.

Are Ken and Kim cheapskates who lead lives of high deprivation in the hope of being rich one day? No, they are not. After setting aside a regular amount each month, they spend most of the money they earn. They wear nice clothes, live in a nice home, dine in fine restaurants, take vacations, and enjoy many of the good things money can buy. They simply realize something that the Borrowers and Consumers either don't know or choose to ignore. By making a long-term commitment and having a financial plan to build wealth over time, the odds are they will always have more money than they need, and someday may have more than they want.

TAKE THESE STEPS BEFORE YOU START INVESTING

The fact that you are taking time to read this book tells us that you are concerned about your financial future. You want to learn the basics of sound investing to achieve important life goals, such as living in a nice home, paying for your children's college education, and having a comfortable retirement. At the same time, you want to have enough spending money to be able to enjoy the present. Millions of others have achieved all these goals, and you can, too. But before we discuss the basics and you begin investing, we strongly recommend that you do the following three things, if you haven't already done so:

1. Graduate from the paycheck mentality to the net worth mentality.
2. Pay off credit card and high-interest debts.
3. Establish an emergency fund.

Graduate from the Paycheck Mentality to the Net Worth Mentality

From the time we are old enough to understand, society conditions us to confuse income with wealth. We believe that doctors, CEOs, professional athletes, and movie actors are rich because they earn high incomes. We judge the economic success of our friends, relatives, and colleagues at work by how much money they earn. Six- and seven-figure salaries are regarded as status symbols of wealth. Although there is a definite relationship between the income and wealth, they are very separate and distinct economic measures.

Income is how much money you earn in a given period of time. If you earn a million in a year and spend it all, you add nothing to your *wealth*. You're just living lavishly. Those who focus only on net income as a measure of economic success are ignoring the most important measuring stick of financial independence. It's not how much you make, *it's how much you keep.*

The measure of wealth is net worth: the total dollar amount of the assets you own minus the sum of your debts. So, the first thing we want you to do is calculate your net worth. Calculating your net worth is very simple. First, add up the current dollar value of everything you own. Such items include the following:

- Cash in checking and savings accounts, credit unions, or money market funds
- The cash value of your life insurance
- Your home and any other real estate holdings
- Any stocks, bonds, mutual funds, certificates of deposit, government securities, or other investments
- Pension or retirement plans
- Cars, boats, motorcycles, or other vehicles
- Personal items such as clothing, jewelry, home furnishings, and appliances
- Collectibles such as art or antiques
- Your business, if you own one and were to sell it
- Anything else of value that you own

Once you have the total current value of what you own, add up the total amount of all debts that you currently owe. These include the total amount due on the following:

- The mortgage on your house or any real estate holdings
- Credit cards
- Car loans
- Personal loans
- Educational loans
- Life insurance loans
- Home-equity loans
- Accounts payable in your business
- Any other debts

Subtract what you owe from what you own, and that's your net worth. Simply go to Google.com, type "net worth calculator" in the search box, and you will get links to literally thousands of net worth calculators. Choose one, fill in the blanks, and your net worth will be calculated for you.

Once you calculate your net worth, you may find it useful to see how it measures up against the net worth of others in your age and income category. Every three years the Federal Reserve surveys household net worth in the United States. The latest figures available are for 2010. At that time, the median family net worth in the United States (meaning half had less, half had more) was $77,300.

As you might expect, odds favor the well educated and self-employed. Families headed by a college graduate had a median net worth of $195,200, compared to $56,700 for families headed by a high school graduate. And the self-employed enjoyed the highest median net worth of $285,600.

Not surprisingly, median net worth tends to rise with age and with income, as illustrated:

MEDIAN NET WORTH AS IT RELATES TO AGE

AGE	MEDIAN NET WORTH
Less than 35	$ 9,300
35–44	$ 42,100
45–54	$117,900
55–64	$179,400
65–74	$206,700
75 and more	$216,800

MEDIAN NET WORTH AS IT RELATES TO PERCENTILE OF HOUSEHOLD INCOME

PERCENTILE OF INCOME	MEDIAN NET WORTH
Less than 20	$ 6,200
20–39.9	$ 25,600
40–59.9	$ 65,900
60–79.9	$ 128,600
80–89.9	$ 286,600
90–100	$1,194,300

Make it a habit to calculate your net worth once a year. Charting a course to financial freedom begins with and requires knowing where you are.

Pay Off Credit Card and High-Interest Debts

Our greatest hope is that when you calculate your net worth, you have no high-interest debts or revolving credit card balances. However, if you do, you should probably pay them off before you start investing.

We recommend doing that simply because it's the highest, risk-free, tax-free return on your money that you can possibly earn. Credit card balances are the most insidious of all. You might think you are outsmarting the credit card companies when you transfer existing balances from one card to another promising you a low interest rate for the next several months. Don't fall for it. Pay them off. By maintaining a revolving balance, you are making the credit card companies richer and you poorer.

For example, let's assume a household carries a credit card balance of $8,000, makes the minimum monthly payment of $160, and is being charged an interest rate of 18.9 percent. If no additional charges are added to the balance, it will take about 8 years and more than $7,000 in interest charges to pay it off. That means the credit card holder will spend more than $15,000 to buy $8,000 worth of goods and services. If you think that's a good deal, seek medical attention.

Have you ever read the very fine print in the contracts that credit card companies send you? If you do, you may be shocked to learn just how much power they have. Miss one payment and that bargain interest rate of 6 percent can skyrocket to 25 or 30 percent or more without informing you. Thanks to credit reporting services, they can check to see if you are paying your other outstanding debts on time. Be late with a payment on your mortgage, another credit card, or any other debt, and they reserve the right to raise your interest rate to any level that they choose. You have no say in the matter, and there is no federal limit on the interest rate a credit card company can charge. By agreeing to their terms, you risk placing your financial future in the hands of companies with the power to become legalized loan sharks.

Do you realize that over the course of a lifetime, your total income will likely be in the millions of dollars? Well, the banks and credit card companies sure do, and they want a piece of it. Every high-interest debt you don't pay off is siphoning off dollars from your potential net worth and shifting it to the net worth of lending companies. Maybe that's why they own large skyscrapers. Maybe that's why they bombard us with TV commercials and endless pieces of junk mail offering us credit cards with all kinds of perks, such as airline miles, cash rebates, and the like. Maybe that's why they can afford to sponsor high-profile major sporting events and we can't. By paying off your credit cards, you get a guaranteed, tax-free return of 12, 18, 30, or more percent.

If you're on the credit card merry-go-round, get off. If the balances are very large and you own your home, consider taking out a home-equity loan to pay off the credit cards. The interest rate will probably be lower and the interest will be tax deductible.

Once the revolving balances are paid, pay off the balances due each month so you don't incur any interest charges. If carrying credit cards causes you to overspend, cut them up and close the accounts. Pay cash or switch to debit cards. Let somebody else keep the lenders in high cotton. Trust us; they will do just fine without your help.

Establish an Emergency Fund

The final prerequisite to investing is to have a readily accessible source of cash on hand for emergencies. Accidents, natural disasters, illness, job loss, widowhood, and divorce can wreak financial havoc. Worse yet, financial emergencies have a way of showing up when least expected. The two ways to minimize their damage is to carry the proper types and amount of insurance and have a cash cushion handy in case it's needed. The basics of insurance are covered in Chapter 21.

How big of an emergency fund you need depends largely on your net worth and job stability. On the one hand, if you have a very stable job, such as that of a tenured university professor, a cash reserve of as little as three months' living expenses may be more than ample. On the other hand, if you are self-employed or work in a profession where layoffs are common, you may want to have as much as a year's worth of living expenses stashed away. For most people, six months' living expenses is probably adequate.

Keep your emergency fund in an account that is safe and liquid. Bank savings accounts, credit union accounts, or money market mutual fund accounts are all satisfactory. With a good emergency fund you'll sleep better at night. It also lessens the possibility that you will have to invade funds invested toward achieving your long-term financial goals.

If you know your net worth, have paid off your high-interest debts, and have established a ready cash reserve, congratulations! You are now ready to become a Boglehead investor.

CHAPTER TWO

Start Early and Invest Regularly

Adding time to investing is like adding fertilizer to a garden: It makes everything grow.

—Meg Green
Miami, Florida, Certified Financial Planner

In February 2005, Jack Bogle and a small number of Bogleheads met for an informal dinner in Orlando, Florida. During the course of conversation, Mr. Bogle mentioned receiving a letter from a Vanguard shareholder some weeks back. The person writing reported that he had been investing since the mid-1970s with Vanguard. Since that time, the value of his portfolio had grown to $1,250,000. But here is the interesting part: He never earned more than $25,000 per year in his lifetime.

Did that get your attention?

You may be asking, "How is that possible? Is he a stock market wizard? Did he have a great advisor? Did he win the lottery? Did he rob a bank? Did he inherit a bundle? Was he just lucky?"

We don't know the person or anything about his investing history. But the likely truth is that he accumulated a small fortune through consistently saving and investing over time. Anyone can do it, although very few choose to do it. It turns out that an investment of $601 at the beginning of each month in stock index funds, coupled with an average annual return of 10 percent, grows to the sum of $1,249,655 in 30 years. Incidentally, $601 a month is approximately 28.9 percent of a yearly salary of $25,000. And in case you might be wondering, yes, the math works the same for everybody.

THE MAGIC IS IN THE COMPOUNDING

Most people earning $25,000 a year believe that their only shot at becoming a millionaire is to win the lottery. The truth is that the odds of anyone winning a big lottery are less than the odds of being struck twice by lightning in a lifetime. However, the power of compound interest and the accompanying Rule of 72 illustrate how anyone can slowly transform small change into large fortunes over time.

The Rule of 72 is very simple: To determine how many years it will take an investment to double in value, simply divide 72 by the annual rate of return. For example, an investment that returns 8 percent doubles every 9 years (72/8 = 9). Similarly, an investment that returns 9 percent doubles every 8 years and one that returns 12 percent doubles every 6 years.

On the surface that may not seem like such a big deal, until you realize that every time the money doubles, it becomes 4, then 8, then 16, and then 32 times your original investment. In fact, if you start with a single penny and double it every day, on the thirtieth day it compounds to $5,338,709.12. Are you starting to understand the power of compound interest? No wonder Einstein called it the greatest mathematical discovery of all time.

Let's assume a child is born today. For the next 65 years, she or her parents will deposit a certain amount into a stock mutual fund that pays an average annual return of 10 percent. How much do you think they need to deposit each day in order for her to have $1 million at age 65? Five dollars? Ten Dollars? In fact, a daily deposit of only 54 cents compounds to more than $1 million in 65 years. It really helps to start early.

Here's another illustration of the power of starting early: If a portfolio earns an average annual return of 8 percent after expenses and taxes, the amounts someone has to invest just one time at various ages, in order to have $1 million at age 65 is shown:

AMOUNT NEEDED AT 8 PERCENT ANNUAL RETURN TO ACCUMULATE $1 MILLION AT AGE 65

AGE	INVESTMENT
15	$ 21,321.23
20	$ 31,327.88
25	$ 46,030.93
30	$ 67,634.54
35	$ 99,377.33
40	$146,017.90
45	$214,548.21
50	$315,241.70
55	$463,193.49
60	$680,583.20

Source: Copyright Portfolio Solutions, LLC.

Most us don't have large sums of money to make one-time deposits when we are young. However, all is not lost. If a 25-year-old wants to have a million by age 65, it's easily achievable. Simply deposit $4,000 a year at the start of every year in a Roth IRA and get an average annual return of 8 percent. At age 65, the portfolio will be worth $1,119,124 tax-free from saving just $11 a day. However, if that same person waits until age 35 to begin investing $4,000 a year, the portfolio will be worth $489,383 at age 65—a tidy sum, but far short of a million. A young married couple who deposits $8,000 for 40 years at 8 percent will be multi-millionaires from their annual Roth investment.

Here's another example to illustrate the enormous benefit of getting an early start. At age 25, Eric Early invests $4,000 per year in a Roth IRA for 10 years and stops investing. His total investment is $40,000. Larry Lately makes yearly deposits of $4,000 in his Roth IRA starting at age 35 for 30 years. His total investment is $120,000. Assuming both portfolios earn an 8 percent average annual return, at age 65, Eric's IRA will be worth $629,741, but Larry's IRA will be worth only $489,383. By starting 10 years earlier and making one-third of the investment, Eric ends up with 29 percent more.

We have all heard the old clichés:

- If I only knew then what I know now.
- We are too soon old and too late smart.
- Youth is too precious to be wasted on the young.

If you are a young person, we strongly encourage you to use the leverage of your youth to make the power of compounding work for you. And if you are no longer young, it's even more important. Use the time you have to make the Rule of 72 work for you.

THIS ABOVE ALL:
SAVING IS THE KEY TO WEALTH

As you will soon learn, the Boglehead approach to investing is easy to understand and easy to do. It's so simple that you can teach it to your children, and we urge you to do so. For most people the most difficult part of the process is acquiring the habit of saving. Clear that one hurdle, and the rest is easy.

What's that? You want an investment system where you don't have to save and can get rich quickly? Dream on. Sure, you can buy stocks on margin by putting as little as 20 percent down. But what if their value goes down? Are you prepared to come up with the cash to cover a margin call? In 1929 a lot of investors ran into that very problem. The consequences ushered in the historic stock market crash and the Great Depression. To our way of thinking, buying on margin isn't a prudent risk.

Bogleheads are investors, not speculators. Investing is about buying assets, holding them for long periods of time, and reaping the harvest years later. Sure, it requires taking risks, but only when the odds are in your favor. Speculating is similar to gambling. Speculators buy an investment with the hope of selling it quickly and turning a fast profit. Like gamblers, some speculators do win, but the odds are stacked against them.

Being a Boglehead requires planning, commitment, patience, and long-term thinking. If there really were easy, quick secrets to getting rich, there would be many more wealthy people than there are today. Promises of fast, easy money are the stuff of flim-flam men on late-night TV infomercials. As financial writer Jason Zweig so aptly put it, "The problem with getting rich quick is you have to do it so often."

If you want to achieve your financial goals in less time, here's one of the simplest, best pieces of advice that we can give you:

When you earn a dollar, try to save a minimum of 20 cents.

Some diligent savers actually strive to save 50 cents of every dollar they earn. The more you save, the sooner you achieve your financial goals. There is no substitute for frugality. Deciding how much to save is the most important decision you will ever make because you can't invest what you don't save.

In 2000, the National Bureau of Economic Research published a paper titled "Choice, Chance and Wealth Dispersion at Retirement." The paper reports the results of a study done by economists Steven Venti and David Wise that compared the lifetime earnings of several thousand American households with their net worth at retirement. The purpose of the study was to determine what factors influence the accumulation of wealth.

As you might suspect, Venti and Wise found some households with high lifetime earnings and relatively low net worth at retirement. Conversely, they also found households with modest lifetime earnings and relatively high net worth at retirement. Their next step was to determine why some people accumulated more wealth than others. Was it because some people enjoyed better health? Were some people smarter or luckier in their choice of investments? Was it due to receiving large inheritances? The economists concluded from their research that none of these factors had a significant impact on wealth at retirement. They only found one significant factor: Some people choose to save more than others.

You have a choice about what to do with every dollar that comes into your life. You can spend it today or save and invest it to make more dollars tomorrow. The key to successful money management lies in striking a healthy balance between the two.

FINDING THE MONEY TO INVEST

The late actor George Raft explained how he blew about $10 million this way: "Part of the money went for gambling, part for horses, and part for women. The rest I spent foolishly." All good wealth builders have just one thing in common: They spend less than they earn. There are two basic ways to find money to invest: You can either earn more money or spend less than you currently earn. We recommend doing both. Here are some ideas to get you started.

Pay Yourself First

You've heard it before and you'll hear it again. If you wait until you have a few extra dollars to invest, you'll likely wait forever. The first rule of saving/investing is to take it off the top of your paycheck. How much you save is up to you. We recommend a bare minimum of 10 percent. Very few people save over a third of their income, but the few that do are the ones most likely to retire early. There are no magic formulas for acquiring wealth. The earlier you start and the more you invest, the sooner you reach financial freedom.

If you are currently spending all of your income, begin by saving just 1 percent this month and increase it by 1 percent every month for the next year. In a year you will have established the habit of saving 12 percent of your income.

Reducing your spending is financially more efficient than earning more money. For every additional dollar of earnings you plan to save, you will likely have to earn $1.40 because you have to pay income taxes. However, every dollar you don't spend is a dollar that can be invested. Once again, frugality pays.

Create a Tax-Free Fortune for Just $15 a Day

Find a way to reduce your spending by $15 a day and you'll have almost $5,500 ($5,475) a year to invest in a Roth IRA. Carry a notepad with you for a month and write down the cost and description of everything you spend money on. You will be amazed at the dollars that slip through your fingers every day. Can you cut back on the number of restaurant meals and visits to the gourmet coffeehouse? Can you walk or bicycle to work instead of driving, taking a bus, or riding a taxi? Brown bag your lunch and you'll likely save $5 to $7 a day or more. Make the gourmet coffee at home for 50 cents instead of paying $4 and you save $3.50. Rent a video instead of taking the family to the movies and calculate how much that saves. Watch the big game at home on TV instead of spending a fortune on tickets, parking, and concessions.

If you're under the age of 50, the maximum you can contribute to a Roth IRA annually is $5,500. People over 50 can contribute up to $6,500. These contribution limits will be adjusted for inflation, so be sure to check to see if they've increased. You must have earned income, and your adjusted gross income must not exceed the current limits in order to be eligible to contribute the maximum amount. If you exceed the adjusted gross income limits, you are ineligible. Tax laws change over time, so check to see if you are eligible. No matter how much or little you can contribute, don't pass up this opportunity to build tax-free wealth if you can. A 25-year-old who invests $5,000 in a Roth IRA once a year for 40 years reaches age 65 with a tax-free fortune of $1,625,149.

Similarly, it's common for some employers to match employee contributions to their tax-deferred retirement plan. If that's the case where you work, be sure to participate. If you take all of your salary now without saving, you're passing up free money and effectively giving yourself a pay cut. Don't take the money and run. Take the money and save!

Commit Future Pay Increases to Investing

Many people find it difficult to save because they're in the habit of spending all they earn to maintain their current lifestyle. If that's the case with you, then resolve to channel at least half of all future take-home pay increases to investing. That way you'll be able to maintain your standard of living, enjoy some of the benefits of a raise, and invest, too.

If you change jobs and it comes with a handsome pay increase, go on living at the spending level you have become accustomed to and channel the new money into buying your financial freedom. Someday you will thank yourself profusely.

Shop for Used Items

If you make a habit of buying some items used, it's possible to pay less than half the new price for many of them. Adopting that habit can be better than doubling your salary. A used hammer or screwdriver works just a well as a new one. Shop at thrift stores or garage sales and read the want ads for items you need. At used clothing and furniture stores you can find excellent items for a fraction of their original cost. The resale value of a new computer plummets in a year. One that's a year or two old will probably do all that you want it to do for a fraction of the cost. Nobody has to know it's used but you. Which brings us to the most important item to consider buying used.

Don't Drive Yourself to the Poor House

The habit of buying a new car every few years has the potential to decrease your future net worth more than any other buying habit, including credit card debt. Worse yet, most cars are bought on credit, making them even more costly. General Motors makes more profit from car loans than from cars.

Take a look at how super-rich owners of professional sports franchises made their fortunes. If you do, you will find that a good number of them own or owned a chain of auto dealerships. Just like credit card companies, auto manufacturers and dealers look at all that money we are going to make in a lifetime and do a great job of getting a piece of it. The result is that they end up owning an NFL, NBA, or major league baseball franchise, and we end up owning an expensive bucket of bolts that loses about 25 percent of its value each year.

The way to lower your cost of driving is to buy a good used car and pay cash for it. A good rule of thumb is that the annual cost of driving a new, mid-priced car is about $2,500 higher than driving a three-year-old used car. If you buy a new luxury car or a gas-guzzling SUV, the increased cost can easily be double that or more.

Let's assume that a 19-year-old makes it a lifetime habit to buy three-year-old mid-priced cars. If she takes the $2,500 yearly savings and invests it at the beginning of the year in a balanced portfolio earning 8 percent a year, the savings compounds to $1,129,750 by age 65. You can double the amount for a two-car family. Lowering the cost of driving over the course of a lifetime can literally be the difference between retiring a millionaire and retiring broke. If legendary billionaire investor Warren Buffett drives an old pickup truck, and if Mr. Bogle can drive to our Boglehead Reunion in his six-year-old Volvo, why should we feel it's necessary to buy a new car to impress our neighbors?

Move Where the Cost of Living
Is Cheaper

You can accomplish this two ways: Move to less expensive housing in the same area, or move to another part of the country where the cost of living is lower. The result of doing either or both can provide you with more money to invest. Moving to a smaller home reduces your property taxes, mortgage payment, utility bills, and cost of maintenance. At the same time, proceeds from the sale of your previous home may give you a nice chunk of equity to invest.

If you live on the East Coast between Washington and Boston, or on the West Coast between San Diego and San Francisco, there can be a huge financial payoff in moving to a region where the cost of living is cheaper. For example, a move from Newport Beach, California, to almost any Florida coastal city will lower your cost of living by more than 50 percent according to the salary calculator at homefair.com (www.homefair .com/homefair/calc/salcalc.html). If you are tired of New England winters and long to be where you can play golf almost every day, a move from Boston to Phoenix lowers your cost of living 41 percent according to the cost-of-living calculator at bestplaces.net (www.bestplaces.net/col/). And if you live in the Bay Area, you may be singing, "I Left My Wealth in San Francisco." A move to almost anywhere in the continental United States is guaranteed to lower your cost of living substantially.

The most desirable place to live is a matter of personal taste, but differences in the cost of living between neighborhoods, cities, and regions are a matter of fact. Some people can't imagine living anywhere other than Manhattan. However, one former resident remarked, "New York is a place where you earn enough money to buy yourself out of problems that don't exist elsewhere." You may be able to lower your cost of living, have more money to invest, and increase your quality of life simply by moving.

Create a Side Income

Creating additional sources of income is an excellent way to find money to invest. Ralph (not his real name) is a classic example. He's 28, has a wife, a new baby, and a full-time job with a Fortune 500 company. Hoping to become financially independent someday, Ralph started his own carpet-cleaning business that he operates on weekends. He also owns a single-family rental home in the warm-weather climate where he lives. During the winter the property garners premium rates, and when the price is right, he plans to buy a few more properties. Income from the carpet-cleaning business and a positive cash flow from rental income give Ralph the wherewithal to invest in mutual funds. He is also maxing out his matching 401(k) at work, and is investing the maximum allowable amount in Roth IRAs for him and his wife. Incidentally, Ralph recently bought a three-year-old family sedan in excellent condition for a little more than half of its blue-book value. Is there any doubt Ralph is on the right path to becoming wealthy?

In addition to providing investment income, side incomes make us less vulnerable to layoffs, downsizings, office politics, and obnoxious bosses. Just as it makes sound economic sense to diversify your investments, it makes sense to diversify your sources of income.

If you decide to create added sources of income, do your homework. The secret of any successful business lies in fulfilling unmet needs and wants. Find a need and fill it. Find a problem and solve it. Find a hurt and heal it. People pay money for goods and services that make them feel good and solve their problems. Odds of success are good if you choose an activity that's in step with your educational background, previous job experiences, aptitudes, and interests.

One final word of caution: Be very wary of people and advertisements touting great wealth by signing up for their investment secrets seminar, real estate seminar, home-based business opportunity, or network marketing operation. The overwhelming majority of them are scams that will only leave you poorer. To quote an old proverb from the racetrack, "When a man with experience meets a man with money, the man with money gets the experience, and the man with experience gets the money."

Not All Debt Is Bad Debt

Although consumer debt is to be frowned on, it's important to realize that debt is not inherently bad. In fact, there are times when debt is an excellent investment. Low-interest loans to finance the cost of a home, a rental property, education that will boost earning potential, and to start a new business are all examples of good debt. Many of the best things in life would not be possible if it were impossible to borrow money. The key is to keep interest rates low, preferably tax deductible, and borrow funds only when the expected payoff is higher than the cost of borrowing.

For example, there are times when carrying a mortgage on your home is a better option even when you have the funds to pay it off. Let's assume you are borrowing at an effective, fixed rate of 5 percent. At the same time, you believe that you can earn an average annual return of 8 percent in a balanced portfolio over the long term. Paying off the mortgage is a can't-miss 5 percent return. However, investing the money at 8 percent earns an average of 3 percent more per year. With the money invested in liquid assets, you have access to it if needed, and the value of the house will likely appreciate whether it's mortgage-free or not. Or, perhaps you would rather spend the money than leave a mortgage-free home to your heirs. Is it a risk? Yes, but it's a calculated risk, and one where the odds are likely to be in your favor. Whether it's a risk worth taking is for you to decide.

SUMMARY:
THE MOST IMPORTANT THINGS

When he was 23, Eric Haban, a Boglehead and regular contributor to the forum, expressed the idea beautifully when he wrote:

> *What most young people don't understand is that SAVING is more important in the beginning than finding the best performing investment. Having the ability to "Pay yourself first," manage your debt load, and determine a*

vision of what you want to accomplish is vital to your success. I read an article last week that stated 40 percent of Americans don't know where their earnings go. The simplicity of saving, coupled with the power of compound interest, is something to be very happy about.

Before becoming Bogleheads, all three of us made our share of poor investments. It was the habit of saving through the years, coupled with learning sound investment strategies, that made financial freedom a reality for us.

CHAPTER THREE

---◆---

Know What You're Buying: Part One

Stocks and Bonds

Only buy something that you'd be perfectly happy to hold if the market shut down for 10 years.

—Warren Buffett

Before we start on our investing journey, we need to know something about the various mainstream investment options that are available to us. In this chapter, we'll learn about stocks, bonds, mutual funds, funds-of-funds, exchange-traded funds (ETFs), and annuities.

Although you may never choose to invest in an individual stock or bond, if it's your intention to invest in mutual funds, you still should have an understanding of the underlying investments that are in your mutual funds. Therefore, we'll try to cover some of the various products you can invest in directly, as well as investment options that are probably best left to investing via mutual funds. We're somewhat biased, of course, and feel that mutual fund investing is the best route for most investors in most situations. (Notice we did not say *all* investors or *all* the time!)

Because bonds and bond funds seem to be one of the least understood investment options, we'll spend a lot of time on that subject. We'll try not to get too technical, but hopefully we'll cover the subject in enough detail to make you comfortable with your investment decisions.

STOCKS

Stocks represent an ownership interest in a corporation. When a company issues stock, it's actually selling a small fractional share of its business to each person who purchases shares of the stock. A stock certificate of ownership is issued to the purchaser, indicating the number of shares owned, and the proceeds of the stock issue are then used to fund the business affairs of the corporation.

Once the initial stock offering is completed, stock shares can then be exchanged (bought and sold) on the stock exchange where the company is listed. Sales and purchases of these shares are made through stockbrokers, who charge a commission or fee for their services. The value of these shares can and will vary over time, and they're revalued on a continuing basis when the stock markets are open for trading. The stock's value at any given time depends on how much another buyer is willing to pay for a share of that company's stock, and how much the seller is willing to accept. On one hand, if the outlook for the company is good or improving, buyers might be willing to pay more than you paid for your share of stock, and if you sold it at the higher price, you'd make a profit. On the other hand, if you had to sell at a time when the price of the stock was lower than you paid, you'd lose money. Investors who decide to hold their shares of stock, rather than sell them, expect to profit from the dividends the company pays them from time to time, and/or from the increase in the value of their stock shares as the company (they hope) grows and prospers.

Inasmuch as these stock shares represent partial ownership of a single company, it's usually not a good idea to invest all of your funds in just one company, since your entire portfolio's investment performance would be tied to the fortunes of that particular company. If the company experienced problems, the value of your stock would most likely fall, and you could possibly even lose your entire investment, should the company go bankrupt. We'll talk more about this later, when we discuss mutual funds and diversification.

BONDS

When you purchase individual bonds at initial issue, you're actually lending a specific amount of your money to the bond issuer. In return for

lending your money to the issuer, you're promised a return on your investment that is the bond's yield to maturity and the return of the face value
of the bond at a specified future date, known as the *maturity date*. These
maturity dates can be short-term (1 year or less), intermediate-term (2 to
10 years), and long-term (10 or more years). So, in reality, a bond is nothing more than an IOU or promissory note that pays interest from time to
time (usually semiannually) until maturity.

Bonds are issued by a number of entities, including the U.S. Treasury,
government agencies, corporations, and municipalities.

Treasury Issues

Treasury issues are considered the safest bond investments, since they're
backed by the full faith and credit of the U.S. government. Treasury issues
include Bills, Notes, Bonds, Treasury Inflation-Protected Securities
(TIPS), and two types of U.S. Savings Bonds (EE Bonds and I Bonds).
Treasury interest income is exempt from state and local taxes.

T-Bills, T-Notes, and T-Bonds
Treasury issues of one year or less are known as Treasury Bills, or *T-Bills*.
Currently, *T-Bills* are being issued for 13-, 26-, and 52-week periods.
Issues of 2, 3, 5, and 10 years are called *T-Notes*. Issues for periods greater
than 10 years are known as *T-Bonds*. Together, all of these issues are often
simply referred to as *Treasuries*.

TIPS
In 1997, the Treasury introduced Treasury Inflation-Indexed Securities
(TIIS). Shortly after their introduction, they became widely known in the
investment community as TIPS (Treasury Inflation-Protected Securities).
As its name implies, TIPS offer protection against the ravages of inflation.
We'll discuss TIPS in greater detail in Chapter 5, when we discuss inflation-
protected bonds.

U.S. Savings Bonds
The Treasury also currently issues two different types of U.S. Savings
Bonds—I Bonds and EE Bonds. Both I and EE Bonds have a minimum
one-year holding period, which means they can't be cashed in during the

first year you own them. After satisfying that first-year holding period requirement, they can be cashed in any time between the start of the second year and 30 years, with no loss of principal. However, if you redeem your Savings Bonds prior to five years, you'll lose the last three months' interest.

Each May and November, the Treasury announces a new yield figure for both I and EE Savings Bonds. On newly issued bonds, you'll start to earn the new rate immediately. On older bonds with variable yields, you'll earn that newly announced yield for six months, starting on your Savings Bond's six- or twelve-month anniversary of issue. However, I Bonds and EE Bonds differ in the way the yield is set. We'll cover I Bonds in greater detail in Chapter 5 when we talk about inflation-protected bonds, but we'll discuss EE Bonds now.

EE Bonds purchased from May 1997 through April 2005 earn a market-based rate that's calculated to yield 90 percent of the previous six-months' average yield for five-year Treasuries. This rate then remains in effect for the next six months, and that pattern continues until the EE bond reaches its original maturity.

EE Bonds purchased on or after May 1, 2005, have a fixed rate that's set by the Treasury. The Treasury does not disclose the formula used in setting the rate, so there's no way to know in advance what the new rate might be. Unlike older EE Bonds, which had a market-based variable rate that changed every six months, the yield on the new EE Bonds is fixed, much like a CD, and the rate that's in effect when you purchase these EE Bonds remains the same for 20 years. The fixed rate for future EE Bonds will be set by the Treasury and announced each May and November.

EE Bonds come with a minimum guaranteed yield of 3.526 percent if held for 20 years, since they are guaranteed to at least double in that time period. If the market-based rates of the older EE Bonds (90 percent of the preceding six-months' average of the five-year Treasury) or the fixed rates of the newer EE Bonds haven't doubled the value of your EE Savings Bonds in 20 years, the Treasury will make a one-time adjustment to your account to make up for any shortage.

Other Benefits of Savings Bonds

Even though EE and I Savings Bonds are purchased with after-tax money for your taxable account, they are tax-deferred for up to 30 years. This makes Savings Bonds an ideal candidate for your portfolio when you need to hold bonds in your taxable account, but don't need current income from your bond holdings. Like other Treasury issues, Savings Bonds are free from state and local taxes.

Furthermore, if you meet the income requirements in effect at the time you redeem the bonds to pay tuition expenses for you, your spouse, or your children, you can use any EE Savings Bonds purchased after 1989 and all I Bonds, regardless of purchase date, tax-free, for all qualifying educational expenses. However, to qualify for this tax-free educational benefit, the Savings Bonds *must* be registered in one or both parents' names. If the child is listed as an owner or co-owner, the bonds do not qualify for the tax-free educational benefit. However, the child can be listed as a beneficiary, and the bonds will still qualify. We'll talk more about this in Chapter 14 when we cover savvy ways to fund a college education.

How to Buy Treasury Issues

T-Bills, T-Notes, T-Bonds, and TIPS are sold at regularly scheduled auctions. You can buy Treasury issues at auction in a number of ways:

- You can have your bank purchase them for you. (It may charge you a fee.)
- You can have your broker purchase them for you. (He/she may charge you a fee.)
- You can open a TreasuryDirect account at www.treasurydirect.gov and use that account to make your purchases.
- *Note:* If the Treasury issues are being purchased for your tax-deferred account, then you can't use any of these methods for purchasing your Treasuries. Rather, your IRA custodian must purchase the Treasuries for your account at the auction.

U.S. Savings Bonds can be purchased online at TreasuryDirect (www.treasurydirect.gov). Savings Bonds purchased via TreasuryDirect are held in book entry form only; the Treasury does not issue statements on these accounts. So while the Savings Bond purchases and redemptions are easily handled online, it's up to you to keep a paperwork trail. The easiest way to do this is to print out updated account statements while you're online. When you use TreasuryDirect for your Savings Bond purchases, the Treasury will take the funds for your purchase directly from your bank account, and they'll deposit any redemption proceeds back into your bank account.

Government Agency Securities

There are a number of government agencies that issue pools of mortgage-backed securities (MBS) that investors can purchase, either directly or via bond mutual funds. Some of these better-known agencies include the Government National Mortgage Association (GNMA, called Ginnie Mae), the Federal National Mortgage Association (Fannie Mae), and the Federal Home Loan Mortgage Corporation (Freddie Mac). The purpose of these agencies is to stimulate and facilitate home ownership by low- and moderate-income Americans.

The U.S. government established the GNMA within the Department of Housing and Urban Development (HUD). This agency's mission is to guarantee that MBS investors will receive the timely repayment of both principal and interest on GNMA-backed securities (Ginnie Maes). GNMAs actually represent an investor's financial interest in a repackaged group of individual mortgages, which are known as mortgage-backed securities. The underlying mortgages in these repackaged pools, which are sold to investors, are insured by other federal agencies, such as the Federal Housing Authority (FHA) and the Department of Veterans Affairs (VA).

GNMA uses the full faith and credit of the U.S. government to back up its guarantee of timely payments of both principal and interest to those who invest in GNMA-backed securities. However, this guarantee does not mean that the value of the mortgage-backed securities that investors purchase will not fluctuate. They can and they will, depending on interest rates.

For instance, when interest rates rise, homeowners will continue to hang on to their lower-cost mortgages. This means that investors in those lower-yielding GNMA securities will have to endure a longer period of lower interest payments, since homeowners don't have any financial incentive to prepay their mortgages. As a result, this can lower the value of the GNMA bond as well as GNMA bond funds holding this bond.

Conversely, when interest rates fall, homeowners tend to refinance their mortgages, thus paying off the investors in the underlying higher-yielding GNMA securities. That means, of course, that the GNMA investors will have to put the prepaid money back to work sooner than expected, and at a lower yield. Again, this impacts the value of the GNMA bond and the GNMA bond funds that own this bond.

GNMA securities tend to perform best when interest rates remain relatively steady for a long period of time. Without interest rate fluctuations, the GNMA securities investor will receive a stream of income approximately equal to what he/she expected to get when they first bought the security.

Fannie Mae and Freddie Mac package and resell pools of existing mortgages to investors. The securities of these agencies, which have the "implied" backing of the United States, are not, in fact, guaranteed by the "full faith and credit of the United States," as are GNMAs. Rather, they are guaranteed by government departments, such as the VA or the FHA. Basically, they are similar to GNMAs, in that they're packages of individual mortgages, and are, therefore, mortgage-backed securities. However, they don't carry the extra layer of protection that comes with the GNMA guarantee. This adds a small additional element of risk to Fannie Mae and Freddie Mac securities. As a result, investors need to be aware of it, and should expect to be compensated by higher yields for any additional risk.

Corporate Bonds

As the name implies, *corporate bonds* are issued by corporations that need additional funds for various business purposes (expansion, new equipment, new product introduction, etc.). The yield of the newly issued corporate bond will be primarily determined by four factors:

1. The creditworthiness of the corporation issuing the bonds
2. The current yield of bonds with comparable safety ratings and maturities
3. The demand for the bonds
4. The call feature of the bonds

Credit ratings are assigned to corporate bond issues by a number of rating agencies, including Standard & Poor's, Moody's, and Fitch. Normally, the higher the credit rating, the lower the bond's yield. For example, Standard & Poor's Investment-grade bonds include AAA (the highest rating), AA, A, and BBB. In addition, Standard & Poor's assigns bond ratings pluses (+) and minuses (-). A BBB- is the lowest of the investment grade bonds. Bonds with ratings lower than BBB- are considered speculative, and pay a higher interest rate since there's a greater risk that the issuing companies might not be able to repay investors. These lower-rated bonds are known as *junk bonds, high-yield bonds,* and *non-investment-grade bonds.*

Municipal Bonds

State and local governments sell bonds to pay for various government and/or government-approved projects. These municipal bonds are normally free from federal taxation, and they are usually also free from taxes in the state of issue. For investors who live in a city with a local tax, owning municipal bonds issued by their local government can be triple tax-free, since they'd pay no federal, state, or local taxes on the income from those bonds. Because of these tax advantages, municipal bonds, which normally yield less than comparable taxable bonds, can make sense for investors in the higher tax brackets (usually 25 percent and above). However, you'd need to check the tax-free bond's yield against other available taxable bond choices to see which would give you the greatest after-tax return. Since there are federal, state, and possibly even local tax issues at play in an investor's decision, covering every possible scenario is beyond the scope of this book. Rather, you should consult with your tax advisor or use an online calculator to determine if municipal bonds make sense for you.

Here are two free online calculators that can help you determine which type of bond or bond fund (muni or taxable) would give you the greatest after-tax return:

1. Visit https://investor.vanguard.com/home and search for "taxable-equivalent yield calculator" (without the quotes).
2. Visit www.TRowePrice.com and search for "Tax-Free Equivalent Yield Calculator" (without the quotes).

After using the calculators, if it appears that municipal bonds may be suitable for your portfolio, you need to be aware that some municipal bond issues are subject to the IRS Alternate Minimum Tax (AMT). Therefore, if you're subject to the AMT, you'll want to check carefully before making your municipal bond or muni bond fund purchase, in order to determine if/how you might be impacted by owning munis that are subject to this tax.

Finally, if you're going to buy municipal bonds, you want to be aware that some individual municipal bond issues carry insurance that promises to cover both the interest and the principal payments, should the bond issuer have problems. However, municipal bond investors should know that this guarantee is only as good as the financial strength of the insurer. Additionally, some bonds are backed by the full taxing authority of the issuer, while others are guaranteed only by the revenue generated by the particular project that the bonds were issued to finance.

In summary, as an investor, you need to realize that all municipal bonds and/or municipal bond funds are not created equal, and just as with any other bond investment, you should expect to get a higher yield for taking on additional risk.

Maturity and Duration

Individual bonds have a maturity date (the date that investors are repaid the principal amount of the bond). Bond mutual funds don't, since they're constantly buying new bonds to replace bonds that are maturing. Therefore, an intermediate-term bond fund might hold some longer-term bonds, some intermediate-term bonds, and some shorter-term bonds that are nearing maturity. So it's the weighted average maturity of all of their bond holdings that puts the bond fund in the intermediate-term bond fund category. Over time, the longer-term bonds become intermediate-term bonds, the intermediate-term bonds become short-term bonds, and the short-term bonds eventually mature and are replaced with new bonds.

Even though bond funds don't have a maturity date, they do have a measure to help bond fund investors determine if a particular bond fund might be appropriate for them, considering their time horizon and risk tolerance level. The term for that measure is *duration*.

Duration is stated in whole and partial years, such as 4.3 years. Most nontechnical bond and bond fund investors simply use the duration figure to predict a bond or bond fund's price volatility in a rising or falling interest rate environment. The higher the duration figure, the more volatile the bond or bond fund would be in a changing interest rate environment.

Bond and bond fund values move in the opposite direction of interest rates. When interest rates increase, the value of bonds and bond funds decreases. And, when interest rates fall, bond and bond fund prices rise. Using the 4.3-year duration figure, a bond or bond fund investor should expect a decrease in their investment's value of approximately 4.3 percent if interest rates were to increase by 1 percent. Conversely, if interest rates were to fall 1 percent, the investor could expect an increase of 4.3 percent in the bond or bond funds' value. An easy way to visualize the relationship between interest rates and bond prices is to picture a seesaw with interest rates on one side and bond prices on the opposite side. When one goes up, the other goes down, and vice versa.

Bond fund investors should understand that while interest rate increases cause a decline in their fund's net asset value (NAV), the yield of their bond fund will increase, and, over time, that increased yield will help to mitigate the loss in value caused by those very same rising interest rates. So, if interest rates rose 1 percent, the time that it would take to make up for the loss in value would be approximately equal to the bond fund's original duration, or 4.3 years. Be aware, though, that a bond fund's duration may change over time, so you'll want to monitor your fund's duration to make sure it continues to match your time horizon.

While we've talked about bonds gaining value in a falling interest rate environment, and losing value in a rising interest rate environment, those are merely "paper" gains and losses. The gain or loss in a bond's value is only realized if you sell your bond in the secondary market, prior to maturity. If you elect to hold your bond to maturity, you'll continue to collect the coupon yield until the bond matures, and there will be no gain or loss. And you would only realize the gain or loss on the bond fund if you sold the fund by redeeming your shares.

You can find a bond or bond fund's current duration by calling either your broker or your mutual fund company. Some fund companies provide bond fund duration figures online. For instance, Vanguard provides a table that lists each Vanguard bond fund's duration (go to vanguard.com).

Selecting the Right Bond Fund

Now that we have a basic understanding of bonds and bond funds, how can we apply what we've learned to help us select a bond fund that's appropriate for us? Here are some simple guidelines you might use:

1. *Find a bond fund that matches your investment time horizon.* For example, if you'll need the money in two or three years, then you'd want to choose a short-term bond fund. It's important that you don't invest in a fund with a duration that's longer than your time horizon.
2. *Don't time interest rate hikes.* Rather, simply invest in a fund that matches your desired characteristics with the intention of holding it for at least the fund's duration or longer.

3. *Match your fund to your risk tolerance.* If you're going to worry about temporary losses in value, select funds with a shorter duration.

Why Should I Invest in Bonds?

It's important to understand that bonds and bond funds have a low correlation (they don't always move in the same direction at the same time) to stocks, so bonds can be a stabilizing force for a portion of your portfolio. For example, in the bear market of 2008, while equity fund losses of 30 percent to 60 percent were common, Vanguard's Total Bond Market Index Fund *gained* 5.05 percent.

How Much Should I Invest in Bonds?

Determining how much of your portfolio should be invested in bonds and how much should be held in equities (stocks) is an asset allocation decision. You'll learn how to go about establishing your own personal asset allocation plan in Chapter 8. However, here are a couple of general guidelines that you might find useful:

1. Mr. Bogle suggests that owning your age in bonds is a good starting point. So, a 20-year-old would hold 20 percent of his/her portfolio in bonds. By the time this investor reaches 50, the bond portion of the portfolio would have gradually increased, in 1 percent increments, to now represent 50 percent of his portfolio.
2. Increase your percentage of bond holdings if you are a more conservative investor, and decrease your percentage of bond holdings if you want to be more aggressive with your portfolio.

Should I Own Individual Bonds or a Bond Mutual Fund?

Because there are no bond funds that hold U.S. Savings Bonds, they must be purchased as individual bonds. However, most of the other bond investments we've discussed offer you the choice of buying either individual bonds or a bond fund that holds a number of bonds of the type you're interested in. Let's consider some of the advantages and disadvantages of both choices. Table 3.1 shows the advantages and disadvantages of owning individual bonds. Table 3.2 shows the advantages and disadvantages of owning bond mutual funds.

We've certainly covered a lot of ground in our discussions on bonds. Hopefully we've helped make you feel more comfortable about making your bond investing decisions. It's hard to go wrong with any good quality, low-cost short- or intermediate-term bond fund.

TABLE **3.1**   OWNING INDIVIDUAL BONDS

ADVANTAGES	DISADVANTAGES
Since you're guaranteed the return of your principal at maturity, you know you won't lose money if you plan to hold the bond to maturity.	Most non-Treasury bond issues must be purchased through a broker, and that involves commissions.
Once your bond is purchased, there are no ongoing expenses for owning the bond, as there are with bond funds.	If you have a bank or broker buy Treasuries for you, they may charge you a fee.
	Establishing a diversified bond portfolio requires a larger investment, since individual bonds have higher minimums.
	You can't reinvest the dividends. You'll have to find a place to invest the proceeds of the dividend checks you receive.
	You must use your tax-deferred account custodian to purchase bonds for your tax-deferred account. This usually involves fees or commissions.
	You can pay hidden markups and spreads if you buy or sell bonds in the secondary market.

TABLE 3.2   OWNING BOND MUTUAL FUNDS

ADVANTAGES	DISADVANTAGES
There are no costs for buying or selling no-load bond funds.	Your pay the fund's costs and expenses all the time you own the fund.
The bond fund holds a large number of bonds, so you get instant diversification.	Since a bond fund doesn't have a maturity date, you can't be assured of getting your principal back when you sell.
Some bond funds allow check writing.	The bond fund manager can make mistakes by selecting the wrong bonds or making bets on the direction of interest rates.
You can arrange to have your bond fund dividends reinvested automatically.	
Most bond funds have smaller investment minimums.	
Professional research and management.	

———◆———

CHAPTER FOUR

Know What You're Buying: Part Two

Mutual Funds, Funds of Funds, Annuities, and ETFs

I've found that when the market's going down and you buy funds wisely, at some point in the future you will be happy. You won't get there by reading, "Now is the time to buy."

—Peter Lynch

MUTUAL FUNDS

Mutual funds pool money from lots of investors to buy securities. Those securities can be stocks, bonds, or money market instruments, as well as other types of investments. As an investor in a mutual fund, you actually own a small fractional interest in the underlying pool of securities purchased by the managers of your mutual fund.

Mutual funds are governed by the Investment Company Act of 1940, and in most cases by the states where they do business.

Mutual funds are available in many varieties. There are equity mutual funds that invest in stocks, bond funds that invest in (you guessed it!) bonds, and funds that invest in a combination of both stocks and bonds (*hybrid* or *balanced* funds). There are also money market funds, whose goal is to offer a stable $1 per share value.

Within each type of mutual fund (equity fund, bond fund), there are a number of funds with differing investment objectives. For instance, equity mutual funds include these funds:

- Aggressive growth funds
- Growth funds
- Growth and income funds
- International funds
- Sector and specialty funds (such as REITs [Real Estate Investment Trusts] and health care)

Just as with equity mutual funds, bond fund investors have a wide range of bond mutual funds to choose from. There are bond funds that invest only in investment-grade bonds (those with higher safety ratings), and there are high-yield (*junk*) bond funds that invest in bonds that are rated below investment grade. Some bond funds invest in only U.S. Treasury issues, while other funds invest strictly in corporate bonds. Still others invest in municipal bonds.

Depending on the maturity dates of the bonds the funds invest in, various term bond funds are available. The most common are these three:

1. Short-term bond funds (1- to 4-year maturity)
2. Intermediate-term bond funds (4- to 10-year maturity)
3. Long-term bond funds (10-year or greater maturity)

Within each of these categories, there are taxable bond funds as well as tax-exempt municipal bond funds.

Some mutual funds invest in both equities and bonds within the same fund. These funds are known as *balanced funds*. However, not all balanced funds hold the same percentage of stocks and bonds. For example, one balanced fund might hold 60 percent stocks and 40 percent bonds (probably the most common mix), while others might hold only 40 percent in equities and 60 percent in bonds.

MUTUAL FUND MANAGEMENT STYLES

There are two major types of mutual fund management styles: active management and indexing. With *indexing,* the fund attempts to replicate as close as possible the return of a particular benchmark, such as the S&P 500, the Wilshire 5000, or the Barclay's Capital Aggregate Bond Index. The index fund managers generally do not buy stocks and bonds that are not in their benchmark, and they hold individual stocks and bonds in proportion to the weight of the stock or bond in the benchmark.

Active managers attempt to select stocks and bonds that they hope will result in their fund outperforming their benchmark, or achieving returns similar to the benchmark but with less risk. Because of the higher costs associated with many actively managed funds, active managers have a much higher hurdle to overcome in order to outperform their lower-cost index fund counterparts. Although some active managers do succeed in outperforming their index fund counterparts each year, over long periods of time, very few managers consistently outperform.

The real problem an investor has is trying to identify, in advance, those active managers who will outperform their index over the long haul. It's not an easy task. However, you can increase the odds of doing so by selecting a good low-cost, actively managed fund, such as those offered by Vanguard and other low-cost providers.

Read the Prospectus. The mutual fund prospectus is the single best way to find out about the objectives, costs, past performance figures, and other important information about any mutual fund you're considering investing in. Although reading a prospectus may cause your eyes to glaze over, it's a very important step to help you determine if a particular fund satisfies your investment objectives (risk, return, etc.). Since you are planning on investing for the long-term (you are, aren't you?), reading a prospectus and understanding what you're investing in will be well worth the time and effort. We can't emphasize it enough: *Read the fund's prospectus and understand what you're investing in!*

Advantages of Mutual Funds. There are at least 10 advantages:

1. *Diversification.* The costs involved in purchasing a diversified portfolio of individual stocks and bonds could be prohibitive for most investors. However, since each mutual fund invests in a large number of stocks, bonds, or both, you get instant diversification when you buy a mutual fund.
2. *Professional management.* Whether your fund is an index fund or an actively managed one, there are professional managers at the helm.
3. *Low minimums.* Although each mutual fund establishes its own minimum purchase requirements, you can actually purchase some mutual funds by promising to invest as little as $50 per month. More normal fund purchase minimums are in the $1,000 to $3,000 range.
4. *No loads or commissions.* Many mutual funds offer their products with no sales commissions (loads). You can buy the funds directly from the mutual fund company without having to use a broker or advisor.
5. *Liquidity.* Since open-end mutual funds stand ready to redeem your fund shares for the current net asset value (NAV) any day the market is open for trading, you've got a ready buyer any time you need to sell.

6. *Automatic reinvestment.* If you wish, you can arrange for your fund's dividends and capital gains to be automatically reinvested in the fund, or directed to other funds.
7. *Convenience.* You can buy and sell most mutual funds by mail, phone, or online. You can set things up so that the proceeds from any fund's redemptions or distributions will be deposited into your bank account. Automatic purchases from your bank account or money market mutual fund can also be arranged, as can periodic withdrawals. And money market funds offer a good place to park your money while it's waiting to be invested.
8. *Customer service.* If you have a question or a problem, you can call your mutual fund's customer service folks and they'll be glad to help you. Most mutual fund companies offer extended hours for their customer service, well beyond the normal market trading hours.
9. *Communications and record keeping.* You'll receive statements on a regular basis, showing any activity on your account, as well as tax-reporting information at the end of each year. Many mutual funds even calculate tax-reporting information for you. You'll also receive semiannual and annual reports on your funds from the fund managers, which contain important information about your fund.
10. *Variety.* Finally, because of the wide selection of funds available, you can probably find a fund to fit just about any investment needs you might have.

So, as we've seen, mutual funds have a lot to offer. We feel strongly that they should be the investment of choice for most individual investors.

Funds of Funds

In an attempt to simplify investing, a recent trend has developed that allows investors to obtain a nicely diversified portfolio by choosing a single mutual fund that meets their desired asset allocation. These offerings invest in other mutual funds, normally from the same company, and usually include stock, bond, and money market mutual funds—thus the name *funds of funds*.

Some of these funds maintain a fairly stable ratio of stocks, bonds, and cash at all times, so it's up to investors to switch to a more conservative fund as they get older and closer to retirement. The various LifeStrategy funds offered by Vanguard are good examples of these types of funds. Let's take a look at the composition of a couple of these funds.

The Vanguard LifeStrategy Growth Fund has a fairly aggressive target asset allocation of 80 percent stocks and 20 percent bonds. This fund of funds invests in four Vanguard funds:

1. Total Stock Market Index Fund
2. Total Bond Market Fund
3. Total International Stock Index Fund
4. Total International Bond Fund

The Vanguard LifeStrategy Conservative Growth Fund has a more conservative target asset allocation of 40 percent stocks and 60 percent bonds. This fund of funds invests in four Vanguard funds:

1. Total Stock Market Index Fund
2. Total Bond Market Fund
3. Total International Stock Index Fund
4. Total International Bond Fund

There are two other funds in the Vanguard LifeStrategy series that offer differing asset allocations. They include the LifeStrategy Moderate Growth Fund, which has a target asset allocation of 60 percent stocks and 40 percent bonds, and the LifeStrategy Income Fund, with a very conservative target asset allocation of 80 percent bonds and 20 percent stocks. So there's a good chance that one of these funds of funds might meet your desired asset allocation.

The more recent products introduced by some fund companies include life-cycle funds of funds that automatically get more conservative as time goes by. As with other funds of funds, the investor simply picks the nicely diversified fund that satisfies their present desired asset allocation. However, unlike other funds of funds that maintain a fairly constant percentage of stocks, bonds, and cash, these life-cycle funds lower the percentage of stocks and increase the percentage of bonds and cash over the years. With the introduction of these life-cycle funds, the mutual fund companies are attempting to simplify things for investors by relieving them of the need to rebalance on a regular basis. And with these funds, there's no need for an investor to have to change their portfolio as they age and get closer to retirement. The Target Retirement series of funds from Vanguard and the Freedom series of funds from Fidelity are good examples of this type of fund.

ANNUITIES

Annuities are an investment with an insurance wrapper. They are available in several different varieties, including fixed annuities, variable annuities, and immediate annuities.

Fixed Annuities

A fixed annuity is similar in some ways to a bank CD, but it's actually an insurance product that agrees to pay you a specific rate of return (say 4 to 6 percent) for a specified period of time (usually one to five years) on the money that you originally invest in the contract. After that specified period of time, your rate of return will revert back to *market rates,* as determined and set by the insurance company that issued the annuity contract.

Most fixed annuities have a low guaranteed *minimum* rate that they'll pay on your investment. Often, the fixed annuity offers a short-term (perhaps one year) initial rate that is set to pay a much higher rate than you could get if you were to purchase a bank CD at that time. (These are known as *teaser* rates.) However, the higher-than-normal initial rates on these fixed annuities are often accompanied by "gotcha" lower subsequent rates and high surrender fees. You might think of an annuity's *surrender fee* as being similar to an early withdrawal penalty on a bank CD. However, these annuity surrender fees (penalties) can be very costly, with some set at more than 10 percent of the withdrawal. Surrender fees can last for up to 10 years or even longer, depending on which insurance company issued your annuity. These fees are normally reduced by 1 percent for each year you own the annuity until they eventually disappear. As a result of these surrender fees, which are often not explained to the annuity buyer, once the expiration date of the initial high-rate period has passed, they can make it financially impractical for you to withdraw your money. That's true even if you find that the new interest rates the insurance company offers are not competitive with what you could receive elsewhere. Now you understand why it's called a *gotcha.*

The money you invest in a fixed annuity is mingled with the insurance company's operating funds, so if the insurance company has financial problems, you may have problems, too. Fixed annuities offer tax deferral, even when purchased with nonqualified (after-tax) funds.

Variable Annuities

A variable annuity is an insurance contract that allows you to invest in a number of sub-accounts. Sub-accounts are basically just clones of mutual funds, with some insurance coverage thrown in. We'll use the two terms interchangeably here.

Most variable annuities have surrender fees, often lasting for many years. So, once you've purchased your annuity, even if you're not satisfied, you can't get all of your money back without paying the surrender fee that's in effect at the time of withdrawal.

In addition, variable annuity fund expenses tend to be much higher than their nonannuity mutual fund counterparts. For example, Morningstar's Principia annuity database shows that nearly 9,500 variable annuity sub-accounts have total annual expenses that are greater than 2.5 percent, more than 4,500 sub-accounts have total annual expenses greater than 2.75 percent, and nearly 2,000 variable annuity sub-accounts have total annual expenses that are greater than 3.0 percent. In our opinion, that's simply outrageous, since that's more than 15 times the cost of a low-cost broad-based mutual fund such as Vanguard's Total Stock Market Index, which has total annual expenses of 0.17 percent.

Variable annuities from one insurance company might offer only a limited number of sub-accounts to choose from, while an annuity from another company may have a very long list of mutual funds. You can own several funds and switch between these funds in your variable annuity without any tax consequences. The value of your variable annuity will depend on the performance of the mutual funds that you choose to invest in.

Fixed annuities and variable annuities have some similarities and some differences. For example, like fixed annuities, variable annuities offer tax deferral, even when purchased with after-tax funds. However, unlike fixed annuities, the money you invest in a variable annuity is segregated from the insurance company's operating funds. Thus, the safety of your investment is not tied to the financial strength of the insurance company that issued your annuity.

Since variable annuities are already tax-deferred, if you have a choice, there's typically no benefit to investing in an annuity inside an already tax-deferred retirement plan, such as a 401(k), 403(b), or IRA. You wouldn't be gaining any additional tax-deferral benefit from paying the higher expenses of the variable annuity. That's like wearing two raincoats when one will suffice!

Immediate Annuities

An immediate annuity is a contract between you and an insurance company. In exchange for a sum of money from you, the insurance company will promise to pay you a specific amount of money, on a regular basis, for the remainder of your lifetime. And if you're willing to accept smaller payments, the insurance company will guarantee that those payments will continue for the remainder of both your and your spouse's lives or for a specified period of time. You cannot outlive this income stream, even if you live to be 100 plus.

As with fixed annuities, these payment guarantees are backed by the financial strength of the insurance company you purchase the annuity from. Therefore, it's very important that you check on the safety ratings of the insurance company prior to purchasing an immediate annuity. You should know, too, that not all immediate annuities will pay you the same amount, so you'll need to shop around for the best deal, again considering the financial strength of the various insurance companies. Unlike fixed and variable annuities, there are no surrender charges involved, since once you make the decision to purchase an immediate annuity and start receiving payments, you can't normally get your money back.

Because of their high costs and surrender fees, and the decreased tax benefits of annuities in relation to more tax-efficient investments available, annuities really don't have much to offer most investors. It's probably safe to say that most annuities are *sold* and not *bought*. We've heard horror stories about unscrupulous annuity sales folks who sold inappropriate annuities with high surrender fees to trusting older folks who were in a low (or no) tax bracket and had absolutely no need for a high-priced tax-deferred annuity product. There are a number of other lower-cost, tax-deferred, and tax-free investment options available, such as 401(k) plans, IRAs, Roth IRAs, and other retirement plans. Investors should fund these retirement plan options before ever considering a variable annuity.

And now, with the lower tax rates on qualified dividends and long-term capital gains, once they've funded their retirement plans, most investors would probably be better served by investing any extra money they have in their taxable account, rather than in a variable annuity. However, it should be noted that Vanguard and a few other companies do offer low-cost variable annuities with no sales charges or surrender fees. So, if you already own a high-cost variable annuity, and the surrender fees have expired, or are very low, you might want to consider doing a tax-free transfer (they're known as 1035 exchanges) to a low-cost annuity provider. And, if you don't currently own one, but you feel that an annuity does have a place in your portfolio, then you'd definitely want to invest your hard-earned money in a low-cost annuity, such as those offered by Vanguard.

The Securities and Exchange Commission (SEC) has an excellent primer where you can get more information on variable annuities at www.sec.gov/investor/pubs/varannty.htm#wvar.

EXCHANGE-TRADED FUNDS

Exchange-traded funds (ETFs) are basically mutual funds that trade like stocks on an exchange. They are bought and sold continuously throughout the day when the stock market is open. The ETF's stocklike features appeal to a wide range of investors, including long-term buy-and-hold investors, as well as short-term traders. Perhaps one of the biggest benefits of owning ETFs is the low cost. ETF expenses can be as low, or even lower, than many mutual funds that track the same index.

ETFs are available that follow both foreign and domestic equity indexes. There are ETFs that follow bond indexes, as well. Although many ETFs track a particular index, there are an increasing number of actively managed ETFs.

Unlike regular mutual funds, which are priced at net asset value (NAV) only once a day at the close of business by the fund company, based on the value of the securities owned by the fund, ETFs are priced continuously throughout the day, by an open market system, as are stocks, whenever the stock market is open. This makes ETFs attractive to those investors who wish to trade during the day and know the exact price of their trade.

There are some downsides to ETFs. First, you have to use a broker each time you buy and sell, and that usually means you'll be charged a commission for each transaction. Needless to say, the shorter the holding period, the more these added commission costs could negate any benefits of the ETF's lower expenses. As a result, ETFs are not suited for investors who make a number of smaller purchases, such as with dollar-cost averaging, since they'd have to pay a commission on each purchase. Rather, these investors should stick with low-cost, open-end index mutual funds.

Another potential downside is the difference between the market value of an ETF share and the NAV of the underlying securities that make up the ETF. Because ETFs are market traded, they can trade at a slight premium or discount to the value of the underlying securities held in the fund. Generally, the premium or discount is not very large, but you need to be aware of it.

However, ETFs may be appropriate for investors who can make large, one-time purchases with the intention of holding them for a long period of time. In this situation, the one-time commission may well be more than offset by the reduced expenses incurred over a long period of time. In addition, ETFs may also be appropriate for investors who can't find a low-cost index fund to cover a particular segment of the market that they're interested in.

It's important to note that Vanguard offers their low-cost ETFs commission-free, eliminating the previously mentioned downside associated with having to pay commissions to buy and sell ETFs.

When used properly, low-cost ETFs can certainly play an important role in a long-term investor's buy-and-hold portfolio. On the other hand, investors are likely to shoot themselves in the foot if they plan to use ETFs as day trading or market timing vehicles.

WHAT WE'VE LEARNED

We hope you now have a better understanding of some of the various mainstream investments available to you, and how they may, or may not, fit into your investment plans. You can learn more about these various investments by doing additional reading, as well as by making use of the wealth of free information available on the Internet, starting with the Bogleheads Forum (www.bogleheads.org).

The three of us made a number of mistakes early in our investing careers, and we learned a lot from those mistakes. Through experience and investor education, we've become more knowledgeable over the years. At the end of that journey, we've come to the conclusion that low-cost mutual funds should be the primary investment of choice for most investors.

CHAPTER FIVE

Preserve Your Buying Power with Inflation-Protected Bonds

Control your destiny or somebody else will.

—Jack Welch

I nflation is like a silent thief in the night that comes, sight unseen, and steals our valuables. Unlike the burglar who takes our visible assets, inflation is much more insidious because it steals something that we can't really see—our future buying power.

If we were to start with $1,000 and end up with $1,000 10 years later, some investors would say they hadn't lost anything. They couldn't be more wrong! The $1,000 is merely an exchange medium, and its only value is the amount of goods or services that someone will give us in exchange for that $1,000. So what's really important is not the dollar *amount*, but rather its *purchasing power*, or what it will buy.

Inflation erodes the future spending power of our present dollars, so we'll need more dollars at some future date to purchase the same amount of goods and services in order to offset the effects of that inflation.

In Chapter 2, we learned how the power of compounding works *for* us. However, that same power of compounding works *against* us when it comes to inflation. An inflation rate of 3 percent means that when a 25-year-old investor retires in 40 years, she'll need $3,262 to buy the same basket of goods and services that she can buy for $1,000 today. If inflation were 4 percent over that same period, she'd need $4,801. Of course, if inflation were still higher, it follows that the amount needed to purchase those same goods and services would be even greater.

Since some of us will live an additional 20 to 30 years in retirement, we're talking about a 25-year-old investor having to deal with the effects of inflation eroding the future buying power of her savings for perhaps as long as 60 to 70 years.

We used official U.S. Department of Labor, Bureau of Labor Statistics inflation figures and an online calculator provided by the Federal Reserve Bank of Minneapolis to create Table 5.1. It shows the effects of inflation over different time periods in the United States, as well as the amount we would have needed at the end of each of these various time periods to equal the buying power of $1,000 at the beginning of the period.

These inflation figures are sobering, perhaps even a bit scary. They show, in rather dramatic fashion, how destructive the ravages of inflation can be on the future spending power of our current assets. We hope you now understand what you're up against, and just how important it is for you to invest not only to protect your principal, but to protect and hopefully increase your future spending power as well. But just how do we go about it?

Conventional wisdom states that equities should be the investment of choice for outstripping inflation. However, conventional wisdom doesn't come with any guarantee, and there have been overlapping periods when both small-company stocks (as defined by the Center for Research in Stock Prices), and large-company stocks (as defined by the S&P 500 Index), have failed to outpace inflation.

There have also been long periods when some ultrasafe Treasury investments, such as one-month Treasury Bills and long-term Government Bonds, haven't posted positive *real returns*. (Remember, we said earlier that *real return* is the amount we have left after we subtract inflation from our rate of return.) If we look at the top line on Figure 5.1, we can see what the nominal annualized return (before inflation) of T-Bills has been. That line might give us the impression that T-Bills have been a winning investment over the years. However, when we look at the lower line, we see that the annualized T-Bill's *real return* has been negative for many years. During those negative years, T-Bill investors actually lost spending power, and that was *before* taxes.

TABLE **5.1**   EFFECTS OF INFLATION OVER VARIOUS TIME PERIODS

TIME PERIOD	NUMBER OF YEARS	AMOUNT NEEDED IN 2005 TO EQUAL $1,000 AT BEGINNING OF PERIOD
1935–2005	70	$14,255
1940–2005	65	$13,950
1945–2005	60	$10,850
1950–2005	55	$ 8,103
1955–2005	50	$ 7,287
1960–2005	45	$ 6,597
1965–2005	40	$ 6,200
1970–2005	35	$ 5,033
1975–2005	30	$ 3,630
1980–2005	25	$ 2,370
1985–2005	20	$ 1,815
1990–2005	15	$ 1,494
1995–2005	10	$ 1,281
2000–2005	5	$ 1,134

So where can an investor turn to for a *guaranteed* positive real return? The U.S. Treasury currently offers two choices that satisfy this need— I Bonds and Treasury Inflation-Indexed Securities, commonly referred to as TIPS (Treasury Inflation-Protected Securities). We've mentioned both in previous chapters, but let's now examine how they work in more detail.

FIGURE  5.1   T-BILL RETURNS

Source: Copyright Portfolio Solutions, LLC.

I BONDS

I Bonds (the "I" stands for Inflation) are U.S. Savings Bonds. They're issued by the U.S. Treasury, and are backed by the full faith and credit of the U.S. government, which means that they are risk-free. I Bonds are issued with a fixed rate that is guaranteed to provide a *real return* equal to the fixed rate of the bond at the time of issue.

The I Bond's yield is made up of two parts:

1. The first component of the yield is the fixed or *real rate* that's in effect when you purchase the I Bond. This *real rate* is the amount you'll receive over and above inflation, and it remains the same for the life of the bond (up to 30 years).
2. The second component of the yield is a variable inflation-adjustment rate that's recalculated and announced twice annually, in May and November. This variable rate is based on the rate of inflation over the six-month measuring period just prior to the adjustment dates, as measured by the CPI-U.

Adding these two components (the fixed rate and inflation adjustment) together gives you the current yield for the next six-month period following the announcement date. For example, if the guaranteed *real rate* on the I Bond is 1.2 percent at the time of issue, and the previously announced inflation figure at the time of purchase was 3 percent, you'd earn 4.2 percent (1.2 percent fixed plus 3 percent inflation) for the first six months that you owned the I Bond. Then, if inflation rose to 4 percent during the first six months, you'd start earning 5.2 percent (1.2 percent fixed plus 4 percent inflation) for the second six months. Interest is recalculated twice annually, and that pattern continues for 30 years, unless you redeem the bonds prior to that.

Therefore, since the Treasury adds the rate of inflation to the I Bond's fixed rate to determine the total yield, the before-tax return on I Bonds is guaranteed to be equal to or higher than inflation.

The only drawback in this scenario is that Uncle Sam not only takes his portion of our *real return*, but he also benefits from the inflation portion of the yield on our I Bonds, since the IRS taxes *both parts* of our return. As a result, it's possible that some investors who buy I Bonds with very low guaranteed real return rates and then cash them in when they're in a high tax bracket could possibly end up with less spending power than they started with. However, since I Bonds are tax-deferred for up to 30 years, many investors should be able to postpone cashing in their I Bonds until after they're retired and are in a lower tax bracket.

Let's take a look at how various I Bond fixed interest rates, tax brackets, and inflation rate scenarios play out. Table 5.2 shows the after-tax, inflation-adjusted spending power for I Bond investors in various tax brackets. We compare the performance of two I Bonds, one issued with a 1 percent fixed rate (top half of the table) and one issued with a 1.5 percent fixed rate (bottom half of the table). The inflation rate used in this example is 2 percent.

We can see in Table 5.2 that, with the exception of the 35-percent-tax-bracket investor who only holds a 1 percent fixed-rate I Bond for five years, all tax brackets and all time frames provide a *positive real after-tax* return. Naturally, the lower the investor's tax bracket, the higher the after-tax real return, since Uncle Sam is getting less and we're keeping more. We can also see that the 1.5 percent fixed-rate I Bond overcame even the highest tax bracket and shortest holding period to produce a positive after-tax real return.

Now let's change the inflation rate to 4 percent in Table 5.3 and see how these same I Bonds perform.

Table 5.3 illustrates how the taxation on the higher inflation rate takes its toll on the higher-tax-bracket investors. With the 1 percent fixed-rate I Bond, investors in the 33 percent and 35 percent tax brackets can't

TABLE 5.2 REAL AFTER-TAX RETURN OF $1,000 1% I BOND AND $1,000 1.5% I BOND WITH 2% INFLATION OVER DIFFERENT TIME PERIODS

TAX BRACKET	FIXED RATE	INFLATION RATE	5 YRS.	10 YRS.	15 YRS.	20 YRS.	25 YRS.	30 YRS.
10.00%	1.0%	2%	$1,036	$1,074	$1,116	$1,161	$1,210	$1,261
15.00%	1.0%	2%	$1,028	$1,060	$1,095	$1,134	$1,176	$1,222
25.00%	1.0%	2%	$1,014	$1,032	$1,054	$1,080	$1,110	$1,143
28.00%	1.0%	2%	$1,010	$1,023	$1,042	$1,064	$1,090	$1,119
33.00%	1.0%	2%	$1,002	$1,009	$1,021	$1,036	$1,056	$1,080
35.00%	1.0%	2%	$ 999	$1,004	$1,012	$1,026	$1,043	$1,064
10.00%	1.5%	2%	$1,059	$1,123	$1,195	$1,272	$1,357	$1,450
15.00%	1.5%	2%	$1,050	$1,107	$1,170	$1,239	$1,316	$1,400
25.00%	1.5%	2%	$1,033	$1,073	$1,119	$1,173	$1,233	$1,300
28.00%	1.5%	2%	$1,028	$1,063	$1,104	$1,153	$1,208	$1,270
33.00%	1.5%	2%	$1,020	$1,046	$1,079	$1,119	$1,166	$1,220
35.00%	1.5%	2%	$1,016	$1,039	$1,069	$1,106	$1,150	$1,200

Real After-Tax Return of $1,000 1% I Bond and $1,000 1.5% I Bond with 4% Inflation over Different Time Periods

Tax Bracket	Fixed Rate	Inflation Rate	5 Yrs.	10 Yrs.	15 Yrs.	20 Yrs.	25 Yrs.	30 Yrs.
10.00%	1.0%	4%	$1,026	$1,058	$1,094	$1,135	$1,181	$1,230
15.00%	1.0%	4%	$1,015	$1,037	$1,064	$1,098	$1,136	$1,179
25.00%	1.0%	4%	$ 992	$ 994	$1,005	$1,022	$1,046	$1,076
28.00%	1.0%	4%	$ 985	$ 981	$ 987	$1,000	$1,020	$1,046
33.00%	1.0%	4%	$ 974	$ 960	$ 957	$ 962	$ 975	$ 995
35.00%	1.0%	4%	$ 970	$ 952	$ 945	$ 947	$ 957	$ 974
10.00%	1.5%	4%	$1,049	$1,106	$1,171	$1,244	$1,325	$1,414
15.00%	1.5%	4%	$1,036	$1,082	$1,137	$1,200	$1,272	$1,352
25.00%	1.5%	4%	$1,011	$1,034	$1,069	$1,113	$1,167	$1,230
28.00%	1.5%	4%	$1,004	$1,020	$1,048	$1,087	$1,135	$1,193
33.00%	1.5%	4%	$ 991	$ 996	$1,014	$1,043	$1,082	$1,131
35.00%	1.5%	4%	$ 986	$ 987	$1,000	$1,025	$1,061	$1,107

TABLE 5.4 REAL AFTER-TAX RETURN OF $1,000 1.8% I BOND AND $1,000 2.0% I BOND WITH 4% INFLATION OVER DIFFERENT TIME PERIODS

Tax Bracket	Fixed Rate	Inflation Rate	5 Yrs.	10 Yrs.	15 Yrs.	20 Yrs.	25 Yrs.	30 Yrs.
10.00%	1.8%	4%	$1,063	$1,136	$1,220	$1,314	$1,420	$1,537
15.00%	1.8%	4%	$1,049	$1,110	$1,183	$1,266	$1,362	$1,469
25.00%	1.8%	4%	$1,023	$1,059	$1,109	$1,171	$1,246	$1,332
28.00%	1.8%	4%	$1,015	$1,044	$1,087	$1,143	$1,211	$1,291
33.00%	1.8%	4%	$1,001	$1,018	$1,050	$1,095	$1,153	$1,223
35.00%	1.8%	4%	$996	$1,008	$1,035	$1,076	$1,130	$1,196
10.00%	2.0%	4%	$1,072	$1,156	$1,253	$1,363	$1,486	$1,625
15.00%	2.0%	4%	$1,058	$1,130	$1,214	$1,313	$1,425	$1,551
25.00%	2.0%	4%	$1,022	$1,060	$1,114	$1,182	$1,264	$1,361
33.00%	2.0%	4%	$1,008	$1,034	$1,075	$1,131	$1,202	$1,288
35.00%	2.0%	4%	$1,003	$1,023	$1,059	$1,111	$1,178	$1,259

overcome the higher taxes to realize positive real returns, even if they hold an I Bond for 30 years. And the 1.5 percent fixed-rate I-Bond investors in the higher tax brackets have to hold their bonds for at least 15 years in order to achieve positive after-tax real returns.

In Table 5.4, we've increased the I Bond fixed rates to 1.8 percent and 2.0 percent to see how they perform with the same 4 percent inflation rate we used in Table 5.3.

With the higher fixed rates, even with 4 percent inflation, the I Bonds are still able to overcome the taxes and provide a positive after-tax real return in all tax brackets and for all time frames except for the 35-percent-tax-bracket investor who only holds the 1.8 percent fixed-rate I Bond for five years.

Hopefully the pattern is becoming clear. The higher the I Bond's fixed rate, the lower your tax bracket, and the longer the holding period, the better the odds are that you'll realize a higher after-tax real return. With

TABLE **5.5**   I BOND FIXED-RATE HISTORY

DATE	FIXED RATE	DATE	FIXED RATE	DATE	FIXED RATE
SEP 1, 1998	3.40%	NOV 1, 2003	1.10%	MAY 1, 2009	0.1%
NOV 1, 1998	3.30%	MAY 1, 2004	1.00%	NOV 1, 2009	0.3%
MAY 1, 1999	3.30%	NOV 1, 2004	1.00%	MAY 1, 2010	0.2%
NOV 1, 1999	3.40%	MAY 1, 2005	1.20%	NOV 1, 2010	0%
MAY 1, 2000	3.60%	NOV 1, 2005	1.00%	MAY 1, 2011	0%
NOV 1, 2000	3.40%	MAY 1, 2006	1.4%	NOV 1, 2011	0%
MAY 1, 2001	3.00%	NOV 1, 2006	1.4%	MAY 1, 2012	0%
NOV 1, 2001	2.00%	MAY 1, 2007	1.3%	NOV 1, 2012	0%
MAY 1, 2002	2.00%	NOV 1, 2007	1.2%	MAY 1, 2013	0%
NOV 1, 2002	1.60%	MAY 1, 2008	0%	NOV 1, 2013	0.2%
MAY 1, 2003	1.10%	NOV 1, 2008	0.7%	MAY 1, 2014	0.1%

low or zero fixed rates, high inflation, short holding periods, and high tax brackets, investors are more likely to realize a negative after-tax real yield. Nevertheless, at times, even 0 percent fixed-rate I Bonds may offer better after-tax returns than other available risk-free options.

Even though we've seen I Bonds issued with fixed rates as high as 3.6 percent in the past, we probably shouldn't expect to see fixed rates increasing substantially any time soon. Table 5.5 clearly shows the pattern of declining I Bond fixed rates over time. Should the Treasury increase the fixed rates enough to make it profitable to do so, many investors holding lower-yielding I Bonds would simply cash them in with no loss of principal, pay the taxes due, and then reinvest in the new, higher-yielding bonds. Since the Treasury is well aware of this, we may have to deal with lower-yielding I Bonds for a long time.

TIPS

TIPS offer investors another U.S. Treasury-issued inflation-protection option. Unlike I Bonds, where the Treasury sets the fixed rate, the guaranteed rate on TIPS is established by the marketplace at the Treasury's TIPS auctions. Since they are a marketable security, we have more investment options available to us with TIPS than we do with I Bonds:

- Purchasing TIPS at the Treasury auctions
- Purchasing TIPS in the secondary market
- Investing in a TIPS fund, such as Vanguard's VIPSX or Fidelity's FINPX

If you're looking for guaranteed inflation protection from TIPS, with no risk of principal, buying your TIPS at the Treasury auction and holding them to maturity would be your best choice, since there's always the risk of some loss of principal with the other two options. For many investors, however, the flexibility and benefits of a TIPS mutual fund more than offset the risk of possible loss of principal, just as it does with any other bond mutual fund.

Location, Location, Location

TIPS-guaranteed rates are usually higher than I Bond fixed rates. Therefore, if you have room for them in your tax-deferred account, that's where they should go, because you'd get tax-deferred inflation protection without risking principal. This assumes that you purchase them at auction and hold them to maturity. If you buy or sell TIPS in the secondary market, you may get back more or less than you paid.

What if you don't have enough room for TIPS in your tax-deferred account? If your tax bracket is low, and the difference between the TIPS guaranteed rate and the I Bond fixed rate is large enough, it's possible that placing the TIPS in your taxable account might provide a slightly higher yield than would a lower-yielding I Bond.

When you own TIPS in your taxable account, the major downside is that you have to deal with the issue of paying annual taxes on some income that you won't receive until maturity. That's why it's called *phantom income*. On the plus side, though, if you live in a state with a high income tax, the interest from TIPS in a taxable account isn't subject to state and local taxes, whereas it may be subject to your state's income tax upon withdrawal from a tax-deferred account. Therefore, you'll have to work that into the equation.

Remember, with TIPS, you only receive the fixed-rate portion of the yield on the inflation-adjusted par value on a semiannual basis. The inflation adjustment gets applied to your TIPS principal, but you won't receive that until the bond matures. Therefore, the higher the rate of inflation, and the higher your tax bracket, the more taxes you'll be paying on both the income portion that you actually do receive, and on the inflation-adjusted portion that you haven't received. And, when fixed rates on TIPS are low, it's even conceivable that you could owe more in taxes than you receive in interest payments in a year when inflation is very high, especially if you're in a higher tax bracket.

In Table 5.6, we compare a 1 percent fixed-rate $1,000 tax-deferred I Bond to a 1.5 percent fixed-rate $1,000 10-year TIPS, purchased at auction and held to maturity in a taxable account. We use a 4 percent inflation rate.

As we can see in Table 5.6, the taxable 1.5 percent TIPS outperform the tax-deferred 1 percent I Bond in every tax bracket. The margins of victory for the TIPS range from $8 to $37 after 10 years.

Cautions for Investing in TIPS

There are a few caveats to the comparison in Table 5.6. First, if you had used a broker to purchase the TIPS for you, rather than purchasing it yourself at auction, then the TIPS might have actually underperformed the I Bond, once you factor in the broker's fee.

Additionally, the TIPS figures assume that after paying your annual taxes, you can then reinvest the remainder of the semiannual interest payments you received in another investment that earns the same real rate of

TABLE 5.6 $1,000 1% BOND VERSUS $1,000 1.5% 10-YEAR TIPS

TAX RATE	INFLATION RATE	AFTER-TAX REAL VALUE OF 1% I BOND AFTER 10 YEARS	AFTER-TAX REAL VALUE OF 1.5% TIPS AFTER 10 YEARS
10.00%	4.00%	$1,058	$1,095
15.00%	4.00%	$1,037	$1,067
25.00%	4.00%	$ 994	$1,012
28.00%	4.00%	$ 981	$ 996
33.00%	4.00%	$ 960	$ 970
35.00%	4.00%	$ 952	$ 960

return as the TIPS, and that may not always be possible. Finally, while the I Bond can be cashed in any time after one year with no loss of principal, the TIPS must be held to maturity in order to guarantee no loss of principal. That I Bond flexibility might be worth a slightly lower return to some investors.

SUMMARY: I BOND VERSUS TIPS

Using various rates of inflation up to and including 9 percent, the I Bond outperformed in some situations, and the TIPS outperformed in others. However, the difference between the returns of the 1 percent I Bond versus the 1.5 percent 10-year TIPS over 10 years was always less than $50, regardless of whether the TIPS or the I Bond outperformed. So basically, when comparing a 1 percent I Bond and a 1.5 percent TIPS, for all practical purposes, it's a toss-up.

Next, in Table 5.7, we compare a 1 percent fixed-rate I Bond with a 1.75 percent 20-year TIPS, purchased at auction and held to maturity in a taxable account. In this scenario, we use a 4 percent inflation rate.

In Table 5.7, we can see that the wider spread in the fixed yields (.75 percent) helps the taxable TIPS outperform the lower-yielding I Bond by $116 for those investors in the lowest tax bracket. While the $116 difference over 20 years may not be important to those with smaller

TABLE **5.7**   **$1,000 1% I BOND VERSUS $1,000 1.75% 20-YEAR TIPS**

TAX RATE	INFLATION RATE	AFTER-TAX REAL VALUE OF 1% I BOND AFTER 20 YEARS	AFTER-TAX REAL VALUE OF 1.75% TIPS AFTER 20 YEARS
10.00%	4.00%	$1,135	$1,252
15.00%	4.00%	$1,098	$1,185
25.00%	4.00%	$1,022	$1,062
28.00%	4.00%	$1,000	$1,027
33.00%	4.00%	$ 962	$ 972
35.00%	4.00%	$ 947	$ 951

amounts to invest, for investors with $50,000 or $100,000 to invest in the TIPS, the total difference might be more meaningful. Table 5.7 also shows that the taxable TIPS outperform by $10 and $4 over the 20-year period for investors in the 33 percent and 35 percent tax brackets. In this scenario, for all intents and purposes, it's a virtual toss-up between I Bonds and TIPS in a taxable account for investors in the highest tax brackets.

As we've seen in this chapter, I Bonds and TIPS can help an investor protect the future spending power of their current dollars.

CHAPTER SIX

How Much Do You Need to Save?

You really don't need to begin saving for retirement before you reach 60. At that point, simply save 250 percent of your income each year and you'll be able to retire comfortably at 70.
—Jonathan Pond

The answer to this question is probably uppermost in the minds of most investors who are trying to plan for their retirement. Some (perhaps most?) investors don't have the foggiest idea of where to start. They just hope and pray that things will work out in the end, and that they'll somehow be able to enjoy a comfortable retirement. However, since they're not sure just how much they'll need to retire comfortably, there's always that nagging feeling in the back of their minds that they might not be saving enough. Needless to say, this causes them to worry that they might not be on track to reach their retirement goals.

In this chapter, we'll give you some helpful guidelines and tools that you can use when you're doing your retirement planning. While the results won't be precise, these tools and guidelines will help to give you a better idea of how much you'll need to be financially secure once you reach retirement age.

There are a number of factors that will help us determine the amount we need to accumulate to achieve the retirement of our dreams:

1. The amount we save. Obviously, the more we save, the better off we'll be.
2. Our current age. This helps to determine how many years we have to save and invest, and how long our retirement investments will be able to work for us. Of course, the earlier we start saving and investing, the better chance we have of reaching our goals, thanks to the powerful effect of compounding over a larger number of years.
3. The age at which we plan to retire.
4. How many years we'll have to live off our retirement account, based on our life expectancy.
5. Whether we plan to leave an estate, or if we simply want to make sure that we don't run out of money before we run out of breath.
6. The expected rate of return on our investments.
7. The rate of inflation over our accumulation period.
8. Whether we can expect an inheritance prior to retirement.
9. Our other sources of income in retirement. These would include pensions, Social Security, reverse mortgage, and part-time work.

Although some of these variables are easy enough to determine (our current age and how much we're currently saving), many of these factors are more difficult to nail down.

Retirement Age

For some, the age at which we plan to retire depends a lot on when and if we have enough money to do so. Others may find that they enjoy their job or profession enough to want to continue to work as long as they possibly can. If you're not sure, perhaps it would be wise to simply choose the age at which you'll first be eligible to apply for full Social Security benefits (assuming you believe it's still going to be around), or when you can start collecting your pension, if you're entitled to one.

Years in Retirement

When planning for retirement, many investors use 65 as their retirement date, and then figure they'll spend another 25 years or so in retirement. However, with the continuing improvements in medicine and the growing longevity of the general population, we feel it might be more prudent for those investors who like to be more conservative in their planning to figure on funding 30 years in retirement. It's much better to have saved a bit too much, rather than not enough. In the end, though, each investor will have to elect to use a number they feel most comfortable with, based on their genetics and other factors they feel are important to them.

Leaving an Estate

Determining whether you want to leave an estate is a very personal decision. When pondering this question, you do need to remember that your first task is to accumulate enough to take care of you and, if you're married, your spouse, for the remainder of your days. Only after you've determined that you can surpass that milestone can you even think about leaving a legacy. If you're lucky enough to have sufficient income to take care of all your current needs, including funding the kids' college, your retirement needs, and a legacy, that's fine. If not, then you need to concentrate first on finding ways to save enough for your own needs, since you can't borrow for retirement.

After seeing how hard their parents worked and sacrificed for them, most children want to see their parents enjoy their retirement years, and they wouldn't enjoy receiving an inheritance if they knew it came at the expense of their parents' happiness in their golden years. Remember, one of the greatest gifts you can give your children is to be financially independent in your old age, thus ensuring that you won't become a financial burden to them.

Estimating Future Returns

Estimating the future returns on our portfolio may seem like an impossible assignment to many investors. It can be the single most daunting task we'll have to face when it comes to determining all of the variables we'll need to use as input to help us determine approximately how much we'll need to fund our retirement. Therefore, we'll spend a bit more time on this issue.

If we had a clear crystal ball, we could use it to easily (and accurately) determine, ahead of time, what the future rate of return on our investments would be. But, since most of our crystal balls are pretty foggy, we'll have to find some other means to come up with a working estimate. Finding these other means, though, can be the hardest part of this task, especially if we don't know where to start looking. However, arriving at the best approximation of our portfolio's expected return is well worth the time and effort required, since it's going to have a big impact on our calculations. We've all heard the phrase "Garbage in, garbage out," and it applies here as well.

Fortunately, there's a much better way to arrive at a reasonable portfolio return estimate than checking our foggy crystal balls or throwing darts.

Bogleheads Forum regular contributor, author Richard Ferri, CFA, of Portfolio Solutions, LLC, has prepared a 30-year market forecast, which Rick has graciously allowed us to share with you. It can be viewed online at www.portfoliosolutions.com.

Rick arrived at his estimated return figures by analyzing a number of economic and market risk factors, including Federal Reserve forecasts, inflation forecasts derived from inflation-protected securities, and the volatility of asset classes, styles, and categories.

You can use Rick's market-return forecast figures as a guide to help you estimate the expected returns from your portfolio, based on your portfolio's percentage of holdings in each of the individual asset classes and categories listed. Although it's not guaranteed to be bulletproof, a lot of work went into these figures, so they're a good starting point. Obviously, you'll have to monitor your actual returns and compare them with your estimated returns from time to time. You may even need to make adjustments along the way, either in your asset allocation, or in the amount you need to save to reach your goals. However, you've at least got some reasonable working numbers to start out with.

Table 6.1 shows some of Rick's estimated return figures that you might find useful as a starting point in calculating your portfolio's expected return. The table includes both estimated total returns as well as estimated *real returns* (total return minus inflation). Numbers are based on 2 percent inflation.

Using these estimated total return figures, you'd then apply each percentage to the proportion that it represents in your portfolio.

Here's an example of how you would calculate the expected return on a portfolio that contained 30 percent U.S. large-cap stocks, 10 percent U.S. small-cap value stocks, 20 percent international developed country stocks, 10 percent REITs, and 30 percent intermediate-term high-grade corporate bonds.

1. U.S. large caps expected return = 2.1 percent (30 percent × 7 percent)
2. U.S. small caps expected return = 0.73 percent (10 percent × 7.3 percent)
3. International expected return = 1.48 percent (20 percent × 7.4 percent)

TABLE 6.1   ESTIMATED RETURNS

Asset Class and Category	Estimated Total Return	Less Estimated Inflation	Equals Estimated Real Return
T-Bills	2.1%	2%	0.1%
Intermediate Treasury Notes	3.9%	2%	1.9%
Intermediate High-Grade Corporate Bonds	4.6%	2%	2.6%
U.S. Large-Cap Stocks	7.0%	2%	5.0%
U.S. Small-Cap Stocks	7.3%	2%	5.3%
U.S. Small-Cap Value Stocks	8.0%	2%	6.0%
REITs	7.0%	2%	5.0%
International Developed Country Stocks	7.4%	2%	5.4%

Source: © Portfolio Solutions, LLC.

4. REIT expected return = 0.7 percent (10 percent × 7 percent)
5. Intermediate-term corporate bond expected return = 1.38 percent (30 percent × 4.6 percent)

So, in this example, the portfolio's total expected return would be 6.39 percent (2.1 percent + 0.73 percent + 1.48 percent + 0.7 percent + 1.38 percent).

If these estimated return figures seem low to you, especially in light of the exceptionally high returns you might have experienced in the previous bull market, you're most likely a victim of recency bias (projecting recent events into the future). To overcome any recency bias, you need to be aware of and understand the powerful magnetic market force known as *reversion to the mean* (*RTM*).

Although there are no absolute guarantees with RTM, usually asset classes that have outperformed for a period of time are likely to underperform for another period of time. For example, during the period from 1993 to 2012, the volatile emerging markets segment of the market was at or near the top for 11 years and at or near the bottom for 8 years. You can get an excellent visual presentation of RTM by viewing the Callan asset class performance charts at www.callan.com. Hopefully this will cure any recency bias, and we can move on to the next item on our list, inflation.

Inflation

Since we just covered inflation in Chapter 5, you should realize that it erodes the future spending power of our current assets, so we need to account for inflation in our calculations. If not, we'll most likely find ourselves well short of the amount we'll need at retirement. You can use any inflation number you're comfortable with, but if you're not sure, perhaps it will help to know that over a very long period of time (1914 to 2013), inflation averaged 3.22 percent in the United States. From 1964 to 2013, inflation averaged 4.18 percent, while the average inflation from 2004 to 2013 was 2.47 percent. While there have been periods where inflation was both higher and lower than the average for each period, these figures will give you a good starting point.

Inheritance

If you're hoping for an inheritance to fund the major part of your retirement, it's important to understand that doing so could be dangerous to your financial health. The inheritance you hoped to get could well disappear when one or both of your parents have to spend an extended period of time in a long-term-care facility. Or you might find yourself at retirement age with two very healthy parents who are having the time of their lives and who have no immediate plans to depart this earth. So, for most investors, we'd recommend not using any expected inheritance in your initial planning. Rather, if it turns out that you actually do get the inheritance later, simply consider it to be a windfall. If and when you do get a windfall, and you plan to use some or all of it for your retirement needs, then you can recalculate your retirement needs at that time, based on these new funds.

Other Income

Our final variable includes any income from such sources as Social Security, pensions, part-time employment, sale of a home when downsizing, and reverse mortgages. If you'll be receiving installment payments from the sale of a business or farm, that would be included here as well. All of these various sources of income can be used to help pay for current living expenses in retirement. The income from these sources will reduce the amount that you need to withdraw from your portfolio, and the less you need to withdraw, the less you'll need to save.

PUTTING WHAT WE'VE LEARNED TO WORK

Now that we've talked about the input variables we need to consider, it's time to apply what we've learned and try to answer the question, "How much do I need to save?"

There are lots of different financial calculators available on the Internet that you can use at no charge. Some require you to input your estimated portfolio returns, while others use an assumed rate of return in their calculations. That's why it's important to know your portfolio's estimated return, even if the calculator you use has an expected rate of return built in. Remember, the assumptions the calculator uses may be entirely different than the expected return number you arrived at for your portfolio, when you use the method we discussed earlier in the chapter. Therefore, it's important that you use a calculator that allows you to input your own estimated return data, or that uses assumptions that are more in line with your return expectations.

Some calculators, like the one at www.bloomberg.com, will use your current portfolio value and annual contributions to calculate your expected total value at retirement. So, if you know how much you'll need to save from previous calculations, this calculator will let you know if you're on track to reach that goal, given your present age, your retirement age, the current value of your portfolio, and your expected rate of return.

Others, like the one at www.bankrate.com, will tell you how much you have to invest today to reach your future goal, assuming you had a lump sum that you could invest today and leave invested for a specific period of time. This would be ideal for those who receive a windfall, and want to invest it for their retirement. It's also good for those who want to know if they've already saved enough to reach their goal without further contributions.

It's important for you to understand that some calculators allow you to plug in the expected rate of inflation, while others use an assumed rate that you may or may not feel comfortable with. Some calculators will give their results in inflation-adjusted dollars, while still others will give you

FIGURE 6.1   ONLINE CALCULATOR FOR REQUIRED SAVINGS
              FOR RETIREMENT

[ ]	Annual income required (today's dollars)
[ ]	Number of years until retirement
[ ]	Number of years required after retirement
[ ]	Annual inflation
[ ]	Annual yield on balance (%) (fixed rate)
HTML Tables ▾	

answers in today's dollars, and you'll have to adjust the figures to allow for inflation.

One of the simpler online calculators you might want to try can be found at www.bankrate.com/calculators/retirement/retirement-calculator .aspx. The input screen uses a number of the variables we discussed earlier, and looks like Figure 6.1.

We ran numerous calculations, using various expected rates of return (5 percent, 6 percent, 7 percent, and 8 percent), and changed the "Number of years until retirement" by five in each subsequent calculation. We kept "Annual income required (today's dollars)" constant at a $1,000.00 multiplier, "Annual inflation" constant at 3 percent, and "Number of years required after retirement" constant at 30. (Funding 25 years of retirement rather than the 30 years we used in our calculations, would, of course, reduce the amount needed.)

We feel it's important that you understand these figures shouldn't be taken as gospel, but rather as a ballpark number that you can use as a starting point in your planning. In fact, the online calculator results are accompanied by a warning, which we feel everyone should be aware of. It says: *This calculator is for illustrative purposes only. We do not guarantee that calculations are accurate. Always consult your accountant or a professional advisor before making personal financial decisions.*

Given these parameters and the warning, Tables 6.2 to 6.7 are the results of the various calculations we ran. The results are for each $1,000 of retirement income needed. To arrive at the total amount you'll need to accumulate, simply locate the table that corresponds to the number of years to your retirement and then use the figure next to your expected

T A B L E **6.2**   FIVE YEARS TO RETIREMENT

Required income (current dollars)	$ 1,000
Required income (future dollars)	$ 1,159
At 5% annual return, you will need ≈ (per $1,000)	$26,681
At 6% annual return, you will need ≈ (per $1,000)	$23,650
At 7% annual return, you will need ≈ (per $1,000)	$21,122
At 8% annual return, you will need ≈ (per $1,000)	$19,000

annual return. You then multiply that number by the number of thousands of dollars you'll need to withdraw at retirement.

For example, let's consider the needs of someone who's five years from retirement and has an expected annual portfolio return of 7 percent. Looking at the "Five years to retirement" table, Table 6.2, we find that an individual with a 7 percent annual return would need to have accumulated approximately $21,122 for each $1,000.00 of retirement income he or she will need, over and above pension, Social Security, and any other sources of income the person expects to receive. So, if the individual needed to withdraw $30,000 per year from the retirement fund, he or

T A B L E **6.3**   TEN YEARS TO RETIREMENT

Required income (current dollars)	$ 1,000
Required income (future dollars)	$ 1,344
At 5% annual return, you will need ≈ (per $1,000)	$30,931
At 6% annual return, you will need ≈ (per $1,000)	$27,417
At 7% annual return, you will need ≈ (per $1,000)	$24,487
At 8% annual return, you will need ≈ (per $1,000)	$22,027

TABLE **6.4**   FIFTEEN YEARS TO RETIREMENT

Required income (current dollars)	$ 1,000
Required income (future dollars)	$ 1,558
At 5% annual return, you will need ≈ (per $1,000)	$35,857
At 6% annual return, you will need ≈ (per $1,000)	$31,784
At 7% annual return, you will need ≈ (per $1,000)	$28,387
At 8% annual return, you will need ≈ (per $1,000)	$25,535

TABLE **6.5**   TWENTY YEARS TO RETIREMENT

Required income (current dollars)	$ 1,000
Required income (future dollars)	$ 1,806
At 5% annual return, you will need ≈ (per $1,000)	$41,568
At 6% annual return, you will need ≈ (per $1,000)	$36,847
At 7% annual return, you will need ≈ (per $1,000)	$32,908
At 8% annual return, you will need ≈ (per $1,000)	$29,602

TABLE **6.6**   TWENTY-FIVE YEARS TO RETIREMENT

Required income (current dollars)	$ 1,000
Required income (future dollars)	$ 2,094
At 5% annual return, you will need ≈ (per $1,000)	$48,189
At 6% annual return, you will need ≈ (per $1,000)	$42,715
At 7% annual return, you will need ≈ (per $1,000)	$38,150
At 8% annual return, you will need ≈ (per $1,000)	$34,317

TABLE **6.7** THIRTY YEARS TO RETIREMENT

Required income (current dollars)	$ 1,000
Required income (future dollars)	$ 2,427
At 5% annual return, you will need ≈ (per $1,000)	$55,864
At 6% annual return, you will need ≈ (per $1,000)	$49,519
At 7% annual return, you will need ≈ (per $1,000)	$44,226
At 8% annual return, you will need ≈ (per $1,000)	$39,782

she would need to have accumulated approximately $633,660.00 ($21,122 × 30) at retirement.

Next, let's use Table 6.7 to calculate the needs of someone who is 30 years from retirement and has an expected return of 8 percent. If that person needed to withdraw $30,000 per year from a retirement plan when he or she retired, that individual would need to have accumulated approximately $1,193,460 ($39,782 × 30) by the retirement date.

As we can see from these tables, the higher expected return obviously reduces the amount needed per $1,000, but that lower figure assumes the same rate of return throughout the 30 years of our retirement. In reality, younger investors tend to be more aggressive by holding a higher percentage of their portfolio in equities. As a result, they should expect a higher rate of return for taking on this additional risk. Then, as we get older and closer to retirement, we need to get more conservative. This means we'll be taking on less risk by lowering the percentage of equities in our portfolio and increasing the percentage of bonds, so we should expect lower returns. As a result, we should revisit the calculators from time to time, and adjust our input variables to get a more updated picture of where we stand in our renewed quest to answer the question, "How much do I need to save?"

CHAPTER SEVEN

Keep It Simple

Make Index Funds the Core, or All, of Your Portfolio

There is a crucially important difference about playing the game of investing compared to virtually any other activity. Most of us have no chance of being as good as the average in any pursuit where others practice and hone skills for many, many hours. But we can be as good as the average investor in the stock market with no practice at all.

—Jeremy Siegel, Professor of Finance,
Wharton School, University of Pennsylvania,
and author of *Stocks for the Long Run*

In his outstanding book, *The Four Pillars of Investing*, William Bernstein writes: "The stockbroker services his clients in the same way that Bonnie and Clyde serviced banks." While most won't publicly admit it, the vast majority of stockbrokers, mutual fund managers, sellers of investment products, and money managers don't earn their keep. In fact, most of them build substantial wealth at their clients' expense. More than one broker has been heard to remark, "We make millionaires—out of multimillionaires."

What's that? You say your money guy is making you a fortune? We sincerely hope that's the case. However, with a very simple, no-brainer investment strategy called *passive investing* you have, at the very least, a 70 percent chance of outperforming any given financial pro over an extended period of time. And over some 20-year periods, passive investing outperforms as many as 90 percent of actively managed funds. The reason is because this system allows you to keep more of your money working for you, which means less money for the brokers, investment houses, mutual fund managers, money managers, and the government. It may sound too good to be true, but this time it really is true, and it's backed up with a preponderance of empirical evidence.

HOW INVESTING IS DIFFERENT FROM MOST OF LIFE

Through education and experience, most of us come to learn and practice certain life principles that serve us well. For example:

- *Don't settle for average.* Strive to be the best.
- *Listen to your gut.* What you feel in your heart is ususaly right.
- *If you don't know how to do something, ask.* Talk to an expert or hire one and let the expert handle it. That will save you a lot of time and frustration.
- *You get what you pay for.* Good help isn't cheap and cheap help isn't good.
- *If there's a crisis, take action!* Do something to fix it.
- *History repeats itself.* The best predictor of future performance is past performance.

Well, guess what? Applying these principles to investing is destined to leave you poorer. As an investor, you can be well above average by settling for slightly less than the index returns. Listening to your gut is the worst thing you can do. Although it sometimes pays to hire an expert, you may get less than you pay for. Trying to fix a perceived investment crisis by taking action is usually a recipe for poor returns. And using yesterday's results to pick tomorrow's high-performing investments or investment pros is another losing strategy. Investing has a whole new set of rules, and if we are to be successful, we need to play by these new rules.

According to Dalbar, Inc. of Boston, from 1993 to 2012, the S&P Index 500 averaged a gain of 8.21 percent per year. However, during that same 20-year period, the average equity fund investor had an average annual gain of only 4.25 percent. Put another way, had the average equity fund investor just bought a low-cost S&P 500 Index fund and held it, he/she would have almost doubled their rate of return. The study found that the underperformance was due to investor behavior such as market timing and chasing hot funds. Had these investors been long-term, buy-and-hold investors, they would have earned close to the market's returns. When the average investor underperforms the index by such a significant amount, it's clear that most are playing with a bad set of guidelines or none at all. A one-time investment of $10,000 invested at 8 percent compounds to $46,610 in 20 years. The same $10,000 invested over the same period at 4.25 percent compounds to only $22,989.

The reason why so many common life principles don't apply to the world of investing is very simple: The short-run performance of the stock market is random, unpredictable, and for most people, nerve-racking. The next time you hear someone saying that he/she knows how the stock market or any given stock is going to perform in the next few weeks, months, or years, you can be sure they are either lying or self-delusional.

There is more than 200 years of U.S. stock market history and the long-term trend is up. Over the long term, stock market performance has been rather consistent. During any 50-year period, it provided an average, after-inflation return of between 5 and 7 percent per year. That means if you invested in a well-diversified basket of stocks and left them alone, the purchasing power of your investment would have doubled roughly every 12 years.

Although long-term returns are fairly consistent, short-term returns are much more volatile. Stocks over the long-run offer the greatest potential return of any investment, but the short-run roller-coaster rides can be a nightmare for those who don't understand the market and lack a sound investment plan to cope with it. The 1990s were stellar years for stocks but the 1930s were a disaster.

INDEX INVESTING: IT PAYS TO BE LAZY

Index investing is an investment strategy that Walter Mitty would love. It takes very little investment knowledge, no skill, practically no time or effort—and outperforms about 80 percent of all investors. It allows you to spend your time working, playing, or doing anything else while your nest egg compounds on autopilot. It's about as difficult as breathing and about as time-consuming as going to a fast-food restaurant once a year.

Here is the crux of the strategy: Instead of hiring an expert, or spending a lot of time trying to decide which stocks or actively managed funds are likely to be top performers, just invest in index funds and forget about it! As we discussed in Chapter 4, an index fund attempts to match the return of the segment of the market it seeks to replicate, minus a very small management fee. For example, Vanguard's Index 500 seeks to replicate the return of the S&P 500; the Total Stock Market Index seeks to replicate the return of a broad U.S. stock market index; and the Total International Index seeks to replicate the return of a broad cross-section of international stocks. In addition to stock index funds, there are bond index funds that seek to replicate the performance of various bond indexes. There are also index funds of funds that hold various combinations of stock and bond index funds.

WHY INDEXING IS SO EFFECTIVE

Index funds outperform approximately 80 percent of all actively managed funds over long periods of time. They do so for one simple reason: rock-bottom costs. In a random market, we don't know what future returns will be. However, we do know that an investor who keeps his or her costs low will earn a higher return than one who does not. That's the indexer's edge. More specifically, here are the cost and other advantages of indexing:

1. There are no sales commissions.
2. Operating expenses are low.
3. Many index funds are tax efficient.
4. You don't have to hire a money manager.
5. Index funds are highly diversified and less risky.
6. It doesn't much matter who manages the fund.
7. Style drift and tracking errors aren't a problem.

Let's look at these advantages in more detail.

No Sales Commissions

Purchasing a load fund from a broker usually means incurring a sales charge of 4 to 6 percent. That money goes straight into the brokerage firm's pocket instead of going to work in your account. Your money gets a very nice haircut before it's invested. With a no-load index fund, all of your money is put to work for you. Of course, the broker will likely tell you that his or her funds are managed by some of the top pros in the business and you're paying for their wise counsel and guidance. However, the research shows that load funds don't perform any better than no-load funds. If you subtract the cost of commissions, they perform even worse. More than likely, you are paying for the broker's Mercedes.

Low Operating Expenses

Actively managed funds typically have a yearly expense ratio of 1 to 2 percent. That means that between 1 and 2 percent of the balance of your investment is deducted each year to pay the fund manager and other expenses of running the fund. By contrast, managing an index fund is very cheap and easy. Nobody has to decide which funds to buy or sell or when to buy or sell them. The manager simply replicates the index. It's easily managed with the help of a computer. As a result, most index funds have expense ratios well under 0.5 percent, and many are 0.2 percent or lower. If you don't think those miniscule costs matter, consider this: Let's assume someone puts $10,000 in a mutual fund, leaves it there 20 years, and gets an average annual return of 10 percent. If the fund had an expense ratio of 1.5 percent, the fund is worth $49,725 at the end of 20 years. However if the fund had an expense ratio of 0.5 percent, it would be worth $60,858 at the end of 20 years. Just a 1 percent difference in expenses makes an 18 percent difference in returns when compounded over 20 years.

Tax Efficiency

Every time an active fund sells a profitable stock, it creates a taxable event that's passed on to the investor. What that means to you is that you get a tax bill that subtracts from the return on your investment. Unless you are holding the fund in a tax-deferred or tax-free account, this can add up over time to serious dollars for Uncle Sam and less dollars for you. Broad market index funds, by contrast, have very little turnover. Since they only replicate all or most of the stock market, you're far less likely to be surprised with a large tax bill.

No Need to Hire a Money Manager

Index investing is so simple that there really isn't a need to hire a money manager to monitor your portfolio, unless you simply feel compelled to do so. Typical money managers take anywhere from 0.75 percent to as much as 3.0 percent a year to manage your portfolio. Once again, that's money going into someone else's account and compounding instead of staying and compounding in your account.

Higher Diversification and Less Risk

As we'll discuss in Chapter 12, diversification is the key to reducing investment risk. The fastest way to get rich in the stock market is to own the next Microsoft. The fastest way to lose all your money is to own the next Enron. Identifying them in advance is impossible. However, you don't have to identify them in advance to make a healthy return on your investment. If you buy an S&P 500 index fund, your investment is highly diversified and its performance will match that of 500 leading U.S. corporations' stocks. Is it possible to lose all of your money? Yes, but the odds of that happening are slim and none. If 500 leading U.S. corporations all have their stock prices plummet to zero, the value of your investment portfolio will be the least of your problems. An economic collapse of that magnitude would make the Great Depression look like *Lifestyles of the Rich and Famous*.

Greg Baer and Gary Gensler, authors of *The Great Mutual Fund Trap*, did a study comparing the risk of actively managed domestic funds to the Wilshire 5000 Index, a broad total stock market index that covers the U.S. equity market. They found that for the 10-year period ending December 31, 2001, the standard deviation (a measure of risk) for actively managed funds was 19.4 percent, compared to 16.2 percent for the more diversified total stock market index.

Little Consequence as to Who Manages Fund

Just like any other profession, some active fund managers are better than others. They all aren't Warren Buffett and Peter Lynch. Lynch managed the Fidelity Magellan fund from 1978 to 1990, posting average annual returns of 29 percent. For the 10-year period ending 12-31-12, Standard & Poor's data shows that actively managed funds underperformed their index in all categories. Furthermore, consistently high-performing managers are so rare that some investment scholars attribute their consistent performance to luck. Many of yesterday's superstar managers and funds are today's underperformers, and vice versa. Once again, identifying them in advance and knowing when they will do well is the problem. When it comes to index funds, who's managing the fund is a nonissue. All the manager has to do is track the appropriate index.

Style Drift and Tracking Errors Not a Problem

With active funds, there is always a possibility of some of the stocks in a fund moving from one classification to another. Inasmuch as index funds are designed to replicate a particular segment of the market, such as large-cap growth or small-cap value, there is no possibility of the funds drifting into another category.

Due to their simplicity, low cost, and ease of manageability, investing in index funds is an excellent choice for nearly every investor. Due to their higher costs, most active fund managers have to outperform their respective index by an average of 2 percent per year just to match the performance of an index fund, and that's very difficult for most managers to do. A lot of very smart people spend countless hours every day trying to analyze, time, and beat the market, but very few do it over the long haul. And knowing who tomorrow's star performers will be is next to impossible. A few investors will get it right, but many more will get it wrong and underperform those who simply index their investments.

In school, it usually takes a lot of work to earn an A, less work to earn a B, and so on. In investing, if you spend lots of time and effort studying the market, or pay someone to manage your investments, you have less than a 20 percent chance of being an A investor. However, if you know nothing about investing, spend minimal time on your investments, and buy index funds, you have a 100 percent chance of being a B investor. In a world where most investors get a D or worse, B is beautiful.

READ WHAT OTHERS SAY

Most of the world's leading investment researchers, scholars, authors, and almost anyone who isn't trying to sell you their investment products agree that low-cost, passive investing is an excellent strategy for most or all of your portfolio. Following are what many of them have to say on the subject of passive versus active investing:

Frank Armstrong, author of *The Informed Investor*: "Do the right thing: In every asset class where they are available, index! Four of five funds will fail to meet or beat an appropriate index."

Gregory A. Baer and **Gary Gensler,** authors of *The Great Mutual Fund Trap*: "With returns corrected for survivorship bias, the average actively managed funds trail the market by about 3 percentage points a year."

William Bernstein, PhD, MD, author of *The Four Pillars of Investing*, frequent guest columnist for Morningstar, and often quoted in the *Wall Street Journal*: "An index fund dooms you to mediocrity? Absolutely not: It virtually guarantees you superior performance."

John C. Bogle, founder and former chairman, The Vanguard Group: "If you go back to 1970, there were only 355 equity funds. Only 169 of them survive today, so right away you are dramatically skewing the numbers by not counting the losers. Of those 169 survivors, only nine beat the S&P 500 through 1999. Three by 1 percent to 2 percent per year, four by 2 percent to 3 percent, and only two by more than that. I would say that 2 percent isn't really statistically significant, but let's leave that aside. Then there are taxes. After tax, maybe only those top two truly beat the market. That means it's just a game of chance and a bad one at that."

Jack Brennan, chairman, The Vanguard Group: "With an index fund, the certainty of keeping up with the market is a very worthwhile trade-off for the possibility of beating it."

Warren Buffett, chairman of Berkshire Hathaway and investor of legendary repute: "Most investors, both institutional and individual, will find that the best way to own common stocks is through an index fund that charges minimal fees. Those following this path are sure to beat the net results (after fees and expenses) delivered by the great majority of investment professionals."

Jonathan Clements, author and writer of the popular *Wall Street Journal* column "Getting Going": "I am a huge, huge, huge fan of index funds. They are the investor's best friend and Wall Street's worst nightmare."

Douglas Dial, portfolio manager of the CREF Stock Account Fund of TIAA-CREF: "Indexing is a marvelous technique. I wasn't a true believer. I was just an ignoramus. Now I am a convert. Indexing is an extraordinarily sophisticated thing to do."

Paul Farrell, columnist for CBS MarketWatch and author of *The Lazy Person's Guide to Investing*: "So much attention is paid to which funds are at the head of the pack today that most people lose sight of the fact that, over longer time periods, index funds beat the vast majority of their actively managed peers."

Richard Ferri, author of *Protecting Your Wealth in Good Times and Bad*: "When you are finished choosing a bond index fund, a total U.S. stock market index fund, and a broad international index fund, you will have a very simple, yet complete portfolio."

Walter R. Good and **Roy W. Hermansen,** authors of *Index Your Way to Investment Success*: "Index funds save on management and marketing expenses, reduce transaction costs, defer capital gain, and control risk—and in the process, beat the vast majority of actively managed mutual funds!"

Arthur Levitt, former chairman of the Securities Exchange Commission and author of *Take on the Street*: "The fund industry's dirty little secret: Most actively managed funds never do as well as their benchmark."

Burton Malkiel, professor of economics, Princeton University and author of *A Random Walk Down Wall Street*: "Through the past 30 years more than two-thirds of professional portfolio managers have been outperformed by the unmanaged S&P 500 Index."

Moshe A. Milevsky, author of *The Probability of Fortune*: "I am somewhat skeptical about anyone's ability to consistently beat the market."

Jane Bryant Quinn, author of *Making the Most of Your Money*: "Indexing is for winners only."

Ron Ross, author of *The Unbeatable Market*: "Carhart evaluated 1,892 equity funds for the period 1962 to 1993 for the equivalent of 16,109 'fund years.' He concluded, 'The results do not support the existence of skilled or informed mutual fund portfolio managers.'"

Paul Samuelson, first American to win the Nobel Prize in Economic Science: "The most efficient way to diversify a stock portfolio is with a low-fee index fund. Statistically, a broadly based stock index fund will outperform most actively managed equity portfolios."

Bill Schultheis, author of *The Coffeehouse Investor*: "Once you remove yourself from Wall Street's complete and total obsession with trying to beat the stock market average and accept the fact that approximating the stock market average is a rather sophisticated approach to the whole thing, building a successful common stock portfolio becomes an immensely gratifying experience."

Charles Schwab, founder and chairman of the board of The Charles Schwab Corporation: "Only about one out of every four equity funds outperforms the stock market. That's why I'm a firm believer in the power of indexing."

Douglas A. Sease, author of *Winning with the Market* and former financial editor of the *Wall Street Journal*: "You will never see an S&P index fund leading the best-performance charts in the *Wall Street Journal*. But—and this is the point—your fund's returns will almost certainly beat those of the majority of actively managed funds over a period of five years or more. And you will never see an S&P index fund at the bottom of the *Wall Street Journal* performance charts, either."

Chandan Sengupta, author of *The Only Proven Road to Investment Success*: "You should switch all your investments in stocks to index funds as soon as possible, after giving proper consideration to any tax consequences."

William F. Sharpe, Nobel Laureate, STANCO 25 Professor of Finance, Emeritus, Stanford University Graduate School of Business, and Chairman, Financial Engines, Inc.: "I love index funds."

Rex Sinquefield, co-chairman of Dimensional Fund Advisors: "The only consistent superior performer is the market itself, and the only way to capture that superior consistency is to invest in a properly diversified portfolio of index funds."

Larry E. Swedroe, author of *The Successful Investor Today*: "Despite the superior returns generated by passively managed funds, financial publications are dominated by forecasts from so-called gurus and the latest hot fund managers. I believe that there is a simple explanation for the misinformation: It's just not in the interests of the Wall Street establishment or the financial press to inform investors of the failure of active managers."

Andrew Tobias, author of *The Only Investment Guide You'll Ever Need*: "If the professionals do no better than darts—and most do not—then how much is it worth to have them manage your money?"

Jerry Tweddell and **Jack Pierce,** authors of *Winning with Index Mutual Funds*: "You don't have to pay for an expert to invest successfully in index funds. With a very simple and basic understanding of index funds, you can consistently beat 70 percent to 80 percent of all professionally managed mutual funds."

Eric Tyson, author of *Investing for Dummies* and *Mutual Funds for Dummies*: "Why waste your time trying to select and manage a portfolio of individual stocks when you can replicate the market average returns (and beat the majority of professional money managers) through an exceptionally underrated and underused investment fund called an index fund?"

Jason Zweig, senior writer and columnist at *Money* magazine and coauthor of the revised edition of Benjamin Graham's classic, *The Intelligent Investor*: "If you buy—and then hold—a total stock market index fund, it is mathematically certain that you will outperform the vast majority of all other investors in the long run. Graham praised index funds as the best choice for individual investors, as does Warren Buffett."

The next time some investment salesperson tells you, "It's a stock picker's market," or they tell you index funds are just going to earn mediocre returns, you may want to show the salesperson this list of quotes from noted authorities on investing. And if the salesperson counters by telling you that those people don't know the real truth about investing, you may find it useful to quote the words of Jack Nicholson in the movie, *A Few Good Men*: "You want the truth? YOU CAN'T HANDLE THE TRUTH!"

HOW TO BUY INDEX FUNDS

Not all index funds are created equal. There are a number of fund companies that sell index funds. Not surprisingly, many of them will also charge you a healthy sales commission and a high yearly management fee. Do not buy those. Repeat: *Do not buy load index funds with high annual expense ratios*. You are buying an index. You are not buying stock-picking skill, money management, or anything else other than a fund that replicates an index. Cheap is beautiful. Only consider investing in no-load funds with annual expense ratios of 0.5 percent or less, the cheaper the better.

Once you've narrowed the field, you will find two basic types of index funds to choose from: index mutual funds and exchange-traded funds, also known as ETFs. As we said in Chapter 4, we believe that the vast majority of investors will be better off buying index mutual funds rather than ETFs.

As you may suspect, as Bogleheads we are partial to Vanguard due to its rock-bottom costs. However, there are other reputable firms that offer no-load, low-cost index funds. For example, if you are just starting out, you may not be able to afford the $1,000 minimum investment that Vanguard requires for an IRA, or the $3,000 minimum for regular investments. If that's the case, you may want to set up an automatic investment plan with TIAA-CREF (www.tiaa-cref.org). It will waive its minimum investment fee if you agree to deposit as little as $50 a month in an IRA or mutual fund account. Other reputable firms you may want to consider are Fidelity, T. Rowe Price, USAA, and Charles Schwab.

BOGLEHEADS AND ACTIVELY MANAGED FUNDS

From what you have read in this chapter thus far, you might believe we are index zealots who believe all actively managed funds are simply a waste of money. While all three of us believe that indexing is an excellent investment strategy, all three of us own actively managed Vanguard funds, too. Although Vanguard is known as the pioneer of index funds, it also offers a wide variety of actively managed funds, with some having delivered great returns. For example, for the first 20 years of its existence (1984 to 2004), Vanguard's Health Care Fund had the highest annual average return of any mutual fund in the world. And in the past 25 years, a portfolio of Vanguard's actively managed funds outperformed the Wilshire 5000 (the total U.S. stock market index) by an average of 0.9 percent per year. This portfolio's excellent performance has largely been due to a combination of good management coupled with low costs. Vanguard's average expense ratio for actively managed funds is now 0.28 percent.

Does this mean one should abandon passive investing and opt for low-cost, actively managed funds? Not at all! At the same time Vanguard Health Care was doing phenomenally well, Vanguard U.S. Growth was a disaster, turning in a shameful performance during the great bull market of the 1990s. It's also important to keep in mind that investing in a health care fund is placing a sector bet. What if some unforeseen event happens that depresses the market for health care stocks? Do you want to have most of your eggs in that basket? We think not.

Another important point to keep in mind: It's common for actively managed funds to have great before-tax returns and not-so-great after-tax returns, due to the trading that goes on in actively managing the funds. For that reason, we recommend keeping any actively managed funds in tax-deferred or tax-free accounts, such as 401(k)s, SEPs, Keoghs, or Roth IRAs.

By placing your money in actively managed, low-cost funds, there is the possibility of getting greater returns. Nevertheless, it's important to realize that you are taking a greater risk with the accompanying possibility of greater loss. There's no free lunch. That's why we recommend placing the bulk, or all, of your investments in index funds.

CHAPTER EiGHT

◆

Asset Allocation

The Cornerstone of Successful Investing

The most fundamental decision of investing is the allocation of your assets: How much should you own in stocks? How much should you own in bonds? How much should you own in cash reserve?"

—Jack Bogle

Your most important portfolio decision can be summed up in just two words: asset allocation. In this chapter we'll help you design an asset allocation plan based on your goals, time frame, risk tolerance, and personal financial situation. In addition, we'll look at some of the extensive academic research studies on the topic that have led to remarkably similar conclusions.

It was Sancho Panza, Don Quixote's sidekick, who observed: "It is the part of a wise man to keep himself today for tomorrow and not to venture all his eggs in one basket." Asset allocation is the process of dividing our investments among different kinds of asset classes (baskets) to minimize our risk, and also to maximize our return for what the academics call an *efficient portfolio*.

How do we do this? Well, we begin by asking ourselves two questions: "What investments should we select?" and "What percentage should we allocate to each investment?" The academic community has spent a great deal of time and research trying to answer these two questions. They have given us sophisticated theories that we can use to select our investments and combine them in the most efficient manner to give us maximum return with minimum volatility.

THE EFFICIENT MARKET THEORY (EMT)

To understand EMT, we'll go back to the year 1900 when a young French mathematician named Louis Bachelier wrote his PhD thesis, which contained the seeds of the Efficient Market Theory. EMT can be described as "an investment theory that states that it is impossible to 'beat the market' because existing share prices already incorporate and reflect all relevant information."

Another student of the stock market was Alfred Cowles, who came to prominence about 20 years later. Mr. Cowles was an investor who carefully followed the stock market forecasts of professional "experts" and stock market gurus prior to the worst stock market crash the United States has ever experienced. This was the bull market of the 1920s that reached its peak in August 1929, and bottomed in the summer of 1932. Cowles recognized that if the so-called experts could not correctly forecast stock market movements, there must be a reason.

Cowles did a painstaking review of the stock forecasts of 7,500 financial services recommendations made from 1903 through 1929 and then compared their recommendations with his own database of actual stock performance. His results were published in 1933 in an article titled, "Can Stock Market Forecasters Forecast?" His three-word conclusion: *It is doubtful.*

Cowles was not finished. In 1938 he formed the Cowles Commission for Economic Research. The Commission immediately began assembling data on all the stocks traded on the New York Stock Exchange since 1871—a tremendous task in 1938 when computers were unknown. This database remains a valuable resource today.

In 1944 Cowles published a new study of 6,904 market forecasts by investment professionals from 1929 to 1943. The study again found *no evidence of ability to predict successfully the direction of the stock market.*

In the 1960s, a University of Chicago Professor, Eugene F. Fama, performed a detailed analysis of the ever-increasing volume of stock price data. He concluded that stock prices are very efficient and that it's extremely difficult to pick winning stocks—especially after factoring in the costs of transaction fees.

In 1973, Princeton professor Burton Malkiel, after extensive research, came to the same conclusion as Bachelier, Cowles, and Fama. Professor Malkiel published a book with the catchy title *A Random Walk Down Wall Street*. The book is now an investment classic, and updated revisions are published on a regular basis. We think it deserves a place on the bookshelf of every serious investor. Professor Malkiel describes a *random walk* this way:

> *One in which future steps or directions cannot be predicted on the basis of past action. When the term is applicable to the stock market, it means that short-run changes in stock prices cannot be predicted.*

Another, more vivid, description of a random walk:

> *A drunk standing in the middle of the road whose future movements can only be guessed.*

Few academics argue that the stock market is totally efficient. Nevertheless, they agree that stocks and bonds are so efficiently priced that the majority of investors, including full-time professional fund managers, will not outperform an unmanaged index fund after transaction costs. Jack Bogle wrote:

> *I know of no serious academic, professional money manager, trained security analyst, or intelligent individual investor who would disagree with the thrust of EMT: The stock market itself is a demanding taskmaster. It sets a high hurdle that few investors can leap.*

Efficient markets and *random walk* are obscenities on Wall Street, where investors are constantly told that Wall Street's superior knowledge can make it easy to beat the market (for a fee). Nearly all the academic community disagrees, but without advertising dollars their research results are generally unknown by the investing public.

MODERN PORTFOLIO THEORY

Harry Markowitz is credited with being the father of Modern Portfolio Theory (MPT). This is a watershed concept that has changed the way knowledgeable investors structure their portfolios. Markowitz realized the importance of *risk*, which he defined as the standard deviation of expected return. He understood that risk and return are related. This relationship of risk and return is crucial for us to understand if we are to build efficient portfolios—portfolios that offer the highest return with the least amount of risk.

Let us consider an investor choosing between two investments with the same expected return. Investment A increases steadily and without a decline. Investment B fluctuates in value by going up and down as it ends with the same return as investment A. Which investment would you rather own? Obviously, you would choose investment A for its smoother ride. This concept is called *risk aversion* in the financial field. Given the same outcome, investors will always choose the investment with less risk.

The only way to entice our investor to buy Investment B would be to offer a higher expected return. This is an important lesson for every investor: The greater the risk of loss, the greater the expected return. Or to put it another way: "There is no free lunch."

One of Markowitz's greatest contributions to investors was his recognition that a mixture of volatile noncorrelated securities could result in a *portfolio* with lower volatility and possibly higher return. He published his findings in 1952 in the *Journal of Finance*. Thirty-eight years later, in 1990, Professor Markowitz received the Nobel Prize in economics.

The Brinson, Hood, Beebower Study

In 1986, three researchers—Gary Brinson, Randolph Hood, and Gilbert Beebower—teamed up to study the performance of 91 large pension funds during the 10-year period 1974 to 1983. They reasoned that pension fund returns came from four sources:

1. Investment policy (asset allocation) defined as the allocation of stocks, bonds, and cash
2. Individual security selection
3. Market timing
4. Costs

They found that a pension fund's allocation between stocks, bonds, and cash determined 93.6 percent of the variability of pension plan returns. They further found that the portfolio manager's attempts to actively manage their fund cost the average fund a 1.10 percent reduction in return compared to just buying and holding an index composed of the S&P 500 Index, Shearson Lehman Government Corporate Bond Index, and 30-day Treasury Bills (cash).

Needless to say, the Brinson, Hood, Beebower Study was not well received by the financial industry, which enjoys huge profits promoting its ability to beat the market with security selection and market timing. Nevertheless, the importance of asset allocation is now recognized more than ever by both professional and nonprofessional investors alike.

In 2003, The Vanguard Group did a similar study using a 40-year database of 420 balanced mutual funds. It found that 77 percent of the variability of a fund's return was determined by the strategic asset allocation policy. Market timing and stock selection played relatively minor roles. The Vanguard researchers also found that the benchmark indexes had a higher return than the corresponding funds. Finally, the Vanguard researchers found that the returns of the highest-cost funds lagged those of the lowest-cost funds.

Current-day researchers use the findings of Bachelier, Markowitz, Cowles, Fama, and Bogle, together with all the other financial innovations of the past 100 years, to formulate what is called *Modern Portfolio Theory*.

Our brief review of the history of investment research serves two purposes. First, it will help you design an efficient (low-risk/high-return) portfolio. Second, it will give you the knowledge and conviction needed to stay the course. Now, let's start designing our personal asset allocation plan.

1. What are your goals?
2. What is your time frame?
3. What is your risk tolerance?
4. What is your personal financial situation?

What Are Your Goals?

Are you saving for your first home; for your child's college education; or for a comfortable retirement income for you and your spouse? It may be all three or some other goal. It's important to have specific goals so that you know what you are saving for and approximately how much money is necessary.

TABLE 8.1 ANNUALIZED RETURNS OF LARGE DOMESTIC STOCKS FOR DIFFERENT TIME PERIODS 1935–2013

TIME PERIOD	WORST RETURN	BEST RETURN
1 year	–43%	+54%
5 years	–12%	+29%
10 years	–1%	+20%

What Is Your Time Frame?

Stocks are usually unsuitable for short time frames (less than five years). Suppose, for example, that you are investing for your child's college tuition, which is due in three years. Let's assume that at the top of the bull market in May 2008, you had your daughter's college savings in an S&P 500 Stock Index Fund. Unfortunately for her, nine months later her college savings would have been worth only about half its previous value. It's this unpredictability and volatility of stocks that make them unsuitable for short time frames. Table 8.1 shows how stock market declines (and gains) become less and less as investing periods lengthen.

Over the 85-year period from 1929 through 2013, we can clearly see that an investor who picked the worst one-year period to invest in large domestic stocks would have lost 43 percent. However, the same investment over *any* 10-year period would have lost only 1 percent. Now we can understand why stocks are poor investments for short-term goals but can be excellent investments for long-term goals.

What Is Your Risk Tolerance?

The first thing to do when developing an allocation is to come up with a risk profile.
—Errold F. Moody

Knowing your risk tolerance is a very important aspect of investing, and one that the academics have studied extensively. Their experiments prove that most investors are more fearful of a loss than they are happy with a gain.

We all know people who are afraid of investing in the stock market because they know they might lose money. Risk-averse savers keep billions of dollars in CDs and bank savings accounts, despite their low yields. At the other extreme, we know of investors like Donald Trump who think nothing of investing hundreds of millions of dollars in speculative investments—and are seemingly unworried even when bankruptcy looms. Most of us have a risk tolerance that lies somewhere between these extremes.

In order to help determine if your portfolio is suitable for your risk tolerance, you need to be brutally honest with yourself as you try to answer the question, "Will I sell during the next bear market?" Here are some stats that might help you answer that question.

On March 10, 2000, the NASDAQ Composite Index reached an all-time closing high of 5,049. Thirty-two months later, on October 9, 2002, it was down to 1,224—more than a 75 percent loss for investors who sold at that time. At the end of 2006, the NASDAQ Index had struggled back to 2,415, but that was still only half its previous high.

Until you have owned stocks in a severe bear market, it's very difficult to know how far your investments would need to decline before you would decide to sell. Don't fool yourself. There almost certainly is some point during a market decline when you would consider selling.

Imagine that you are in a severe bear market and that you have been watching your hard-earned savings steadily erode for a week, a month, a year, or even longer. You are discouraged. Gloom and doom has set in all around you. You have no idea how much further your investments will decline. Should you sell now, or hope that the market stops its stomach-churning descent?

"Experts" on television proclaim that the market is going to go down further. Writers of newspaper and magazine articles confirm that the worst is yet to come. Your friends are selling their stocks, and they advise you to do the same. Your family, happy when you were making money, begins to lose faith in your investing plan. They also urge you to sell before it's too late. This is what a bad bear market is like. Ask yourself, "What would I do? Would I lose faith and sell, or would I be disciplined enough to stay the course?"

In a situation like this, your emotions can be your worst enemy. One of the chief advantages of an asset allocation plan is that it imposes a discipline that will help you to resist the temptation to sell funds in under-performing asset classes and to resist chasing the current "hot" fund.

If, on the one hand, you think you would sell out of fear because the market is down, your portfolio is unsuitable for you. On the other hand, if you can honestly say, "No, I wouldn't sell because I've learned that U.S.

bear markets have always come back higher than before," your portfolio is probably suitable for your risk tolerance.

The *sleep test* is a great way to help determine if your asset allocation is really right for you. When setting up an asset allocation plan, investors should ask themselves: "Can I sleep soundly without worrying about my investments with this particular asset allocation?" The answer should be yes, since no investment is worth worrying about and losing sleep over. It's important for you to understand that stocks and bonds go up—and they go down, and you need to be comfortable with that fact. These ups and downs are just normal market behavior and should be expected. Experienced investors understand this volatility and accept the inevitable declines. We know that by simply changing our allocation between stocks and bonds, we can lessen the amount of volatility in our portfolio until we reach our comfortable *sleep level*.

Table 8.2 shows the maximum *annual* loss and the average annual return an investor would have incurred during the period from 1926 through 2012, using various stock/bond combinations. Published annual returns do not reveal the huge compounding losses that investors actually suffer in a lengthy bear market. The Dow stocks plunged 17 percent in 1929, 34 percent in 1930, and another 53 percent in 1931. Few investors can tolerate large year-after-year losses (not knowing when they will end). This is the primary reason why we believe that nearly every portfolio should contain an allocation to bonds.

TABLE 8.2   WORST ANNUAL LOSS BASED ON STOCK/BOND ALLOCATION (1926–2012)

ALLOCATION	WORST ANNUAL LOSS	AVERAGE RETURN
100% stocks	–43.1%	10.0%
80% stocks/20% bonds	–34.9%	9.4%
60% stocks/40% bonds	–26.6%	8.7%
40% stocks/60% bonds	–18.4%	7.8%
20% stocks/80% bonds	–10.1%	6.7%
100% bonds	–8.1%	5.5%

If you were invested in stocks during the three-year 2000 to 2002 bear market or the 2007 to 2009 bear market, you undoubtedly have a good idea of your risk tolerance. If you sold losing funds, or if you lost sleep, your portfolio should almost certainly have held more bonds. If you remained unperturbed, you probably had a suitable portfolio. In fact, you might even increase your allocation in stocks if your goal is more than five years away.

If you are new to investing, you should understand that it's one thing to see your portfolio decline on paper. However, it's a much different matter to watch your hard-earned savings slowly melt away in a long bear market. If you are an investor who has not yet experienced a bear market, we suggest that you add from 10 percent to 20 percent more bonds than you think you need for safety. This will be your insurance against worry, and might help prevent you from selling at the wrong time.

What Is Your Personal Financial Situation?

Your personal financial situation has a direct influence on the type and amount of securities you select, and their allocation within your asset allocation plan. For example, the investor with a pension and future social security income obviously does not need to accumulate as large a retirement portfolio as someone without these assets. And someone with significant net worth or a large portfolio does not need to invest in risky investments in search of higher returns.

We know a very successful executive who, upon retirement, put all his investments into high-quality, diversified, municipal bonds. The income from the bonds is more than sufficient for his family's lifestyle. This executive wants to spend his time traveling and on the golf course—not managing a complex portfolio of assorted securities. His simple portfolio may be unusual, but we think it's probably a very suitable portfolio for him. However, most of us want a return greater than is available from savings, CDs, and bonds. This is why we use stocks to provide the growth and additional income needed to meet our goals.

DESIGNING OUR PERSONAL ASSET ALLOCATION PLAN

We have discussed the Efficient Market Theory and Modern Portfolio Theory. We have considered the four elements needed to design an efficient portfolio: your goals, your time frame, your risk tolerance, and your personal financial situation. Now, we will put this all together to design your own personal asset allocation plan.

Choosing Your Investments

Investments in stocks, bonds, and cash have proven to be a successful combination of securities for portfolio construction. At times, you will read about investors who claim great returns from other more exotic securities such as limited partnerships, hedge funds, timber, gold bullion, penny stocks, unit trusts, options, commodity futures, and so on. Our advice is to forget about them. Most of these investments are highly complex and sold to investors who have little idea of the risks involved. Instead, we suggest you heed the advice of author and syndicated columnist Jane Bryant Quinn: "Never buy anything whose price you can't follow in the newspapers—and you shouldn't buy anything too complex to explain to the average 12-year-old."

Remember the Brinson, Hood, Beebower Study that found that the primary determinant (93.6 percent) of a portfolio's risk and return is our allocation between stocks, bonds, and cash? Accordingly, we will concentrate our attention on these three primary asset classes and use three guidelines to allocate between stocks, bonds, and cash:

1. Jack Bogle's rough guide is that bonds should equal our age.
2. Table 8.2 shows the decline we might expect with various stock/bond combinations.
3. Vanguard's online questionnaire and suggested asset allocations in Appendix IV.

Using these three tools and your own experience, you should be able to decide what a suitable stock/bond/cash allocation for your personal long-term asset allocation plan is. *This is the most important portfolio decision you will make.*

Don't worry about exact percentages. Ten percent more or less of an asset class will not make a significant difference in your portfolio performance. Investing is a soft science. It's not engineering, where past performance repeats itself exactly. *The only certainty in investing is that past performance will not repeat.*

Let's assume your goal is to save for retirement. After careful consideration of all the factors we've discussed here, you and your spouse agree on a portfolio allocation of stocks and bonds that seems about right for you. Congratulations! You've just made your most important portfolio decision.

Subdividing Your Stock Allocation

It's important for maximum diversification that our stock allocation contain various subcategories. This is because different types of stocks

TABLE 8.3   VANGUARD TOTAL STOCK MARKET INDEX FUND BREAKDOWN
             (FEBRUARY 2014)

VALUE	CORE	GROWTH	
24%	24%	25%	LARGE
6%	6%	6%	MEDIUM
3%	3%	3%	SMALL

perform differently at different times. No investor wants to own a portfolio that has all of its equity investments in an underperforming asset
class. Accordingly, we want to have some exposure to as many different
types of stocks as is reasonably practical.

Morningstar's Style Box, Table 8.3, is a useful tool that shows how
your portfolio's equity holdings are divided between the different styles
and sizes. You can use the Style Box to analyze your portfolio at no charge
at www.morningstar.com. You will find it listed under "Tools/X-Ray." We
will use the Style Box to show the style and capitalization size of the stocks
in one fund—Vanguard's Total Stock Market Index Fund (VTSMX). We
choose this fund because it closely approximates the entire U.S. stock market, based on the market value of each stock, and also because many
investors choose this one fund for their entire domestic stock allocation.

Morningstar's Style Box is particularly useful for investors using mul-
tiple stock funds so that the total allocation in all funds in the portfolio
does not unintentionally overweight or underweight any particular style
(value, core, growth) or market capitalization (large, medium, small).

If you look closely at Table 8.3, you will notice that large-cap stocks
dominate the U.S. stock market. Many investors believe that overweighting value and small-cap stocks may result in less volatility and higher
long-term returns. This can be accomplished by adding a value and/or a
small-cap fund to a total market index fund.

In recent years, we have seen a proliferation of specialty funds, which
are also known as *sector funds*. Many of these specialty funds were introduced by mutual fund companies to take advantage of investing fads that
were popular at the time. Specialty stock funds include gold, technology,
health, energy, utilities, and many more. Specialty funds are often volatile
because they concentrate on relatively few stocks in specific industries
that often go in and out of favor.

Technology funds are a good example of the dangers in overweighting sector funds. Technology funds led the bull market in the late 1990s, with many boasting annual returns of over 100 percent. This attracted millions of investors who overloaded their portfolios with technology stocks and stock funds. Unfortunately, these same investors suffered serious losses when many technology stocks plunged more than 70 percent, or went into bankruptcy, during the subsequent 2000–2002 bear market. Stock traders often say, "Bulls make money, bears make money, but hogs get slaughtered."

If you decide to add one or more sector funds, we suggest that your total allocation to sector funds not exceed 10 percent of the equity portion of your portfolio. Jack Bogle had this to say: "You could go your entire life without ever owning a sector fund and probably never miss it."

Real Estate Investment Trusts (REITs) are a special type of stock. REIT funds often behave differently than other stock funds. This characteristic of noncorrelation can make them a worthwhile addition to larger portfolios. We suggest that REIT funds not exceed 10 percent of your equity allocation.

International Stocks

U.S. stocks represent about half the value of world stocks, with foreign stocks representing the other half. Foreign stocks offer diversification and possibly higher returns, but they also carry more risk in the form of political instability, weak regulation, higher transaction costs, and different accounting practices. Of particular significance is the fact that a foreign stock investment is really two investments—one in stocks and one in currencies. Both elements provide additional diversification to a domestic portfolio.

The history of the Japanese stock market may provide the best evidence of how diversification among international stocks can be worthwhile. At the end of 1989, the Japanese stock market's capitalized value was the largest in the world. The Nikkei 225 Index reached an all-time high of 39,916. Twenty-two years later, the Nikkei was under 8,500. As of this writing, the Nikkei remains far below its 1989 high. Sad is the Japanese investor who failed to invest in international stocks outside Japan. Who can say that the same thing could not happen to U.S. stock investors? Financial writer Larry Swedroe offers this good advice: "Never treat the highly likely as certain and the highly unlikely as impossible."

Table 8.4 lists the 1998 to 2013 returns of the S&P 500 Domestic Stock Index and the Morgan Stanley Capital International EAFE (Europe, Australasia, and the Far East) Stock Index.

TABLE 8.4 COMPARISON OF DOMESTIC INDEX VERSUS INTERNATIONAL INDEX RETURNS

Year	Domestic	International	Best Performer
1998	28.6%	20.0%	Domestic
1999	21.0%	27.0%	International
2000	–9.1%	–14.2%	Domestic
2001	–11.9%	–21.4%	Domestic
2002	–22.1%	–15.9%	International
2003	28.7%	38.6%	International
2004	10.9%	20.3%	International
2005	4.9%	13.5%	International
2006	15.8%	26.3%	International
2007	5.5%	11.2%	International
2008	–37.0%	–43.4%	Domestic
2009	26.5%	31.8%	International
2010	15.0%	7.7%	Domestic
2011	2.1%	–12.1%	Domestic
2012	16.0%	17.3%	International
2013	32.4%	22.8%	Domestic

We can see that domestic stocks and international stocks behave differently at different times. Over very long periods of time their returns have been quite similar. So what are we to do? Jack Bogle, in *Common Sense on Mutual Funds*, writes: "Overseas investments—holdings in the corporations of other nations—are not essential, nor even necessary, to a well-diversified portfolio. For investors who disagree—and there are some valid reasons for global investing—we recommend limiting international investments to a maximum of 20 percent of a global equity portfolio."

We believe that investors will benefit from an international stock allocation of 20 percent to 40 percent of their equity allocation.

Subdividing Your Bond Allocation

In Chapter 3, we discussed bonds in detail. We will now suggest specific bond funds for your bond allocation.

Bond Funds

A single low-cost short- or intermediate-term, good-quality bond fund should be adequate for small investors. The bond fund should have a duration equal to or less than the expected time frame needed to meet your goal. Keeping your duration less than your time frame reduces the chance of a negative fund return.

We also suggest a broad-based, diversified bond fund such as Vanguard's Total Bond Market Index Fund. This is an intermediate-term bond fund that seeks to match the returns of the Barclay's U.S. Aggregate Float Adjusted Index—a commonly used proxy for the broad investment grade U.S. bond market. This bond fund holds approximately 6,000 individual bonds with an average duration of approximately five years. It has a low expense ratio of 0.20 percent (0.10 percent for Admiral shares). Its worst annual loss since its inception in 1986 was (–2.7 percent) in 1994.

Investors with a short time frame, or who are worried about volatility, should opt for a short-term bond fund. Volatility will be less, but expected return will also be less. Even more than stocks, there is no free lunch in bonds. This is because thousands of experienced and highly trained professional bond managers all over the world are continuously watching their screens to take advantage of what they perceive as a mistake in bond pricing. By immediately buying or selling, these bond professionals almost instantly bring the bond's price back to perceived fair value.

High-Yield Bonds

High-yield bonds, also known as *junk bonds*, appeal to many investors because of their higher yields and sometimes higher returns than their more staid bond cousins. We have not included them in our portfolios for several reasons:

1. *Bonds are primarily for safety.* Stocks are primarily for higher return (and risk). Junk bond funds behave somewhere between traditional high-quality bonds and stocks. This tends to muddy the important distinction between bonds and stocks in a portfolio, thereby making risk control more difficult.

2. *Taxable high-yield bonds are among the most tax-inefficient of all securi-ties.* By placing high-yield bond funds in retirement accounts (where they belong), there is less room for other tax-inefficient funds.

3. *High-yield bond funds often have higher returns (and risk) than other bond funds.* However, we believe that for investors willing to give up the safety of traditional good-quality bonds, it's more efficient (higher return per unit of risk) to invest in stocks, rather than high-yield bonds.

4. *High-yield bond funds are more closely correlated to stocks.* Thus, they offer less diversification benefit than do traditional bond funds. In the 2008 bear market, Vanguard's High-Yield Bond Fund fell –21.3 percent.

For these reasons, our guideline portfolios do not contain high-yield bond funds.

Treasury Inflation-Protected Securities

As your portfolio increases in size, it's time to consider adding a different type of bond—Treasury Inflation-Protected Securities (TIPS). TIPS provide diver-sification and protection from unexpected inflation. Vanguard offers two TIPS funds—an intermediate-term fund (VIPSX) and a short-term fund (VTAPX). If you decide to include a Vanguard TIPS fund in your portfolio, you can choose between VIPSX ($3,000 minimum) with its *higher* expected risk and return, and VTAPX ($10,000 minimum) with its *lower* expected risk and return. There is no free lunch.

Table 8.5 shows the annual returns of Vanguard's Total Bond Market Index Fund (VBMFX) and Inflation-Protected Securities Fund (VIPSX).

The years 2001, 2002, and 2008 were bad bear market years for stocks. The S&P 500 Index declined (12.2 percent) in 2001, (22.15 per-cent) in 2002 and (37 percent) in 2008. Bonds helped smooth out the ride for investors during these difficult years.

PORTFOLIO GUIDELINES

It's difficult to recommend specific portfolios because each investor is unique. As we learned earlier, we each have different goals, time frames, risk tolerances, and personal financial situations. You may also be restricted to investing in only the funds offered in your retirement plan.

We suggest eight simple portfolios depending on your stage in life. Four portfolios use asset classes (not specific funds). These will be useful for non-Vanguard investors. The four remaining portfolios are for inves-tors using Vanguard funds. We assume the investor has emergency cash savings elsewhere equal to 3 to 12 months' income. High-income taxpay-ers should consider tax-exempt (municipal) bonds when tax-advantaged accounts are full.

TABLE 8.5 COMPARISON OF ANNUAL RETURNS FOR VBMFX AND VIPSX

YEAR*	VBMFX	VIPSX
2001	8.43%	7.61%
2002	8.26%	16.61%
2003	3.97%	8.0%
2004	4.24%	8.27%
2005	2.40%	2.59%
2006	4.27%	0.43%
2007	6.92%	11.49%
2008	5.05%	−2.85%
2009	5.93%	10.80%
2010	6.42%	6.17%
2011	7.56%	13.24%
2012	4.05%	6.78%
2013	−2.26%	−8.92%

*2001, 2002 and 2008 were bad bear-market years for stocks. Bonds helped smooth out the ride for investors during these difficult years.

A YOUNG INVESTOR'S ASSET ALLOCATION

Domestic large-cap stocks	55%
Domestic mid/small-cap stocks	25%
Intermediate-term bonds	20%

A YOUNG INVESTOR USING VANGUARD FUNDS

Total Stock Market Index Fund	80%
Total Bond Market Index Fund	20%

A MIDDLE-AGED INVESTOR'S ASSET ALLOCATION

Large-cap domestic stock fund	30%
Small/mid-cap funds	15%
International funds	10%
REITs	5%
Intermediate-term bond fund	20%
Inflation-Protected Securities	20%

A MIDDLE-AGED INVESTOR USING VANGUARD FUNDS

Total Stock Market Index Fund	45%
Total International	10%
REIT	5%
Total Bond Market Index Fund	20%
Inflation-Protected Securities	20%

AN INVESTOR IN EARLY RETIREMENT

Diversified domestic stocks	30%
Diversified international stocks	10%
Intermediate-term bonds	30%
Inflation-Protected Securities	30%

AN INVESTOR IN EARLY RETIREMENT USING VANGUARD FUNDS

Total Stock Market Index Fund	30%
Total International Index Fund	10%
Total Bond Market Index Fund	30%
Inflation-Protected Securities	30%

AN INVESTOR IN LATE RETIREMENT

Diversified domestic stocks	20%
Short- or intermediate-term bonds	40%
Inflation-Protected Securities	40%

AN INVESTOR IN LATE RETIREMENT USING
VANGUARD FUNDS

Total Stock Market Index Fund	20%
Short-Term or Total Bond Market	40%
Inflation-Protected Securities	40%

READ WHAT OTHERS SAY

Jack Bogle, author of *Common Sense on Mutual Funds*: "Asset allocation is critically important; but cost is critically important, too—all other factors pale into insignificance."

Frank Armstrong, CFP, AIF, and author of *The Informed Investor*: "The impact of asset allocation or investment policy swamps the other (investment) decisions."

William Bernstein, PhD, MD, author of *The Intelligent Asset Allocator* and *The Four Pillars of Investing*: "If you really want to become proficient at asset allocation you are going to have to log off the net, turn off your computer, and go to the bookstore or library and spend several dozen hours reading books."

Jonathan Clements, distinguished columnist for the *Wall Street Journal* and author of three financial books, *Funding Your Future; Twenty-Five Myths You've Got to Avoid;* and *You've Lost it, Now What?* "Forget Wall Street's exotic garbage. Instead, stick with stock, bond, and money market funds."

Roger C. Gibson, CFA, CFP, author of *Asset Allocation*: "Asset allocation and diversification are the foundation stones of successful long-term investing."

Gary Ginsler, former under-secretary of the Treasury, and **Gregory Baer**, assistant secretary for Financial Institutions: "Sit down and draft an asset allocation plan. If you don't know how much of your total net worth is allocated to each asset class and why, then you're making about the worst mistake in investing."

AAIII Guide to Mutual Funds: "The stock market will fluctuate, but you can't pinpoint when it will tumble or shoot up. If you have allocated your assets properly and have sufficient emergency money, you shouldn't need to worry."

Walter R. Good, CFA, and **Roy W. Hermansen,** CFA, are coauthors of *Active Asset Allocation*. This quote is from another of their books, *Index Your Way to Investment Success*: "Development of a long-term investment plan constitutes the most important single investment decision that you are likely to make."

Professor Burton Malkiel of Princeton University, former member of the Council of Economic Advisers, former Vanguard director, and author of *A Random Walk Down Wall Street*: "The most important decision you will probably ever make concerns the balancing of asset categories (stocks, bonds, real estate, money market securities, etc.) at different stages of your life."

John Merrill, author of *Outperforming the Market*: "Your portfolio mix of asset classes will be far more important in determining its performance than will be your selection of individual securities or mutual funds."

Jane Bryant Quinn, author of *Making the Most of Your Money*: "People don't pay a lot of attention to asset allocation, but it's the key decision that determines your investment success, not how smart (or dumb) you are at picking stocks or mutual funds."

Bill Schultheis, author of *The Coffeehouse Investor*: "The most important factor when diversifying is to adhere to your asset allocation strategy, because when you stick to your strategy and rebalance your assets at year-end, buy and sell decisions are no longer arbitrary."

Charles Schwab, founder of the discount brokerage company that bears his name, and author of *Charles Schwab's Guide to Financial Independence*: "Choose your asset allocation model carefully. Asset allocation is the biggest factor in determining your overall return."

CHAPTER NINE

Costs Matter

Keep Them Low

The shortest route to top quartile performance is to be in the bottom quartile of expenses.

—Jack Bogle

We are accustomed to believing that the more we pay for something, the more we receive. Sorry; this is not how it works when buying mutual funds. Every dollar we pay in commissions, fees, expenses, and so on is one dollar less that we receive from our investment. For this reason, *it's critical that we keep our investment costs as low as possible.*

Most investors have little idea of the many kinds of costs, disclosed and undisclosed, that are associated with investing. It's estimated that the total of all costs in the U.S. equity market (not just mutual funds) is about $300 *billion* annually. We are talking about advisory fees, brokerage commissions, customer fees, legal fees, marketing expenditures, sales loads, securities processing expenses, and transaction costs. Not included in the $300 billion figure is the cost of taxes. We will discuss taxes in Chapters 10 and 11.

FEES COVERED BY THE PROSPECTUS

It's important that we understand the different mutual fund fees and expenses that are listed in every mutual fund prospectus. Later, we will investigate mutual fund transaction costs that are little known and seldom reported. Stephen Schurr, senior editor of TheStreet.com, writes: "Death by a thousand fees isn't going to show up in a quarterly fund statement." For this reason, we will go over them one by one here so that you will know what to look for, what to minimize, and what to avoid.

Sales Charge on Purchases

Many investors pay a front-end sales commission (load) when they purchase their fund shares. Front-end loads may be reduced for large investors. For example, many mutual fund companies will give a 1 percent reduction of the front-end load if you are investing over $100,000 within 13 months. The more you invest, the greater the reduction (called break-points). For very large investors, the load may be waived entirely.

A significant disadvantage of a front-end load is that the load reduces the amount of money actually invested. For example, if an investor writes a $10,000 check to purchase mutual fund shares, and the fund has a 5 percent front-end sales load, only $9,500 is available for investment. Later, you look in the newspaper and it shows that your fund, in which you made a $10,000 investment, had a 10 percent return. Great, you say to yourself, "I made $1,000 last year." Sorry, you actually made only $950 ($9,500 × 10 percent). Next time you see a list of returns for front-loaded mutual funds, it's helpful to know that the returns you are looking at are almost always overstated because they do not factor in the front-end load.

Deferred Sales Charge

Deferred sales charges are often called *back-end loads*. The most common type of back-end load is a *contingent deferred sales load*, or CDSL. The total amount of the load paid by the investor will depend on how long the investor holds his or her shares. CDSL charges typically decrease to zero if the investor holds his or her shares long enough. Unlike a front-end sales charge, an investor paying a back-end sales charge will have the full amount of his/her check invested immediately. Finally, a fund or class with a contingent deferred sales load will typically also have an annual 12b-1 fee.

This is how a 5 percent deferred sales charge might work. If we assume that the investor holds mutual fund shares for less than one year, the commission load would be 5 percent. If the investor holds shares for at least one year, but less than two, the load would be reduced to 4 percent—and so on each year, until the load eventually goes away. A common belief is that by waiting until the surrender fee is gone the commission is eliminated. Not so! The commission has been paid from the increased 12b-1 fees in this type of fund.

The deferred sales charge is usually assessed on either the original purchase value or the value of the fund shares at redemption—whichever is less. However, some companies only assess their back-end loads on the redemption value, which is often more than the amount invested. The only way to be sure how the redemption fee is assessed in a fund that you're considering investing in is to read the prospectus carefully.

We recommend that mutual fund investors avoid load funds. If financial advice is needed, use a fee-only financial planner—not a mutual fund salesperson who has a conflict of interest.

No-Load Mutual Funds

No-load funds do not charge a commission or sales load. However, all funds (load and no-load) have expenses. To help meet these expenses, funds charge certain fees. A brief description of the fees that mutual funds may assess follows.

Purchase Fees

Purchase fees are sometimes charged to new shareholders to help defray costs associated with a fund purchase. The rationale is that each shareholder purchasing shares should pay the costs involved in his or her purchase. One study estimated that purchase costs exceed 1 percent of the value of the average shares purchased. Purchase fees are paid directly into the fund for the benefit of long-term shareholders.

Exchange Fees

Some funds impose a fee when a shareholder exchanges from one fund to another within the same group of funds. Exchange fees are sometimes used to limit expensive fund transactions, discourage market-timing, and lower fund expenses for long-term investors.

Account Fees

An account fee is a fee that some funds impose separately on investors for the maintenance of their accounts. For example, a shareholder whose fund falls below a stated minimum may be charged a low-balance account fee to help defray the cost of maintaining the account.

Redemption Fees

The redemption fee is a fee that funds may charge shareholders when they redeem (sell) their shares. Redemption fees help discourage market-timers who are costly for a fund's buy-and-hold investors. Redemption fees and purchase fees are paid directly to the fund and not to a broker. Reasonable redemption fees, purchase fees, and exchange fees benefit long-term shareholders and penalize short-term traders.

Management Fees

Management fees are those fees paid from fund assets to the fund's investment advisor or affiliate for portfolio management. Management fees do not include purchase fees, exchange fees, low-balance fees, or redemption fees.

12b-1 Fees

12b-1 fees are fees paid by the fund out of fund assets to cover distribution expenses and sometimes shareholder service expenses. They got their name from the SEC rule that authorized their payment. 12b-1 fees have become controversial, largely because they hide the salesperson's deferred sales commission. The SEC allows funds with 12b-1 fees of less than 0.25 percent to call themselves no-load.

Other Expenses

Included in this category are annual operating expenses not included in management fees or 12b-1 fees. Examples include custodial expenses, legal expenses, accounting expenses, transfer agent expenses, and other administrative expenses.

Together, the last three types of expenses listed (management, 12b-1, and other expenses), make up the fund's Total Annual Fund Operating Expense, which is expressed as a percentage of the fund's average net assets. The *expense ratio* of each mutual fund is available from the mutual fund company, from Morningstar, and it's sometimes included in newspapers and other sources of mutual fund performance data. The fund's expense ratio must be disclosed in every mutual fund's prospectus.

Read the Fund Prospectus

Few funds charge all the fees we have discussed. However, the *only* way to know which of these fees and expenses you will be paying is to read the fund's prospectus. The SEC requires that fee and expense information be displayed in the first few pages of the prospectus.

FEES NOT COVERED BY THE PROSPECTUS

Now we come to the costs of mutual fund ownership we seldom find in the prospectus.

Hidden Transaction Costs

A mutual fund incurs a cost every time it buys or sells a security. Transaction costs, caused by fund *turnover*, include brokerage commissions, bid-offer spreads, and market impact costs. Together, they may easily exceed the expense ratio and other costs disclosed in the prospectus.

Brokerage Commissions

In a study titled, "Portfolio Transaction Costs at U.S. Equity Mutual Funds," researchers Jason Karceski, Miles Livingston, and Edward O'Neal found that the average brokerage commission cost for mutual fund managers was 0.38 percent of fund assets.

Soft-Dollar Arrangements

Some mutual fund companies have *soft-dollar arrangements* with their brokers. This is a situation in which the broker, in addition to receiving a commission for buying and selling securities at the best price, receives a commission for providing added benefits to the fund manager. Investigators found that these soft-dollar commissions were sometimes being used to hide the costs of employees' salaries, travel, entertainment, and meals, which should correctly be included in the mutual fund's expense ratio.

Spread Costs

In addition to the broker's commission, every time a security is bought or sold there is a hidden *spread* that is the difference between the market maker (dealers and specialists) bid and ask prices. A 2004 study prepared for the Zero Alpha Group (ZAG) found that the average annual spread between bid and asked prices was 0.34 percent (0.06 percent for index funds).

Market Impact Costs

Fund managers usually buy and sell securities in large blocks. This frequently forces the fund manager to buy more stocks (or bonds) than is offered at the prevailing price. The result is that the manager and his or her broker will have to raise their offer above the prevailing price in order to attract enough sellers. The reverse is true when selling large blocks of stocks (or bonds). In this situation, the mutual fund manager is often forced to sell at a lower price to attract sufficient buyers.

Barra, a research firm, did a study of market impact cost and found that a stock fund with $500 million in assets and a turnover rate of 80 to 100 percent could lose 3 to 5 percent a year to market impact costs. Another study by Clifford Dow found that market impact costs of a mutual fund transaction may vary anywhere from 0.5 percent to 20 percent of the value of the security traded.

A Word About Turnover

Turnover refers to the amount of buying and selling activity that's done by the fund manager in a given year. A turnover of 100 percent indicates that the manager buys and sells the average stock in the fund portfolio every twelve months. Turnover is expensive, because it includes the cost of brokerage commissions, spreads, market impact costs, and increased management costs, and it usually increases taxes as well. Studies have found that funds with a low turnover (lower costs) have a higher average return than similar funds with high turnover (higher costs). Fund turnover figures are found in the fund prospectus or by asking a fund representative. Morningstar is also a good source for finding out what a particular mutual fund's turnover rate is.

Wrap Fees

Wrap fees, imposed by brokerage firms, are another fee we should mention. Wrap fees are sold to investors who want a private money manager of their own. Wrap fees, sometimes 2 percent or more, are added to the underlying expenses of the selected mutual funds. We feel that it's nearly always a mistake to pay twice for professional management, which is exactly what happens with wrap accounts. Avoid the wrap.

ADDING IT ALL TOGETHER

As you can see, the costs incurred by investors in U.S. equity funds are numerous, and many are hidden. To get a good idea of the total annual cost of the average U.S. equity mutual fund, review the figures prepared by Jack Bogle and the Bogle Research Center:

TOTAL ANNUAL COSTS OF U.S. EQUITY
MARKET FUNDS

AVERAGE EQUITY MUTUAL FUND	PERCENT OF AVERAGE ASSETS
Advisory fees	1.1
Other operating expenses	0.5
Total Expense Ratio	1.6
Transaction costs	0.7
Opportunity cost	0.4
Sales charges	0.6
Total Annual Cost	3.3

From 1926 through 2004 the compound annual return for U.S. stocks was 10.5 percent, according to Ibbotson Associates, a Chicago investment firm. If we subtract the total annual cost (3.3 percent) of the average mutual fund, we find that the average shareholder had a compound annual return of 7.2 percent. In other words, each year the average mutual fund takes nearly one-third of our investment return for itself. It could even be worse! If costs remain the same, and future returns are lower, as many prognosticators believe, the costs of investing (as a percentage of total return) will be even more damaging.

To understand the devastating effect of cost, we will use as an example a young worker named Tad, age 25, starting his first job with zero savings, but determined to invest $3,500 annually into a Roth IRA until retirement at age 65 (40 years).

Using the Bloomberg Retirement Planner calculator (www .bloomberg.com/invest/calculators/returns.html), without inflation adjustment, we find that if Tad had the long-term average stock return of 10.5 percent, he would accumulate $1,961,795. Sounds great! However, if Tad's average return was 7.2 percent because of mutual fund costs, he would accumulate only $788,745—*less than half!*

Of course, Tad will not stop investing at retirement. Assuming Tad continues to earn the market's average return of 10.5 percent on his $1,961,795 portfolio, he would enjoy an average annual return of $205,988. However, if Tad earns only 7.2 percent on a $788,745 portfolio, he will have to get by with an average annual return of $56,790—*less than one-third!*

Do costs matter? You bet they do! As we've stated in other parts of the book, we don't feel it's prudent to plan for returns of 10.5 percent going forward. However, whatever the future stock market returns, lower fees are certainly better than higher fees.

TAKING ADVANTAGE OF LOWER COSTS

Knowing the tremendous advantage of keeping costs low, we need to put this knowledge to good use. Whenever possible, we will use index funds with their low cost and low turnover. ETFs and low cost, low-turnover, managed funds may also be considered. According to Vanguard and Lipper, Inc., in 2012 the average expense ratio for Vanguard funds was 0.19 percent, *which is one-sixth the average fund's expense ratio of 1.11 percent.*

LOW COST AS A PREDICTOR

We have seen how low cost improves return. It's not surprising that low cost is also the most reliable indicator for predicting a mutual fund's future performance. Unfortunately, there is no foolproof system that will enable us to select winning mutual funds in advance. If there were, we would use the magic system to give us a life of leisure and riches. Investing is about probabilities—and the probability is good that by using low-cost mutual funds, we will outperform the majority of other investors.

The Financial Research Corporation conducts research for industry insiders. One of their most important studies was to determine which of 11 common predictors of future mutual fund performance really worked. The predictors studied were Morningstar ratings; past performance; expenses; turnover; manager tenure; net sales; asset size; alpha; beta; standard deviation (SD); and the Sharpe ratio. Their study's conclusion: *The expense ratio is the only reliable predictor of future mutual fund performance.*

In another study, Standard & Poor's examined all diversified U.S. stock funds in nine different Morningstar style-box categories. The study, reported in the September 2003 issue of *Kiplinger* magazine, divided the funds in each Style Box into two groups: funds with above-average costs and funds with below-average costs. The results of the study? In eight out of nine categories, lower-cost funds beat higher-cost funds during 1-year, 3-year, 5-year, and 10-year periods. They also found a similar pattern with bond funds.

CONCLUSION

In this chapter we learned about the critical importance of low cost when selecting mutual funds. Accordingly, we will avoid all load funds and we will favor low-cost index funds. We will *always* read the prospectus to determine the published costs of any fund we are considering. We will *always* know a fund's turnover so that we have an idea of the fund's hidden transaction costs—the higher the turnover, the higher the cost is likely to be. We will not use wrap accounts. We will remember that low cost is the best predictor for selecting funds with above-average performance. Above all, we will remember—*cost matters*.

READ WHAT OTHERS SAY

American Association of Individual Investors Guide to the Top Mutual Funds: "Funds with loads, on average, consistently underperform no-load funds when the load is taken into consideration."

Frank Armstrong, author of *The Informed Investor*: "Wrap fee accounts may be great for the ego, but they're bad economics."

Greg Baer and Gary Gensler, authors of *The Great Mutual Fund Trap*: "Many of the costs of investing are practically invisible—you never have to write a check to anyone for fees or commissions."

William Bernstein, PhD, MD, author of *The Intelligent Asset Allocator* and *The Four Pillars of Investing*: "Make no mistake about it, you are engaged in a brutal zero-sum contest with the financial industry. Every penny of commissions, fees, and transactional cost they extract is irretrievably lost to you."

John Brennan, former Vanguard CEO and author of *Straight Talk on Investing*: "You should care about expenses because they directly reduce the return you receive. It's as simple as that."

Richard Ferri, author of *Protecting Your Wealth in Good Times and Bad*: "Let's face it: Most investment companies are in business to make money from you, not for you. Every dollar you save in commissions and fee expenses goes right to your bottom line."

Arthur Levitt, former chairman of the American Stock Exchange and later chairman of the U.S. Securities and Exchange Commission:

"The deadliest sin of all is the high cost of owning some mutual funds. What might seem to be low fees, expressed in tenths of 1 percent, can easily cost an investor tens of thousands of dollars over a lifetime."

Professor Burton Malkiel, author of *The Random Walk Guide to Investing*: "Let me assure you, many financial services companies make every effort to obscure the total costs you are actually paying. Every extra dollar of expense you pay is skimmed from your investment capital. The only factor reliably linked to future mutual fund performance is the expense ratio charged by the fund."

Jerry Tweddell and **Jack Pierce,** authors of *Winning with Index Mutual Funds*: "Don't assume that because you pay more, you get more. Unlike just about any other business, it's backward on Wall Street: The more you pay for services, the lower your returns are likely to be."

CHAPTER TEN

Taxes: Part One

Mutual Fund Taxation

The profound impact of taxes on fund returns is a subject too long ignored.

—Jack Bogle

In Chapter 9 we learned about the importance of costs and how they reduce mutual fund returns. In this chapter we will discuss the biggest cost of all—taxes. When we understand how taxes are assessed on mutual funds, we can devise ways to significantly reduce the tax drag on our returns. Sir John Templeton rightfully stated, "For all long-term investors, there is only one objective—maximum total return after taxes."

THE DEVASTATING IMPACT OF TAXES

Many studies have been done to determine how federal taxes reduce mutual fund returns to fund shareholders. One of the longest studies, commissioned by Charles Schwab, was for the 30-year period from 1963 to 1992. The study found that a high-bracket taxpayer who invested $1.00 in U.S. stocks at the beginning of that period would have $21.89

at the end of the period if invested in a tax-deferred account. Meanwhile, the same $1.00 would have grown to only $9.87 if invested in a taxable account—*less than half as much.* These figures clearly show that taxes, plus the impact of compounding, make a tremendous difference in after-tax performance.

Jack Bogle did a 15-year study ending March 30, 2009. He found that the average equity mutual fund return was 5.4 percent before taxes and 3.7 percent after taxes—an annual tax-drag of 1.7 percent. During the same period, the more tax-efficient Vanguard S&P 500 Index Fund returned 6.7 percent before taxes and 6.1 percent after taxes.

In a more recent 15-year study ending June 28, 2013, Gerstein Fisher Research examined the tax-drag on mutual fund investors. They concluded that tax-drag ranged from 0.70 percent to 1.20 percent per year for active funds and 0.51 percent per year for passive funds. Fortunately, like expense ratios, minimizing taxes is another cost we can control—if we take the time to learn how. That is what this chapter and the next one are all about.

HOW MUTUAL FUNDS ARE TAXED

If we want to minimize taxes on our mutual funds, it's necessary for us to understand how mutual funds and mutual fund shareholders are taxed at the federal level. We will ignore the different states' income tax rates and regulations in order to keep our discussion as simple as possible.

Two sources of mutual fund income are subject to tax—dividends and capital gains. Each is taxed differently, depending on the type of dividend and the type of capital gain. It's important for us to understand the difference.

Stock Dividends

Stock dividends can be a major source of fund returns. Since 1926, when reliable data first became available, dividends have accounted for approximately 35 percent of total return. In the third quarter of 2013, 84 percent of the stocks in the S&P 500 were paying dividends.

Prior to the Jobs and Relief Reconciliation Act of 2003, stock dividends were taxed at the investor's marginal (highest) income tax rate. However, the Reconciliation Act of 2003 granted relief to most stock dividend recipients. The act reduced the tax on "qualified" dividends, the kind paid by most large U.S. corporations. In 2014, the maximum rate of tax on qualified dividends was:

- Zero percent on any amount that otherwise would be taxed at a 10 percent or 15 percent rate.
- Fifteen percent on any amount that otherwise would be taxed at rates greater than 15 percent but less than 39.6 percent.
- Twenty percent on any amount that otherwise would be taxed at a 39.6 percent rate.

The lower rates on qualified dividends increase the tax-efficiency of stocks relative to bonds whose yield is taxed at ordinary income tax rates. For this reason, and the fact that stocks benefit from the lower capital gains tax rates, we generally recommend placing stocks in taxable accounts and bonds in tax-advantaged accounts.

Tax-aware investors using taxable accounts should check with their mutual fund company to determine if the stock mutual fund they intend to purchase is invested primarily in stocks that pay "qualified" dividends. U.S. corporate dividends are mostly qualified. For example, in 2013, 95 percent of the dividends in Vanguard's Total Stock Market Index Fund qualified for the lower rate. Total International Stock Index Fund dividends were only 68 percent qualified, but international stock funds are eligible for a Foreign Tax Credit as an offset. Both of these total market index funds are very tax efficient and therefore are excellent candidates for taxable accounts.

Bond Dividends

Bond mutual fund dividends are actually bond yields but are described as *dividends* when distributed to shareholders. Bond dividends are not IRS qualified for the lower tax rate. Accordingly, dividends from taxable bond funds in taxable accounts are taxed at the investor's marginal income tax rate—up to 39.6 percent. What do tax-savvy investors do? They place taxable bonds in their tax-sheltered accounts whenever possible.

Capital Gains

Now that we have a general understanding of stock and bond dividends, let's discuss capital gains. A *capital gain* occurs when a stock or bond is sold for a profit. This profit is the difference between the purchase cost of stock or bond shares and their sale price when redeemed (sold). If the stock or bond share is sold below its purchase cost, the difference is a capital loss.

Realized Capital Gains and Losses

A mutual fund manager incurs a *realized* capital gain or capital loss nearly every time a security is sold. At the end of the fund's fiscal year, the manager will add up all the profits and all the losses from the sale of securities in the fund portfolio. If the result is a net profit, the capital gains will be passed on to the fund shareholders and reported on IRS Form 1099-DIV. If the result is a net loss, the fund manager will carry forward the excess losses to offset gains in future years.

Unrealized Capital Gains and Losses

Unrealized capital gains represent the value of profits in the fund's securities that have not yet been sold by the fund manager. If the current market value is more than the manager paid, the unsold security is said to have an unrealized gain. If the current market value is less than the manager paid, the unsold security has an unrealized loss. These unrealized gains and losses are combined and the net unrealized gains or losses can be found in the fund's prospectus and financial statements.

Tax Implications of Unrealized Gains and Losses

Before purchasing a fund for their taxable accounts, investors should determine the amount of the fund's unrealized gains or losses, since un-realized gains can become realized gains—especially in funds with high turnover. Here is a particularly horrible example as related by Jason Zweig in an article in the July 1999 issue of *Money* magazine titled "Mutual Fund Tax Bombs":

> *On Nov. 11 of 1998, a physician in San Francisco invested $50,000 in a mutual fund called BT Investment Pacific Basin Equity. In January, scarcely seven weeks after he had bought the BT fund—he got the shock of his investing life. On his original $50,000 investment, BT Pacific Basin had paid out $22,211.84 in taxable capital gains. Every penny of the payout was a short-term gain, taxable at Dr. X's ordinary income tax rate of 39.6 percent. He suddenly owed nearly $9,000 in federal taxes. As a California resident, he was also in the hole for $1,000 in state tax.*

Jason's article cites an unusual case, but it demonstrates how capital gains distributions can result in large and unexpected tax liabilities.

Unrealized gains shouldn't be used to rule out all funds. Tax-managed funds often have large unrealized capital gains, but they're still very tax efficient. The fund manager accomplishes this tax efficiency by postponing the sale of profitable funds (accumulating unrealized gains) or by selling offsetting losing funds.

Short- and Long-Term Capital Gains

A short-term capital gain is a profit on the sale of a security or mutual fund share that is held for 12 months or *less*. A long-term capital gain is a profit on the sale of a security or mutual fund share that is held for more than one year.

Tax rates for short-term and long-term capital gains are not the same. It's very important for tax-savvy investors to understand the difference. Short-term capital gains are taxed as ordinary income at the shareowner's *highest* marginal income tax rate, while long-term capital gains enjoy a maximum tax rate of 15 percent—*approximately half.*

One of the easiest and most effective ways to cut mutual fund taxes significantly is to hold mutual funds for *more* than 12 months. Buy-and-hold is a very effective strategy in taxable accounts.

TURNOVER AND TAXES

You can see from the previous discussion that there is no capital gains tax on profitable securities within a fund until the security is sold. Accordingly, a tax-savvy investor looks for funds with low turnover. This results in two primary tax advantages:

1. Low turnover indicates that the fund's securities are being held for longer time periods, which results in *fewer* realized capital gains that are subject to tax.
2. The funds that are sold will have *lower* long-term capital gains taxes.

For maximum tax efficiency in taxable accounts, you should do the following:

- Favor funds with low dividends.
- Favor funds with "qualified" dividends.
- Favor funds with low turnover.
- Favor tax-efficient index funds and tax-managed funds.

INVESTING IN TAXABLE ACCOUNTS

Tax-savvy investors first take advantage of tax-sheltered retirement plans, which we'll discuss in the next chapter. Unfortunately, many investors cannot qualify for IRS-approved retirement plans, or if they are qualified, the limitations on maximum contributions may require that additional savings be placed in taxable accounts.

As mentioned earlier, it's very important when using mutual funds in taxable accounts to use tax-efficient mutual funds or ETFs. Tax efficiency is relative. The idea is to locate the least tax-efficient funds in your tax-advantaged accounts and the most tax-efficient funds in your taxable

TABLE 10.1 **RELATIVE TAX EFFICIENCY RANKING FOR MAJOR ASSET CLASSES**

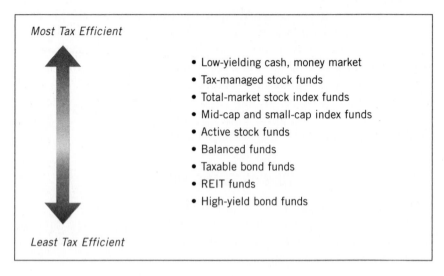

Most Tax Efficient

- Low-yielding cash, money market
- Tax-managed stock funds
- Total-market stock index funds
- Mid-cap and small-cap index funds
- Active stock funds
- Balanced funds
- Taxable bond funds
- REIT funds
- High-yield bond funds

Least Tax Efficient

account. Table 10.1 ranks the *approximate* tax-efficiency of various asset-class funds.

Mutual fund companies are now required to report "before tax" and "after tax" returns in the prospectus. Thus, mutual fund investors should carefully consider the tax efficiency of each fund they plan to hold in a taxable account. A good source for locating a fund's tax efficiency rating is www.morningstar.com. Morningstar provides a "Tax-Cost Ratio," which is the actual percentage *point* reduction in fund return resulting from taxes for an investor in the maximum federal tax bracket. Morningstar reports the Tax-Cost Ratio for 3-, 5-, 10-, and 15-year periods, when available. We recommend using the Tax-Cost Ratio from the longest period so that both bull and bear market cycles are included. Mutual fund tax efficiency, which is generally low in bull markets and high in bear markets, can result in misleading assumptions if measured over short periods of time.

Use only long-term holdings in taxable accounts. It's very important (from both a cost and tax standpoint) to avoid selling or exchanging profitable mutual funds in a taxable account. This is because every sale of shares in a profitable, taxable fund is subject to transaction costs and a capital gains tax. After paying the capital gains tax, you'd end up with that much less for reinvestment in another fund. It's very difficult to pick an alternate fund that is so good that it will earn a superior return on a smaller investment.

Use index or tax-managed funds in taxable accounts. The problem with using managed funds in a taxable account is that the investor cannot be sure that good prior performance will be repeated. We will again use the Fidelity Magellan Fund as an example.

Once the world's largest and best performing fund, the Magellan Fund for many years trounced its benchmark S&P 500 Index. Unfortunately for Magellan shareholders, its more recent performance, despite a succession of carefully selected managers, has been disappointing. As of December 31, 2013, the Magellan Fund had a 10-year annualized after-tax return of 4.0 percent, ranking it in the bottom 2 percent of funds in its category. This compares with the Vanguard S&P 500 Index Fund's after-tax return of 7.29 percent, ranking it in the top 22 percent in its category.

Magellan taxable investors have a *Hobson's choice*. They must continue to pay high annual income and capital gains taxes by holding a tax-inefficient and underperforming fund—or pay a capital gains tax on all past profits, should they decide to exchange to another fund.

The average mutual fund manager remains in his/her position only about five years. This means that if we select a managed fund based on the fund manager's performance, over a long period of time, we are almost certain to find new management at the helm of our fund, with no assurance of continued performance. We suggest that the best solution to this problem in taxable accounts is to use low-cost, low-turnover, tax-efficient index funds that do not depend on the skill (or luck) of stock-picking managers. They are tax efficient and low cost, reflect their benchmark index, and can be held indefinitely.

How Tax-Managed Funds Save Taxes

Most mutual fund performance data is pretax, and nearly all mutual fund managers are compensated on pretax returns. Taxes incurred in the manager's buying and selling of securities is passed on to the fund shareholders. Accordingly, mutual fund managers have little reason to minimize shareholder taxes in their pursuit of higher returns.

The bull market in stocks during the 1980s and 1990s resulted in large gains in many of the stocks held by portfolio managers. Many managers were buying and selling stocks like traders instead of using them as long-term investments.

Many of these managers had turnover exceeding 200 percent, which means that, on average, they only owned each stock for a period of just six months. Every time a manager sold a profitable fund, the gain was passed on to shareholders. It wasn't long before mutual fund shareholders came to realize (about April 15) that a good part of their gains was being seriously eroded by taxes. The result was a shareholder demand for mutual funds that were managed in a manner that would reduce their taxes and result in higher after-tax returns. Enter tax-managed funds.

Tax-managed funds reduce or eliminate shareholder taxes by using a variety of tax-reduction techniques:

- *Low turnover.* Many tax-managed funds use an index-oriented approach to take advantage of indexing's inherent advantages of low cost (higher return) and low turnover (fewer capital gains).
- *Use HIFO (highest-in, first-out) accounting.* Tax-sensitive fund managers sell highest cost shares first, thereby keeping capital gains, which are passed through to shareholders, to a minimum.
- *Tax-loss harvesting.* This is a strategy in which the manager sells losing stocks to accumulate tax losses, which can later be used to offset capital gains from winning stocks.
- *Selecting low-dividend paying stocks.* Dividends are first used to pay fund expenses, and then the balance is passed on to shareholders, resulting in taxes that have to be paid at tax time. Selecting stocks with few or no dividends will minimize annual shareholder taxes.
- *Holding securities for long-term gains.* Short-term gains on the sale of securities held 12 months or less are taxed at about double long-term gains. A tax-sensitive manager will try to hold securities longer than one year.
- *Use redemption fees.* Tax-managed funds frequently require redemption fees in order to discourage shareholders from selling profitable shares, resulting in capital gains and unnecessary trading costs.

Tax-Manage Your Own Portfolio—Strategies You Can Use

Investors cannot control their stock and bond market fund returns. However, investors can control costs—which includes taxes. Most investors simply throw up their hands, saying, "I don't understand taxes—they are too complicated." We believe that by taking the time to understand a few basic rules, most mutual fund investors can dramatically increase their after-tax returns—and that's what really matters. You can use many of the same tax-reducing techniques that are used by tax-aware mutual fund managers when managing your own personal portfolio.

- *Keep turnover low.* We know that buying and selling funds in a taxable account generates capital gains taxes. Therefore, we will try to buy funds that can be held "forever."
- *Use only tax-efficient funds in taxable accounts.* We will try to use only tax-efficient funds in our taxable account(s). This usually means low-turnover index and/or tax-managed funds.
- *Avoid short-term gains.* We know that short-term gains are taxed at about twice the rate of long-term gains. Therefore, we will try to hold profitable shares for more than 12 months before selling.
- *Buy fund shares after the distribution date.* Mutual funds pay taxable distributions at least annually. If we buy a fund shortly before a distribution date, we will have to pay taxes on the distribution. If we wait until after the distribution date, the value of our purchase will still be the same (assuming no market change), but we will avoid the tax on the distribution.
- *Sell fund shares before the distribution date.* There may be a small advantage in selling before the distribution date.
- *Sell profitable shares after the new year.* If shares are sold in December, the tax will be due with that year's return. By simply waiting until January to sell, the tax will be reported a year later. There's usually no sense in paying taxes any earlier than we have to.
- *Harvest tax losses.* This is the practice of selling losing securities in taxable accounts for the purpose of obtaining tax losses to reduce current and future income taxes.

Tax-Loss Harvesting

First Quadrant, LP did a study in which it simulated returns for 500 assets over 25 years to examine the benefits of tax-loss harvesting. They found a huge advantage in tax-loss harvesting versus the passive case. They found that by taking losses, the median portfolio would add about 27 percent, compared to a pure buy-and-hold strategy in typical market conditions. Even after liquidation, the advantage is still an impressive 14 percent.

To understand how tax-loss harvesting works, let's assume it's December. During the year, you sold or exchanged one of your taxable funds for a $2,000 profit. You also have another fund with a $6,000 loss. Here's what you should do:

1. Before the year end, sell the losing $6,000 fund.
2. Use $2,000 of the tax loss to offset the $2,000 gain on the profitable fund. This leaves a $4,000 tax-loss balance.

3. Use $3,000 of the balance (the maximum allowed) to reduce your income reported on the first page of your current income tax return. You are then left with a $1,000 tax-loss balance.

4. This $1,000 balance will be a "capital loss carryover" to the following year's return.

If you decide you want to repurchase your losing fund, you must wait 31 days to avoid a disallowance of your tax loss—called a *wash sale*. During the 31-day interim period, you can put the proceeds from the sale of the losing fund into a money market fund. Some investors fear being out of the market for 31 days. In that case, buy a similar (but not identical) fund during the 31-day waiting period. You can find more detailed information about tax-loss harvesting at the Bogleheads Forum Wiki.

BONDS IN YOUR TAXABLE ACCOUNT

Bonds are deceptively complex and often contain restrictive clauses and hidden fees. Like many things, the more we know, the more we realize we don't know. This is one reason we think most investors are better served by holding bond funds with the oversight of an experienced bond fund manager rather than trying to buy bonds directly. An exception might be Treasury issues purchased directly from the U.S. Treasury Department.

Consider Municipal Bond Funds

A municipal bond fund (frequently called a *muni* or tax-exempt bond fund) invests at least 80 percent of its assets in federal tax-exempt bonds. Single-state municipal bond funds hold the bonds of one state so as to provide its residents with income that is exempt from *both* federal and state taxes. Municipal bonds and bond funds can be very beneficial for higher-income taxpayers who do not have room in their tax-deferred accounts for taxable bonds. Municipal bonds and bond funds generally provide lower yields than comparable taxable bonds. Accordingly, you need to calculate the comparable yield of the tax-exempt bond fund you are considering purchasing and then compare it with the yield of an equivalent taxable bond fund. Here's how you'd do it:

Let's assume you're in the 28 percent federal income tax bracket and are considering a 5.75 percent tax-exempt bond fund. In order to see how this 5.75 percent yield compares with the after-tax yield of a similar taxable fund, you simply divide the yield (5.75 percent) by 0.72 (1 less 0.28). The result is 7.99 percent. If an *equivalent* taxable bond fund is yielding more than 7.99 percent, it's the better buy; if under 7.99 percent, the tax-exempt fund is probably the better choice.

This simple calculation does not include the effect of state income taxes, which should also be considered. The calculation becomes complicated because states have different tax rates and methods of calculations. Fortunately for us, Morningstar.com offers a free tax-equivalent yield calculator that allows input of your state income tax rate when computing a comparison between taxable and tax-exempt bond and bond fund yields. Use the "Tools" link on Morningstar's home page.

U.S. Savings Bonds

U.S. Savings Bonds (both I and EE Bonds) are another tax-smart investment you should consider if you have to put bonds in your taxable account. They're tax-deferred for up to 30 years, and are free from state and local taxes. U.S. Savings Bonds were covered in detail in Chapter 3.

In this chapter, we've learned about the various taxes that impact mutual fund investors, and we've talked about a number of strategies and investments to help us minimize these taxes on our taxable investments. Now let's move on to the next chapter, where we'll explore additional tax strategies that we can employ using tax-sheltered accounts.

CHAPTER ELEVEN

Taxes: Part Two

Managing Your Portfolio for Maximum Tax Efficiency

Of all the expenses investors pay, taxes have the potential for taking the biggest bite out of total returns.

—The Vanguard Group

USE TAX-SHELTERED ACCOUNTS

We think the best way for most investors to minimize taxes is to take advantage of IRS tax-favored retirement plans specifically designed to encourage people to save for their retirement (401(k), 403(b), IRA, etc.). We know that if we don't save for ourselves, our government or our families will be forced to undertake the burden. There are now dozens of tax-reducing retirement plans available to workers and their spouses. Unfortunately, these plans are constantly changing and all are ridiculously complex. For example, the Internal Revenue Service Publication 590 contains the IRA instructions for use in preparing tax returns. It's impossible to give complete details of the many retirement plans available. However, we will take a general look at the various provisions of the most popular plans, so that we can select the best plan(s) for our particular situation.

401(k) Plans

A section 401(k) plan is a type of deferred compensation plan in which an employee can elect to contribute a portion of his or her wages to the plan on a pretax (qualified) basis. The contribution limit is 17,500. Employees age 50 and over are allowed an additional "catch-up" contribution of $5,500, meaning their contribution limit is $23,000. Generally, all deferred compensation plans in which the employee participates must be considered together to determine if the contribution limit is exceeded. Employer contributions to deferred compensation plans are not reported on the employee's W-2 forms and *are not reported as income on the employee's income tax return.* However, they are included as wages subject to Social Security, Medicare, and federal unemployment taxes.

Benefits of 401(k) Plans

Company 401(k) plans are the largest type of individually directed savings plan. 401(k) plans vary between different companies, often substantially; however, nearly all company plans offer these advantages:

- You can have other retirement plans.
- Automatic withholding.
- There is flexibility in the contribution amount.
- Employees are always 100 percent vested in their contributions.
- Most plans offer employer matching contributions.
- Employees can contribute more to 401(k) plans than to IRA plans.
- Choice of investment options (usually mutual funds).
- Loans for hardship withdrawals are often available.
- If you switch jobs, you can roll over your 401(k) into an IRA or a new employer's 401(k) plan. (It's *portable.*)
- There is protection from claims of creditors.

Disadvantages of 401(k) Plans

- Administrative and investment costs are high.
- Some have no matching contribution by employer.
- Many have poor investment options.
- Often, information and advice are inadequate.
- Capital gains are converted into ordinary income.
- Access to your money is restricted.

One of the big problems with many 401(k) plans is their high cost. Many employees (and their employers) don't know the true costs associated with their plan. Most costs never show up on the plan participant's statements.

Fees and expenses generally fall into the following four categories:

1. *Plan administration fees* are the fees used for the plan's record keeping, accounting, legal, and trustee services. These fees can also include costs like telephone voice response systems, access to a customer service representative, educational seminars, retirement planning software, website updates, and so on.

2. *Investment fees* are the largest component of 401(k) plan fees and expenses. They are associated with managing the plan's assets. Investment fees are assessed as a percentage of assets invested. You pay for them in the form of an indirect charge against your account because they are deducted directly from your investment returns.

3. *Individual service fees* are fees that are sometimes charged for individual services not covered by the plan's administrative and investment costs. For example, individual service fees may be charged to a participant for taking a loan from the plan.

4. *Sales commissions* can represent a substantial cost that is often not revealed.

Taken together, it's obvious that even a small 401(k) plan is expensive to administer. As you can imagine, it's the employer who decides who pays these costs—the company, the employee, or both. All too often, it's the unknowing employee who foots the bill in reduced returns and who would be better off investing in an IRA or other tax-efficient investment.

How to Find Hidden Fees and Expenses

If your plan permits you to direct the investment assets in your account, the plan administrator should provide you with a copy of the prospectus, which will show all the fund administrative expenses, including sales charges. Your plan administrator should provide you with a description of any other transaction fees and expenses that will be charged.

Account statements are usually provided at least once a year. If a yearly statement is not forthcoming, ask for it. Failure or delay in receiving account statements is a warning sign that your company plan may be in jeopardy.

Your 401(k) Summary Plan Description (SPD) will tell you what the plan provides and how it operates. It *may* tell you if administrative expenses are paid by your plan (you) or by your employer. If paid by your employer, it's a good sign that the employer cares about his employees. A copy of the SPD should be furnished to every plan participant when that person first enrolls in a 401(k) plan.

Every 401(k) plan files an annual report on a series Form 5500. This official document contains information regarding the plan's assets, liabilities, income, and expenses. It also shows the aggregate administrative fees and other expenses paid by the plan. However, Form 5500 will not show the expenses deducted from investment results, or fees and expenses paid by your individual account. Fees paid by your employer will also not be shown. You are entitled to request a copy from the plan administrator (there may be a charge).

Investment options in 401(k) plans are restricted as to what can be offered. Common investments include stock and bond mutual funds, money market funds, guaranteed investment contracts (GICs), your company's stock, bank accounts, and CDs. A growing number of organizations with traditional 401(k) and 403(b) plans are now also offering Roth 401(k) and Roth 403(b) plans, thanks to the passage of The Pension Protection Act of 2006. Unfortunately, many 401(k) plans do not offer a good selection of low-cost mutual funds that you can use to build a diversified asset allocation plan. If your 401(k) falls short, based on its cost and the criteria we discuss in this book, we suggest you do the following:

1. Invest in your 401(k) up to the company match. The company match is free money you cannot afford to forfeit.
2. If eligible, invest in an IRA up to the maximum.
3. Contribute to the 401(k) up to the maximum.
4. Additional funds should go into tax-efficient mutual funds.

403(b) Plans

Unlike 401(k) plans, which are designed for profit-making entities, 403(b) plans are designed for nonprofit entities such as schools, universities, churches, and certain charitable organizations. According to the Spectrem Group, which tracks the 403(b) industry, approximately 80 percent of the $578 billion invested in these plans is held inside annuities. Most of the remainder is invested in stand-alone mutual funds. A 403(b) plan is the only salary-deferral plan available for public school employees. 401(k) and 403(b) plans are similar in that they both allow employees to defer tax on a portion of their salary. Both allow matching contributions and generally have the same maximum limits.

The major disadvantage of 403(b) plans is their choice of investments. Most offer only high-cost annuities sold by brokerage and insurance firms. It makes no sense (except to the annuity company) to pay the extra cost of the annuity's tax deferral when the 403(b) or other tax-deferred plan already provides the same tax-deferral advantage.

A minority of 403(b) plans offer a variety of options from insurance companies, brokerage companies, and mutual fund companies. This places the 403(b) participant at the mercy of commission-paid salesmen, who often have a serious conflict of interest. Never forget, the more taken from your returns in the form of higher fees and expenses, the less you'll end up with in your retirement account.

If you are a participant in a 403(b) plan, it's important for you to take the time to understand your investments so that you can make changes if you learn that your current choices are less than acceptable. A good source of additional information about 403(b) plans is www.403bwise.com/index.html. If you find that your options are limited and/or high-cost, there is a good possibility that your plan has an escape hatch allowing you to move your money to an outside low-cost 403(b) plan provider such as Fidelity, T. Rowe Price, or Vanguard. This type exchange is referred to as a 90-24 transfer.

Individual Retirement Account (IRA)

A *traditional IRA* is a personal savings plan that gives you tax advantages while saving for retirement. Contributions to a traditional IRA may be tax deductible—either in whole or in part. The earnings on the amounts in your IRA are not taxed until they are distributed. The portion of the contributions that was tax deductible also does not get taxed until it's distributed. A traditional IRA can be established at many different kinds of financial institutions, including mutual fund companies, banks, insurance companies, and brokerage firms.

There are limits as to how much you can contribute. The maximum contribution limit for a single individual to traditional and Roth IRAs is $5,500. The catch-up contribution for individuals age 50 or older is $6,500. Contribution limits are indexed for inflation. If you file a joint return and meet certain requirements (see IRS Pub. 590), it is possible for a couple to make combined contributions that can double the single individual limits. Deductions may be reduced or eliminated for workers covered by a retirement plan at work and will also be reduced or eliminated for workers with higher incomes. See IRS Pub. 590 for the current income limits.

Withdrawing from IRAs

All IRA withdrawals (except for Roths) are taxable at the investor's marginal income tax rates. There is a 10 percent tax penalty for withdrawing money from a traditional IRA if the distribution takes place before the IRA holder reaches age 59½. The law provides several exceptions to the 10 percent withdrawal penalty:

- You have unreimbursed medical expenses that are more than 7.5 percent of your adjusted gross income.
- The distributions are not more than the cost of your medical insurance.
- You are disabled.
- You are the beneficiary of a deceased IRA owner.
- You are receiving distributions in the form of annuity type payments.
- The distributions are not more than your qualified higher education expenses.
- You use the distributions to buy, build, or rebuild a first home ($20,000 maximum for married couples).

Nondeductible Traditional IRAs
The Internal Revenue Service permits contributions into what are called *nondeductible traditional IRAs.* Unfortunately, nondeductible IRAs (Roth IRAs are an exception) have two significant disadvantages in addition to being nondeductible. They turn capital gains into higher-taxed ordinary income, and they require the filing of IRS Form 8606 to track your contributions and tax basis. At each withdrawal, you will use your records and a copy of Form 8606 to determine what percentage of your withdrawal is taxable (the earnings part) and what percentage is not taxable (your prior contributions). If you later decide to convert to a Roth or consolidate IRAs, the tax ramifications can be a nightmare.

The Tax Increase Prevention and Reconciliation Act, signed into law in 1996, removed the modified gross income limitation on rollovers from a traditional IRA (TIRA) to a Roth IRA. Because of this change in the law, high-income individuals who are not eligible to contribute to a Roth IRA can now directly do what's become known as a *back-door Roth.* Here's how it works. If the investor doesn't have an existing TIRA because they weren't eligible to contribute to one due to the income limitations, they would first contribute to a nondeductible IRA and then immediately convert that to a Roth IRA, effectively working around the income limits on a direct Roth IRA contribution. Now you understand why it's called a "back-door Roth."

Roth IRAs

The Roth IRA, like the traditional IRA, is also a personal saving plan, but operates somewhat in reverse. For instance, contributions to a Roth IRA are not tax deductible, while contributions to a traditional IRA may or may not be deductible. For both IRA types—traditional and Roth—securities that remain in the account are not taxed. However, when money is withdrawn, traditional IRA withdrawals will be fully taxed, nondeductible IRA withdrawals will be partially taxed, and Roth IRA withdrawals will not be taxed at all.

Differences between Roth and Traditional IRAs

How is a Roth IRA different from a traditional IRA? Table 11.1 shows some of the major differences between these two types of IRAs.

TABLE 11.1   COMPARISON OF TRADITIONAL AND ROTH IRAS

QUESTIONS	TRADITIONAL IRAS	ROTH IRAS
Is there an age limit on when I can set up and contribute?	Yes. You must not have reached age 70½ by the end of the year.	No. You can be any age.
Is there a dollar limit on how much I can contribute?	Yes. You can contribute up to $5,500 or your taxable compensation, whichever is less. If you are age 50 or older, the maximum is $6,500.	Yes. You may be able to contribute up to $6,500 if you are 50 or older, but the amount may be less, depending on your income, filing status, and if you contributed to another IRA.
Can I deduct contributions?	Yes, depending on your income, filing status, whether covered under another retirement plan at work, and whether you receive Social Security benefits.	No. You can never deduct contributions to a Roth IRA.
Do I have to file a form?	Not unless you make nondeductible contributions. In that case, you must file Form 8606.	No. You do not file a form if you contribute to a Roth IRA.
Do I have to start taking distributions at a certain age?	Yes. You must take required minimum distributions by April 1 of the year following the year you reach age 70½.	No. If you are the owner of a Roth IRA, you do not have to take distributions regardless of your age.
How are distributions taxed?	Distributions from a traditional IRA are taxed as ordinary income. Distributions from nondeductible IRAs are only partially taxed.	Distributions from a Roth IRA are not taxed as long as you meet certain criteria. See IRS Pub. 590.
Do I have to file a form just because I receive distributions?	Not unless you have ever made a nondeductible contribution to a traditional IRA. If you have, file Form 8606.	Yes, File Form 8606 if you received distributions from a Roth IRA (other than a rollover, recharacterization, certain qualified distributions, or a return of certain contributions).

Source: Internal Revenue Service, IRS Publication 590.

Which is better, a traditional or Roth IRA? That can be a difficult question to answer because there are many factors to consider. Here are some of the reasons why you might choose one over the other.

Factors Favoring a Traditional (Deductible) IRA

- Your income is too high for a Roth.
- You expect your income in retirement to be less than it is now.
- You expect your future tax rate to be lower.
- You need the tax deduction now.
- Traditional IRAs *may* provide better protection from creditors.

Factors Favoring a Roth IRA

- You expect your future tax rate to be higher.
- Roth IRA savings are worth more. The reason is that the Roth IRA contains after-tax dollars, which are more valuable than the pretax dollars in a regular IRA.
- You want access to your funds. Roth IRAs incur no penalty on early withdrawal of *contributions*.
- Withdrawals are not reportable income; therefore, they do not affect Social Security payments or increase adjusted gross income.
- No required minimum distribution (RMD) at age 70½. This allows continued growth for the benefit of heirs.
- Eligible contributions can be made at any age, unlike traditional IRAs where contributions must stop at age 70½.
- Heirs pay no income tax on proceeds, as they do with traditional IRAs.

How to Choose What Is Right for You

You can readily see that there are pros and cons for each type of IRA. You or your advisor should decide which IRA is best for your particular situation. Fortunately, you can get help on the Internet in the form of IRA calculators. Two IRA calculators that we like can be found at www .morningstar.com (look under "Tools") and at www.vanguard.com (use "Search"). If you have difficulty making up your mind, don't worry. Your investment in either the traditional (deductible) IRA or the Roth IRA is one of the most tax-efficient ways you can invest for your retirement.

IRA Conversions

Owners of traditional IRAs have the option of converting to a Roth IRA. Uncle Sam, of course, knows that if you hold a deductible IRA, you have never paid any taxes on the earnings in your traditional IRA account. Therefore, if you convert, he is not going to let you switch to a future tax-free account without collecting his share. Accordingly, any amount converted will be added to your adjusted gross income and be subject to income tax in the year you do the conversion.

When should you convert? There are several situations we can think of:

1. *You purchased a traditional IRA because you needed the tax deductions.* Now, you no longer need the annual deductions and realize the tax-free withdrawals of a Roth will be more beneficial.
2. *You think tax rates are going to go up in the future.* The amount being converted will be taxed at today's tax rate instead of the higher taxes you expect later.
3. *You are in a period of low income because you lost your job, took a sabbatical, or perhaps retired and are not yet receiving Social Security.* You are living off savings, borrowing, or other nontaxable income. This could be an excellent time to convert—at least in the amount that brings you up to the top of your current low tax bracket. In this situation, your converted IRA savings were tax-deductible, tax-deferred until converted, and will be income tax free at withdrawal—it doesn't get much better than that!

Deciding if, when, and how much to convert from a traditional IRA to a Roth IRA can be a difficult decision. If you are thinking of converting your traditional IRA into a Roth IRA, we think you will find a conversion calculator very helpful. T. Rowe Price, Vanguard, and Morningstar websites all offer conversion calculators to help make your decision easier.

PLACING FUNDS FOR MAXIMUM AFTER-TAX RETURN

Many investors have only tax-advantage retirement accounts. Others have only taxable accounts. However, there are also many of us who have both tax-deferred and taxable accounts. It's very important that we place the appropriate funds in the appropriate account for maximum after-tax return.

The rule is simple: Place your most tax-inefficient funds into your tax-deferred accounts, then put what's left into your taxable account. The following list provides different type assets in the approximate order of their tax-efficiency, from the least tax-efficient (at the top) to the most tax-efficient.

High-yield bonds
International bonds
Taxable domestic bonds
Inflation-protected securities (TIPS)
Real estate investment trusts (REIT)
Balanced funds
Stock-trading accounts
Small-value stocks
Small-cap stocks
Large-value stocks
International stocks
Large-growth stocks
Most stock index funds
Tax-managed funds
EE and I bonds
Tax-exempt (muni) bonds

We can demonstrate the importance of fund placement with a simple illustration. Suppose you had a $100,000 portfolio of two funds—a $50,000 stock fund and a $50,000 bond fund. However, your tax-deferred retirement account can only accommodate $50,000. Looking at the asset list you can see that a bond fund is less tax efficient than a stock fund, so you'd put the bond fund in your retirement account and what's left (your stock fund) in your taxable account. Now let's look at Table 11.2 to see what happens at the end of 30 years.

We see that the after-tax value after 30 years is more than one million dollars; $1,005,451 to be exact. Now let's look at Table 11.3 to see what happens when you do the reverse—you put the bonds in your taxable account and the stocks in your tax-deferred account.

By putting your stock and bond funds in opposite accounts, your portfolio would amount to $866,078. By placing your two funds in the proper accounts, you were able to increase the after-tax value of your portfolio by $119,021 ($1,005,451 − $886,430). Proper placement of funds is very important.

TABLE 11.2 RESULTS OF FUND PLACEMENT WITH STOCKS IN TAXABLE ACCOUNT

	STOCKS IN TAXABLE	BONDS IN TAX-DEFERRED	TOTAL
Beginning value	$50,000	$50,000	$100,000
Value after 30 years	$820,490	$380,613	$1,201,103
Taxes due on withdrawal	$100,499	$95,153	$195,652
After-tax value	$719,991	$285,460	$1,005,451

Assumptions: Stock return 10%; Dividend yield 1.5%; Dividend and Capital Gain tax 15%; Bond return 7%; Income tax 25%.

TABLE 11.3 RESULTS OF FUND PLACEMENT WITH BONDS IN TAXABLE ACCOUNT

	BONDS IN TAXABLE	STOCKS IN TAX-DEFERRED	TOTAL
Beginning value	$50,000	$50,000	$100,000
Value after 30 years	$232,078	$872,470	$1,104,548
Taxes due on withdrawal	$0	$218,118	$218,118
After-tax value	$232,078	$654,352	$886,430

Assumptions: Stock return 10%; Dividend yield 1.5%; Dividend and Capital Gain tax 15%; Bond return 7%; Income tax 25%.

TAX-SAVVY IDEAS

We suggest 14 tax-reducing ideas for tax-savvy investors. Most are easy to understand and to implement. We can think of no better way for most taxpayers to maximize their after-tax returns.

1. Use tax-advantaged accounts (401(k), 403(b), IRAs, 529 tuition plans, etc.).
2. Buy fund shares *after* the distribution date.
3. Place tax-INefficent funds in retirement accounts, and tax-Efficient funds in taxable accounts.
4. Use tax-managed or tax-efficient index funds in taxable accounts.
5. Avoid balanced funds (stocks and bonds) in taxable accounts.
6. Keep taxable fund turnover low to avoid capital-gains taxes.
7. Avoid short-term gains by holding for more than 12 months.
8. Sell losing shares *before* year-end (tax-loss harvest).
9. Sell profitable shares *after* the new year (to delay tax payment).
10. Determine the most favorable tax-basis method before selling fund shares.
11. Consider municipal bonds and U.S. Savings Bonds for taxable accounts.
12. During years of low income, consider converting to a Roth.
13. Consider gifts to charities of securities with large capital gains.
14. Appreciated holdings in taxable accounts are capital gains and income tax free if left to heirs.

Disclaimer: The advice of a qualified professional accountant or tax attorney is recommended for your particular circumstances.

CHAPTER TWELVE

Diversification

Diversification is a protection against ignorance.
—Warren Buffett

W hen it comes to investing, the old saying, "Don't put all your eggs in one basket," definitely applies. Consider the fate of many now-poor employees who had most or all of their retirement plans invested in the high-flying stock of their former employers, such as WorldCom, Enron, or any one of the many others that have gone bankrupt. Not only did these employees lose their retirement money, they also lost their jobs.

Remember the dot.com mania? At the height of the craze, many investors were reveling in their newfound paper wealth after having invested every penny they could get their hands on in the latest hot dot.com stock that just "couldn't fail." Nevertheless, most of them did eventually fail. Most of these dot.com investors considered it to be the fastest road to early retirement. For a few, it was; but for most of them, it turned out to a very expensive lesson in diversification, or rather, the lack thereof. So, instead of the hoped-for early retirement, many of those undiversified dot.com investors now find themselves having to work well beyond their planned retirement age.

We need to keep the dot.com mania in mind when handling our own investments. There will probably be times when you might be tempted to risk it all and swing for the fences on one or another *sure thing.* So, if you're ever tempted, remember that some of the companies that imploded were considered to be the best in their businesses, and yet investors lost their life's savings. It will happen again in the future; don't let it happen to you. Diversify your portfolio!

Diversification offers two distinct benefits to investors. First, it helps reduce risk by avoiding the "all the eggs in one basket" scenario that we just discussed (all of your money invested in a single company). And, second, you could increase your return at the same time.

In order to diversify your portfolio, you want to try to find investments that don't always move in the same direction at the same time. When some of your investments zig, you want other parts of your portfolio to zag. Although diversification can't completely eliminate market risk, it can help to reduce that risk to a level where you feel comfortable enough to sleep well at night.

When it comes to diversification using individual stocks, there is a widely held belief that you can create a nicely diversified portfolio with as few as 20 to 30 stocks of companies of various sizes, operating in different sectors. However, that number has come under fire recently, and may no longer be valid. Our brilliant friend, author William Bernstein, addressed this subject in the Fall 2000 edition of his *Efficient Frontier,* titled "The 15-Stock Diversification Myth." Here's what he had to say:

> So, yes, Virginia, you can eliminate nonsystematic portfolio risk, as defined by Modern Portfolio Theory, with relatively few stocks. It's just that nonsystematic risk is only a small part of the puzzle. Fifteen stocks is not enough. Thirty is not enough. Even 200 is not enough. The only way to truly minimize the risks of stock ownership is by owning the whole market.

You can read Bill's entire *Efficient Frontier* diversification article online, without charge, at www.efficientfrontier.com, if you'd like to learn more.

It isn't practical for most investors to "own the whole market" by investing in lots of individual stocks, since it would be cost prohibitive. As we stated earlier, we believe that mutual funds offer typical investors the single best option for diversifying their portfolio with the minimum amount of money. Mutual funds own hundreds, and sometimes thousands, of individual stocks, giving investors much more diversification than owning a portfolio of individual stocks. For instance, you can own nearly the entire U.S. equity market relatively inexpensively with just a single equity fund, such as Vanguard's Total Stock Market Index Fund (VTSMX). The minimum purchase price for VTSMX is only $3,000 for both IRA and taxable accounts.

Besides (or in addition to) owning the equity market in a single fund, there are a number of other ways to use mutual funds to create a broadly diversified portfolio of all asset classes. One way to further diversify is to purchase mutual funds that own different segments of the equity markets. There are U.S. equity funds and foreign equity funds. Within each of those major market categories, there are mutual funds that segment the market further by size (large caps, mid caps, small caps, micro caps), or by investment style (blend or core stocks, value stocks, and growth stocks). Some funds focus on a particular sector of the market, such as health care or technology. There are even commodity mutual funds (gold, precious metals, etc.).

Now we need to look beyond an all-stock portfolio for further diversification. That's where bonds and bond mutual funds come in. Since bond values are sometimes rising at the same time that stocks prices are falling, and vice versa, we can smooth the ride out a bit by including both equities and bonds in our portfolio.

Like equities, bonds come in many flavors. There are short-term bond funds, intermediate-term bond funds, and long-term bond funds. Some bond funds invest in government bonds, some in corporate bonds, and others in municipal bonds. While some bond funds invest in highly rated investment-grade bonds, still others invest in lower-rated junk bonds. For more information on the various types of bonds, see Chapter 3.

When investments (like stocks and bonds) don't always move together, they're said to have a low correlation coefficient. Understanding the correlation coefficient principal isn't really that difficult. The correlation numbers for any two investments can range from +1.0 (perfect correlation) to −1.0 (negative correlation). Basically, if two stocks (or funds) normally move together at the same rate, they're said to be highly correlated, and when two investments move in opposite directions, they're said to be negatively correlated. A perfect correlation between two investments (they both go up and down together) would get a rating of 1.0. When two investments each randomly go their separate ways, independent of the movement of the other one, there is said to be no correlation between them, and their correlation figure would be shown as 0. Finally, when two investments always move in the opposite direction, they would have a negative correlation, which would be represented by a rating of −1.0.

In actual practice, you'll find that most investment choices available to you will have a correlation coefficient somewhere between 1.0 (perfect correlation) and 0 (noncorrelated). It's very difficult to find negatively correlated asset classes that have similar expected returns. The closer the number is to 1.0, the higher the correlation between the two assets, and the lower the number, the less correlation there is between the two investments. So, a correlation figure of 0.71 would mean the two assets are not perfectly correlated, but a fund with a correlation figure of 0.52 would offer still more diversification, since it has an even lower number.

Despite what some investors think, simply owning a large number of mutual funds doesn't automatically achieve greater diversification. If a portfolio holds a number of funds that overlap and are highly correlated, there is little benefit. *R*-squared is a simple way the investment community uses to differentiate between investments that are highly correlated and those that are not. For instance, Vanguard's website tells us that each of the mutual funds in Table 12.1 has a high correlation with the Dow Jones U.S. Total Stock Market Index, as shown by their *R*-squared numbers. If an investor owned several of the funds from Table 12.1, it would offer little additional diversification benefit because all of the funds are very similar.

TABLE   12.1   CORRELATION TO DOW JONES U.S. TOTAL STOCK MARKET INDEX (AS OF 11/30/2013)

FUND NAME AND SYMBOL	*R*-SQUARED
Vanguard 500 Index Fund (VFINX)	1.00
Vanguard Growth and Income Fund (VQNPX)	0.99
Vanguard T-M Capital Appreciation Fund (VMCAX)	1.00
Vanguard Total Stock Market Index Fund (VTSMX)	1.00

Let's now take a look at Table 12.2 to see how four of the popular Vanguard funds that are discussed frequently on the Bogleheads Forum have moved in relation to some of the other Vanguard mutual funds. Simply look at the figure where any two funds intersect to find their R-squared over a five-year period. Remember, generally the higher the R-squared, the less diversification benefits we would have gotten by holding both funds during that period. Conversely, the lower the R-squared figure, the greater the diversification benefits of holding both funds. So, to apply the principle of diversification to your portfolio, you would want to add investments that have a low correlation to your other funds. We do have to keep several things in mind regarding correlations. First, they change over time. For instance, an actively managed fund that's been a successful small-cap fund may well attract so much new money that it might have to start investing in larger stocks. Thus, over time, it could become more closely correlated to a large-cap benchmark, and less correlated to its previous small-cap benchmark.

Second, just because two funds have a low correlation to each other doesn't necessarily mean that they're a suitable investment for *your* portfolio. For instance, we can see in Table 12.2 that Vanguard's Precious Metals & Mining Fund has a low correlation to most other funds, but the fund's returns are quite volatile and thus may not be suitable for some investors.

So, creating a well-diversified portfolio of mutual funds can be done relatively easily. It doesn't have to be a daunting or expensive task, and can be done without a broker or paid advisor. You can put the portfolio together yourself using a number of individual funds, or you can just buy a fund of funds like one of Vanguard's Target Retirement funds that does it for you. Either way, you get the diversification you need without putting all of your eggs in one basket.

TABLE 12.2 SAMPLE OF A FIVE-YEAR *R*-SQUARED FUND TABLE

Fund	500 Index	Total Stock Mkt. Index	Total Int'l. Stock Index	REIT Index	Small-Cap Value Index	Tax-Managed International	Tax-Managed Small-Cap	Total Bond Market Index
500 Index		.99	.78	.12	.59	.76	.61	.10
Asset Allocation	.95	.94	.80	.13	.56	.78	.55	.04
Balanced Index	.95	.96	.82	.20	.65	.80	.65	.02
Calvert Social Index	.97	.96	.69	.11	.54	.67	.58	.13
Capital Opportunity	.88	.91	.64	.12	.57	.61	.66	.10
Capital Value	.94	.94	.79	.14	.59	.77	.62	.06
Convertible Securities	.56	.61	.55	.22	.62	.53	.64	.01
Developed Markets Index	.76	.78	1.0	.23	.69	1.0	.64	.02
Dividend Growth	.74	.77	.85	.18	.73	.84	.72	.03
Emerging Mkts. Stock Index	.71	.75	.73	.24	.72	.68	.68	.04
Energy Fund	.24	.26	.39	.06	.35	.39	.32	0
Equity Income	.91	.90	.87	.16	.66	.85	.62	.04
European Stock Index	.79	.80	.92	.13	.64	.92	.60	.04

148

Explorer	.73	.82	.68	.23	.82	.65	.91	.10
Extended Market Index	.78	.86	.74	.26	.84	.71	.91	.09
Global Equity	.79	.83	.89	.23	.77	.87	.73	.02
Growth and Income	.99	.98	.80	.14	.60	.78	.63	.09
Growth Equity	.93	.91	.62	.12	.54	.60	.63	.10
Growth Index	.94	.93	.61	.08	.46	.59	.53	.16
Health Care	.69	.68	.63	.05	.41	.63	.40	.04
International Growth	.82	.85	.96	.23	.76	.95	.72	.04
International Value	.76	.80	.94	.22	.75	.92	.71	.07
International Explorer	.65	.70	.88	.26	.73	.86	.67	.01
Large-Cap Index	1.0	.99	.78	.13	.60	.76	.63	.10
Mid-Cap Growth	.64	.72	.55	.19	.66	.52	.79	.12
Mid-Cap Index	.81	.88	.78	.25	.86	.75	.90	.08

(continued)

Fund	500 Index	Total Stock Mkt. Index	Total Int'l. Stock Index	REIT Index	Small-Cap Value Index	Tax-Managed International	Tax-Managed Small-Cap	Total Bond Market Index
Morgan Growth	.92	.95	.69	.13	.62	.67	.71	.12
Pacific Stock Index	.20	.22	.45	.31	.30	.46	.27	0
Precious Metals & Mining	.07	.09	.16	.19	.24	.15	.21	.05
PRIMECAP	.93	.95	.66	.11	.59	.63	.66	.14
REIT Index	.12	.15	.24	—	.34	.23	.22	.04
Selected Value Fund	.68	.73	.80	.25	.79	.78	.73	.02
Small-Cap Growth Index	.61	.70	.60	.19	.82	.57	.94	.11
Small-Cap Index	.69	.78	.73	.29	.92	.70	.96	.08
Small-Cap Value Index	.59	.67	.72	.34	—	.69	.94	.04
STAR Fund	.90	.93	.87	.23	.72	.85	.72	.01
Strategic Equity	.78	.85	.74	.28	.82	.71	.88	.06
Tax-Managed Balanced	.90	.91	.75	.19	.59	.73	.59	0
Tax-Managed Cap Appr.	.99	.99	.77	.13	.63	.75	.67	.12

Tax-Managed Gr. & Income	1.0	.99	.78	.12	.59	.76	.61	.10
Tax-Managed International	1.0	.78	1.0	.23	.69	—	.64	.02
Tax-Managed Small-Cap	.61	.70	.67	.22	.94	.64	—	.09
Total Bond Market Index	.10	.10	.02	.04	.04	.02	.09	—
Total Int'l Stock Index	.78	.80	—	.24	.72	1.0	.67	.02
Total Stock Market Index	.99	—	.80	.15	.67	.78	.70	.10
U.S. Growth	.88	.88	.60	.11	.46	.58	.53	.17
U.S. Value	.89	.92	.81	.18	.77	.78	.74	.04
Value Index	.95	.94	.87	.17	.66	.86	.64	.05
Wellesley Income	.32	.31	.45	.15	.27	.45	.17	.25
Wellington	.87	.87	.83	.20	.65	.81	.60	.01
Windsor Fund	.96	.97	.82	.16	.67	.80	.67	.07
Windsor II	.85	.87	.87	.18	.70	.86	.67	.02

CHAPTER THIRTEEN

Performance Chasing and Market Timing Are Hazardous to Your Wealth

Don't gamble; take all your savings and buy some good stock and hold it till it goes up, then sell it. If it don't go up, don't buy it.
—Will Rogers

PAST PERFORMANCE DOES NOT PREDICT FUTURE PERFORMANCE

According to an Investment Company Institute study, about 75 percent of all mutual fund investors mistakenly use short-term past performance as their primary reason for buying a specific fund. It doesn't take a rocket scientist to figure out why. The financial media consistently churn out favorable stories about recent winning funds, implying that the fund's managers have some sort of special insight that makes them so successful. Since investors are continually bombarded with these stories about top-performing funds in nearly every financial publication they read, they feel that's the criteria they should use in selecting their mutual funds. Little do they realize that this is simply the hot fund-of-the-month club, and that the performance figures are usually for cherry-picked funds over carefully selected favorable periods of time.

In addition to mutual fund manager "puff" articles, nearly all the leading newspaper and magazines contain lists of funds showing mutual fund past performance. No wonder the uninformed investor assumes past performance is the best way to pick mutual funds—just pick an "A" ranked fund or a five-star fund.

Index funds, by their very nature, are seldom top performers over short periods of time. More importantly, index funds are almost never bottom performers. A wise investor realizes that it's more important to meet financial goals than to take chances in the hope of becoming richer. We have found that it takes a knowledgeable and self-confident investor to select a fund that is not among the current hot performers.

The *Wall Street Journal* publishes one of the more extensive lists of mutual fund performance. In addition to reporting hundreds of daily fund changes, the first week of each month the *Journal* ranks mutual funds in more than 40 categories, based on their 1-month, 1-year, 3-year, 5-year, and 10-year returns. The 20 percent of funds with the highest returns are ranked A, the next highest 20 percent get a B, the middle 20 percent get a C, the next 20 percent get a D, and the bottom 20 percent get an E ranking. If you want past data, the *Journal* is one good place to look. Its sister publication, *Barron's,* is another. Whether all this past performance data is helpful is a question we will answer later.

Morningstar is, by far, the best source of mutual fund information. That research firm uses the well-known star system to rank thousands of mutual funds based on their risk-adjusted performance. The top 10 percent of Morningstar-listed funds earn a five-star rating, the next 22.5 percent get four stars, the middle 35 percent get three stars, the next 22.5 percent get two stars, and the bottom 10 percent get just one star. So should we buy funds based on these star ratings? To find the answer, we turned to Mark Hulbert, author of *The Hulbert Financial Digest,* a well-respected tracker of actual mutual fund performance. He wrote in the February 2, 2004, issue of *Forbes* magazine: "Over the past decade, Morningstar's five-star equity funds have earned an average 5.7 percent against a 10.3 percent return for the Wilshire 5000."

On January 15, 2007, two professors at the University of Amsterdam completed a 10-year study they titled, "The Predictive Performance of Morningstar's Mutual Fund Ratings." Their conclusion: "The predictive performances of the different rating systems used by Morningstar do not beat a random walk."

We are not criticizing Morningstar. It never claimed its star ranking system could predict performance. To the contrary, we greatly admire Morningstar for repeatedly pointing out that the stars *shouldn't* be used to predict future performance. It's the mutual fund companies that have turned the star rating system into a misleading marketing tool—a fact that's understood by most Bogleheads. We routinely see mutual fund advertisements proudly displaying their fund's star ranking, with the implication that the past performance that earned the stars will continue in the future. Only in the smallest print at the bottom of the ad does the fund company admit that past performance is not indicative of future returns.

Matthew Morey, associate professor of finance at Pace University's Lubin School of Business, conducted a study of mutual fund rating services and concluded: "Neither of the ratings systems, nor the alternative ratings systems, are able to successfully predict winning funds."

If the rating services, with their vast databases of mutual fund information, are unable to consistently pick winning funds in advance, it's highly unlikely that we can do any better. Nevertheless, the myth that past performance can be used to pick winning funds persists.

Let's look at some more studies on this counterintuitive subject.

- Mark M. Carhart conducted a study and subsequently published "On Persistence in Mutual Fund Performance" in the March 1997 issue of the *Journal of Finance*. It may be the best and most authoritative study on the subject ever made. He concluded: "Individual funds do not earn higher returns from following the momentum (persistence) strategy in stocks. The only persistence not explained is concentrated in strong underperformance by the worst-return mutual funds. The results do not support the existence of skilled or informed mutual fund portfolio managers."
- Barksdale and Green studied 144 institutional equity portfolios between January 1, 1975, and December 31, 1989. They found that the portfolios that finished the first five years in the top quintile were the *least* likely to finish in the top half over the next five years.
- Barra, a world leader in research and risk management, undertook a lengthy study that looked to answer the question, "Does Historical Performance Predict Future Performance?" The study came to this conclusion: "There is no evidence of persistence of equity fund performance."
- In a 2002 study by Jonathan Berk of the University of California, and Richard Green of Carnegie Mellon University, it was found that "Past performance cannot be used to predict future returns, or to infer the average skill level of active managers."
- Vanguard did a study of past performance for institutional investors. It found that of the top-20 U.S. equity funds during the 10-year period through 1993, *only one* stayed in the top 100 in the subsequent 10-year period.

TABLE 13.1   BEST AND WORST ASSET CLASSES, 1994–2004

YEAR	BEST	WORST
1994	International	Bonds*
1995	Large Caps	International
1996	Large Caps	Bonds
1997	Large Caps	International
1998	Large Caps	Small-Cap Value
1999	Small-Cap Growth	Small-Cap Value
2000	Small-Cap Value	Small-Cap Growth
2001	Small-Cap Value	International
2002	Bonds	Small-Cap Growth
2003	Small-Cap Growth	Bonds
2004	Small-Cap Value	Bonds

*Bonds = Barclay's Capital Aggregate Bond Index.
Large Caps = S&P 500 Index.
Small-Cap Growth = Russell 2000 Growth Index.
Small-Cap Value = Russell 2000 Value Index.

Studies like these tell us in both scientific and easy-to-understand language that past performance cannot be used to predict future performance. Table 13.1 lists the best and worst of five asset classes during one 11-year period. Note that with the exception of large caps, every asset class was both the best and worst performing category during this period.

Not only does mutual fund performance fail to persist, but Table 13.1 makes it clear that asset class performance also fails to persist beyond a few years. Look what happened to investors in some of these funds:

- *44 Wall Street Fund* was the top-performing U.S. diversified stock fund during the 1970s and attracted thousands of eager investors as its fame spread. Unfortunately for these performance chasers, the *44 Wall Street Fund* turned into the worst-performing mutual fund during the 1980s.

- Since the 1960s, the average return of the top-20 mutual funds in each decade was less than the market index return in the next decade.
- Of the 50 top-performing funds in 2000, not a single one appeared on the top-50 list in either 1999 or 1998.
- The Grand Prix Fund ranked in the top 1 percent in fund returns for 1998 and 1999. It finished in the bottom 1 percent for years 2000 and 2001.

Using past performance to pick tomorrow's winning mutual funds is such a bad idea that the government requires a statement similar to this: *Past performance is no guarantee of future performance.* Believe it!

MARKET TIMING

The Motley Fools define *market timing* as "A strategy based on predicting short-term price changes in securities, which is virtually impossible to do."

We don't always agree with the Fools, but this time we think they got it right. Market timing is an obsession in the world of investing. It's nearly impossible to pick up a financial publication without seeing headlines telling us which way the market is headed. The mailman delivers a steady stream of advertisements from financial newsletter writers promising fantastic returns if only we will subscribe to their newsletters and their market timing advice.

It's futile to pick winning funds based on *past* returns, but that certainly doesn't stop investors from trying. Amateurs and professionals alike spend millions of man-hours every year trying to find that elusive secret formula that can pick winning mutual funds in *advance*. This brings us to those financial newsletters that *do* promise to pick winning funds in advance.

FINANCIAL NEWSLETTERS

The definitive study of market timing investment newsletters was made by John Graham, a University of Utah professor, together with Campbell Harvey, a professor at Duke University. These two professors tracked and analyzed more than 15,000 market-timing predictions by 237 newsletter writers from June 1980 through December 1992. Their conclusion couldn't be clearer:

There is no evidence that newsletters can time the market. Consistent with mutual fund studies, winners rarely win again and losers often lose again.

One of the interesting sidelights to this study was that by the end of the 12½-year period, 94 percent of the newsletters in the study had gone out of business.

Mark Hulbert, who we mentioned earlier, did a study of newsletter portfolios. His statistics are startling. For example, Mr. Hulbert constructed a hypothetical portfolio made up of each year's top-performing newsletter-recommended portfolio from 1981 through 2003. Over the 12 months following their top showing, these former winners produced an average annualized *loss* of 32.2 percent. Compare this dismal second-year performance to the Wilshire 5000 total stock market index, which, during the same second-year period, had an annualized *gain* of 13.1 percent.

To understand the danger of using newsletter recommendations, consider *The Granville Market Letter,* which produced a phenomenal 245 percent return in 1991. So what happened in 1992? You guessed it! Its 245 percent return during the first 12 months was followed by an 84 percent *loss* during the second 12 months.

You might conclude that a profit of 245 percent and a loss of 84 percent would produce a nice gain of 161 percent (245 percent − 84 percent). Surprisingly, it does not work that way. The actual two-year *loss* is 61 percent. To understand how this is computed, in Table 13.2, we use an example of someone who invested $10,000 in *The Granville Market Letter*'s recommended portfolio at the beginning of 1991.

TABLE 13.2 INVESTING BASED ON *THE GRANVILLE MARKET LETTER*

Amount Invested	$10,000
After 245% Gain	$24,500
After 84% Loss	$ 3,920
Investor Net Loss	−$ 6,080 (−61%)

The January 2001 issue of *The Hulbert Financial Digest* contained this very revealing statistic: *Among the 160 or so newsletters the HFD monitors, the market timing recommendations of only 10 have beaten the stock market over the last decade on a risk-adjusted basis.* We think you'll agree that spending our hard-earned money for a subscription to a newsletter that has perhaps a 1-in-16 chance of beating the market index is a high-risk gamble that's simply not worth taking.

One of the best-known newsletter writers is Doug Fabian. In August 2003, Mr. Fabian confidently announced to Chuck Jaffee on *CBS MarketWatch* that he could produce a 100 percent return in 365 days using a turbocharged version of the system he sells to investors. To prove that his market timing system worked, Fabian publicly invested $500,000 of his own money using his system. Big mistake! Unfortunately for Fabian, his $500,000 investment subsequently lost $192,000, and he was unable to hide that fact from his readers. Not one to be discouraged, he claimed the lost $192,000 "was worth it" for the lessons he learned about investing. One of the primary reasons we're writing this book is to ensure that your lessons about investing will be much less expensive.

Elaine Garzarelli was America's best known market-timer after she correctly called the 1987 market crash when the Dow lost 22.6 percent in *one day*—nearly one-quarter of its value. Shearson Lehman promoted Ms. Garzarelli to the position of chief quantitative strategist and her advice became widely followed. After she made a series of bad calls, Shearson fired her. She then started her own market-timing newsletter. After a number of additional bad calls, her highly touted market timing newsletter quietly disappeared.

In *Common Sense on Mutual Funds,* Jack Bogle wrote:

> *The idea that a bell rings to signal when investors should get into or out of the stock market is simply not credible. After nearly 50 years in this business, I do not know of anybody who has done it successfully and consistently. I don't even know anybody who knows anybody who has done it successfully and consistently.*

Let's face it. Most newsletter publishers are in the business of making money by selling newsletters. Common sense tells us that if they *really* had a secret formula to make money in the markets, they would be using it themselves, rather than spending their time pounding away on their computer keyboard so they could share their secret formula with us (for a fee, of course).

FINANCIAL SHOWS ON TV

Those financial programs we see on television are a good example of the Wall Street marketing machine in action. CNBC and other financial TV programs are filled with commercials promising that if we use their advertised product or service, we can easily outperform other investors and beat the market. All day long, CNBC and other financial stations provide a parade of financial "experts" who, with great assurance, tell us where the market is headed, what interest rates are going to do, and where to invest our money now. We cannot remember ever hearing a TV guest "expert" say, "I don't know." As soon as one of these programs ends, it's easy to imagine listeners rushing to their computer or telephone to act on this "expert" advice—unaware that what sounds so convincing is often a cleverly disguised marketing pitch for the product or service recommended.

WALL $TREET WEEK

The longest-running and most popular financial show on TV was *Wall $treet Week with Louis Rukeyser*. One of the show's most popular features was the market-timing "Elves." Lou's Elves were 10 market-timing experts who would make weekly predictions about where the Dow Industrial Index would be 6 months and 12 months ahead. Their performance was laughable. On July 27, 1990, at a market top, the Elves were bullish when they should have been bearish. On October 12, at the market bottom, the Elves were bearish, when they should have been bullish, and remained bearish through November 1994 as a powerful advance began. It became so embarrassing that Rukeyser actually replaced five bearish Elves with five more bullish Elves. Unfortunately, the newly organized Elves were bullish all through the bear market plunge (21 percent) in July and August of 1998.

A year later, as the stock market bubble was approaching its climax at the end of 1999, only one Elf, Gail Dudack, was correctly bearish. Rukeyser must have gotten tired of her bearishness and announced Dudack's dismissal on a November show. He replaced her with Alan Bond, another stock market bull (sentenced in 2003 to 12 years and 7 months in prison for defrauding investors). Two months later, the three-year bear market began with all 10 market-timing Elves bullish. This was the beginning of the end for the Elves. They were all still bullish when they were dismissed on September 14, 2001, in the middle of the bear market. We don't know how many investors relied on the Elves (and Alan Bond) for advice, but we're sure that those who did wished they had never heard of them.

In addition to the Elves, each week Mr. Rukeyser would invite several well-known Wall Street stock pickers who would confidently announce their best stock picks. To find out how good these stock picks were, we again turn to our friend, Mark Hulbert, who began tracking these expert stock picks in December 1995.

Over the next 10 years, the average expert-picked stocks were up an annualized 8.0 percent compared to the market index return of 9.5 percent. A 1.5 percent difference may not seem like much, but compounded over a lifetime it makes a tremendous difference. For example, if you had invested $10,000 in 1970 at 8.0 percent for 35 years (ignoring taxes), you would have $147,900. The same $10,000 invested in a market index fund returning 9.5 percent would be worth $239,600. In a taxable account, the difference would be even greater because all the profits from the buying and selling of recommended stocks would be taxed each year. In contrast, the majority of profits in an index fund are not taxed annually, but are deferred until the money is withdrawn—and then taxes are paid at the lower capital gains rates.

FINANCIAL MAGAZINES

Smart Money magazine ran a mutual fund contest between two very well-known, experienced portfolio managers, Ron Baron and Robert Markman. The contest began March 30, 2000, and ended a year later on March 2, 2001. These managers were allowed to buy and sell funds during the contest. If you picked Mr. Baron's portfolio, you would have lost 1 percent of your investment. That's excellent, considering that the S&P declined 12 percent during that period. However, if you had mimicked Mr. Markman's portfolio, you would have lost 64 percent of your investment. We have no way of knowing if one manager was good and the other one bad, or if one was just lucky and the other one was unlucky, since the tables could well be turned the following year. It's these types of short-term contests and performance returns that many financial publications focus on. That doesn't serve the reader's best interest, but it does sell magazines.

Forbes magazine has been listing mutual fund performance figures and making specific mutual fund recommendations for more than 40 years. Each year in late August or early September, *Forbes* publishes a special mutual fund issue containing the investment performance of approximately 1,500 mutual funds. The mutual funds the magazine recommends most highly are featured in the "Honor Roll."

Jack Bogle did a study of these carefully selected "Honor Roll" funds for the period 1974 to 1992. He found that $10,000 invested in the *Forbes* "Honor Roll" funds would have grown to $75,000 during that period. This sounds good, until you find out that the same amount invested in the Vanguard Total Stock Market Index Fund would have grown to approximately $103,600. Mr. Bogle's study gives us a good insight into the value of magazine fund selections.

The articles and columns telling you what you really need to know about investing are usually found tucked away within the newspaper or magazine and are rarely mentioned on the front page or the cover. Front page and cover space is reserved for attention-grabbing headlines that sell. The best of investment/personal finance magazines adorn their covers with headlines about the 10 hottest stocks or funds you must own now, prophecy about the future of the stock market, and other nonsense. As you might well imagine, numerous studies back-testing the investment recommendations of cover articles reveal that most badly underperformed the market. Nevertheless, the print media can't stay in business without attracting a crowd and do what they need to do to sell magazines and newspapers. As one anonymous source concluded in his article, "Unfortunately, rational, pro-index-fund stories don't sell magazines, cause hits on websites, or boost Neilson ratings. So rest assured: You'll keep on seeing those enticing but worthless SIX FUNDS TO BUY NOW! headlines as long as there are personal finance media."

THE BOGLEHEADS CONTEST

In December 2000, on the Morningstar Vanguard Diehards Forum, Taylor Larimore announced that he was starting an annual Bogleheads contest. The goal was to forecast the closing price of the Wilshire 5000 Index (Total Market) on December 31, 2001, one year later. Jack Bogle agreed to donate one of his books as a prize. Taylor's purpose in starting the contest was to demonstrate just how difficult stock market forecasting can be. Ninety-nine Bogleheads made an average prediction that the Wilshire's price would *gain* 6.0 percent. At the end of the year it was *down* 18 percent.

The second Boglehead contest started in January 2002 with 177 predictions. Also included were the forecasts of 11 major Wall Street brokerage firms. Here's what happened:

- Seventy-five percent of the Bogleheads predicted a *gain*.
- The S&P *fell* from 1148 to 880—a decline of 23 percent.
- While 25 percent of the Bogleheads correctly predicted the market *direction*, only three of them predicted the index would go as low as it did.
- Only one Wall Street strategist could even guess the *direction* of the stock market.

These results are shown in Table 13.3.

We hope that you are convinced, as we are, that no one can predict what the stock market will do or which mutual fund will outperform in

TABLE 13.3 WALL STREET EXPERTS' 2002 PREDICTIONS

STRATEGIST	FIRM	PREDICTION
Edward Kerschner	UBS Warburg	1570
Thomas Galvin	Credit Suisse	1375
Abby Joseph Cohen	Goldman Sachs	1363
Stuart Freeman	A.G. Edwards	1350
Jeffrey Applegate	Lehman Bros.	1350
Tobias Levkovich	Salomon Smith Barney	1350
Edward Yardeni	Prudential Securities	1300
Steve Galbraith	Morgan Stanley	1225
Richard Bernstein	Merrill Lynch	1200
Thomas McManus	Bank of America	1200
Douglas Cliggott	Brummer & Partners	950
Year-Ending S&P 500		880

the future. This is why we diversify—so that whatever happens we will not have all our money in losing investments.

PREDICTING INTEREST RATES

We've discussed the futility of trying to forecast stock market performance. What about bonds and interest rates? Surely, it's easy to guess where interest rates are headed, isn't it? And if we know the direction of interest rates, we know how to make money moving in and out of bonds. Yes, it does looks easy, and you probably have your own ideas of where interest rates are headed. You have lots of company, since the media "experts" confidently tell us what interest rates will do next. Now, let's look at the record.

For every bond manager or individual investor who expects interest rates and bond yields to go up, there's another manager or individual investor somewhere who believes rates and yields are going to move in the opposite direction. Thousands of highly trained bond managers around the world are sitting in front of their computers right now, looking for the slightest advantage over their competitors. These bond experts will immediately correct any mispricing with buy or sell orders. Mark Hulbert wrote a 1994 article for the *AAII Journal* in which he stated:

> *If you think successfully timing the stock market is difficult—and it is— timing the bond market is virtually impossible.*

How right he is! Of the 33 newsletters offering bond forecasts during the five-year period ending December 31, 2006, only two newsletter editors outperformed the Shearson All-Maturities Treasury Index during the same period.

Twice a year the *Wall Street Journal* polls about 50 of the top economists in the United States for their interest rate forecasts. Jim Bianco of Arbor Research did a study to see how these predictions actually turned out. The results may surprise you. From 1982, the beginning of the Wall Street's Forecasting Survey, through 2006, the "expert" economists have been right in forecasting the direction of interest rates *only about one-third of the time*. Economist John Kenneth Galbraith once said: "There are only two kinds of interest-rate forecasters: those who don't know, and those who don't know that they don't know."

STAY THE COURSE

The logical alternative to performance chasing and market timing is structuring a long-term asset allocation plan and then staying the course. Sticking with our asset allocation plan is hard to do at times. It requires knowledge and confidence—the knowledge to prepare a sound strategy and the confidence to know our strategy will work if we simply give it time by staying the course.

Wall Street can't stand buy-and-hold strategies because brokers need trading activity to make money. For this reason, you can expect to be continually seduced by Wall Street's billion-dollar marketing machine. Realize that Wall Street feeds millions of dollars to the financial media.

They have a symbiotic relationship. The media want readers, viewers, listeners, and most of all, Wall Street's advertising dollars. Wall Street also wants readers, viewers, listeners, and most of all, *your* dollars. Unfortunately, these dollars come straight out of your investment returns.

Journalists have a constant need for something new to write about, and Wall Street is happy to oblige. The one thing a journalist knows is that if he or she focuses on top-performing mutual funds, the journalist will always have something new to write about. Nearly every financial publication features an interview with a current outperforming mutual fund manager. These managers will *always* appear to have a convincing, winning strategy.

With the help of the media, Wall Street has been very successful at getting investors to chase after last year's winning funds and market time. Motivated by greed, investors listen to any sales pitch promoting a perceived can't-lose strategy or hot fund. Meanwhile, the gloom-and-doom forecasters play on investors' fears when urging us to change to safer securities. Wall Street wins because it makes money either way.

Since purchases, sales, and exchanges can now be made with the push of a button, it's hard for many investors to resist the urge to trade more frequently than they should. Of course, when doing so, they're typically buying high and selling low. When emotions run high, logic flies out the window, and performance usually follows.

Terry Odean and Brad Barber, two professors at the University of California, did a study of 66,400 investors between the years 1991 and 1997 to learn how trading affected those investors' returns. They found that buy-and-hold investors outperformed the most active traders by a whopping 7.1 percent a year. The study's results are shown in Table 13.4.

TABLE 13.4   BUY-AND-HOLD INVESTING VERSUS ACTIVE TRADING

TRADING STRATEGY	TURNOVER	RETURNS
Most Active Trader	258%	11.4%
Average Trader	76%	16.4%
Buy and Hold	2%	18.5%

Warren Buffett wrote in his 1996 annual report to shareholders: "Inactivity strikes us as intelligent behavior." We agree—and the studies confirm his intelligent advice.

READ WHAT OTHERS SAY

Regarding Past Performance

American Association of Individual Investors: "Top Performance lists are dangerous."

Jack Bogle: "There is simply no way under the sun to forecast a fund's future returns based on its past record."

Bill Bernstein: "For the 20 years from 1970 to 1989, the best performing stock assets were Japanese stocks, U.S. small stocks, and gold stocks. These turned out to be the worst performing assets over the next decade."

Jack Brennan, former Vanguard CEO: "Fund rankings are meaningless when based on past performance, as most are."

Jason Zweig: "Buying funds based purely on their past performance is one of the stupidest things an investor can do."

Regarding Market Timing

Warren Buffett: "I never have the faintest idea what the stock market is going to do in the next six months, or the next year, or the next two."

Jonathan Clements, author and columnist: "Market timing is a poor substitute for a long-term investment plan."

Pat Dorsey, director of Morningstar Stock Analysis: "Market-timing is bunk."

Elaine Garzarelli: "I've learned that market timing can ruin you."

Benjamin Graham: "If I have noticed anything over these 60 years on Wall Street, it is that people do not succeed in forecasting what's going to happen to the stock market."

Jane Bryant Quinn, author and syndicated columnist: "The market timer's Hall of Fame is an empty room."

Larry Swedroe, author of a number of investment books: "Believing in the ability of market timers is the equivalent of believing astrologers can predict the future."

Regarding Stay the Course

Frank Armstrong, author: "Buy and hold is a very dull strategy. It has only one little advantage—it works, very profitably and very consistently."

Jack Bogle: "No matter what happens, stick to your program. I've said 'Stay-the-course' a thousand times and I meant it every time. It is the most important single piece of investment wisdom I can give to you."

Rick Ferri, author of a number of excellent investment books: "Write down your strategy—then stay the course."

Carol Gould, *New York Times*: "For most investors the odds favor a buy-and-hold strategy."

Michael LeBoeuf, author of *The Millionaire in You*: "Simple buy-and-hold index investing is one of the best, most efficient ways to grow your money to the ultimate goal of financial freedom."

Eric Tyson, author of *Mutual Funds For Dummies*: "Don't trade in and out of funds. Stay invested. Not only does buy-and-hold investing offer better returns, but it's also less work."

CHAPTER FOURTEEN

Savvy Ways to Invest for College

Economists report that a college education adds many thousands of dollars to a man's lifetime income—which he then spends sending his son to college.

—Bill Vaughan

It's a simple fact of life: More education usually means higher earnings over a lifetime. While you may not have seen the official figures, you still know from first-hand experience that most college graduates earn more than high school graduates and high school graduates earn more than high school dropouts. Therefore, when parents sacrifice to save and invest for their children's college education, they're actually making a significant investment in their children's future lifetime earnings, and the payback can be well worth the sacrifice.

Although some may question whether it's worthwhile to spend the extra money to attend and ultimately graduate from one of the more expensive private colleges, rather than a state university, there's little debate as to whether either college graduate will be rewarded with increased earnings over their lifetime. What really seems to matter most when it comes to expected lifetime earnings is going to college and graduating with a well-chosen major.

According to the Bureau of Labor Statistics, U.S. Census Bureau figures show that a college graduate with a bachelor's degree can expect to
earn nearly $1,000,000 more than a high school graduate over their
40-year working lifetime. And those with a master's degree can expect to
make more than twice as much as a high school graduate over their working lifetime. Table 14.1 shows the expected lifetime earnings for various
educational levels.

As Table 14.1 clearly shows, that's a good investment for four to six
years of college. It amounts to an increase in lifetime earnings of more
than $200,000 for each year spent in college. Therefore, an investment in
an affordable state college education for your children can certainly pay
huge dividends.

According to the Bureau of Labor Statistics, even though women
college graduates continue to earn less than their male classmates, male
and female college graduates earn approximately the same 2.5 times

TABLE 14.1   EXPECTED LIFETIME EARNINGS PER
             EDUCATION LEVEL

HIGHEST EDUCATIONAL ATTAINMENT	LIFETIME EARNINGS
Some high school, no diploma	$1,000,000
High school diploma or equivalent	$1,200,000
Some college, no degree	$1,500,000
Associate degree	$1,600,000
Bachelor's degree	$2,100,000
Master's degree	$2,500,000
Doctoral degree	$3,400,000
Professional degree	$4,400,000

Source: U.S. Census Bureau, "The Big Payoff: Educational
Attainment and Synthetic Estimates of Work-Life Earnings."

the weekly salaries of their high school graduating counterparts. Therefore, we need to try to save enough to send all of our children to college.

Parenting and investing can be difficult enough endeavors in their own right, yet investors with children have to combine these two tasks when considering which investment savings vehicle to choose to fund their children's future education. It can certainly be a daunting task, especially when one considers the wide array of investment options available, including some plans that are specifically designed to fund educational expenses.

As with all other aspects of investing, the earlier you start saving for your children's college education, the better chance you have of reaching your goals. In addition, when choosing the appropriate investment to fund your children's education, you need to be aware that each funding option has its own unique set of requirements, limitations, and tax considerations. The choice you make today could well have an impact later on when your child applies for financial assistance.

METHODS OF SAVING FOR COLLEGE

In this chapter we'll touch briefly on some of the more popular investment choices available to parents (and others) for funding educational college expenses. We'll try to at least make you aware of what's available. You can then do additional reading and research on the particular college-funding investments that seem best suited for your situation. The most recent version of Joseph Hurley's *The Best Way to Save for College* is considered by many to be one of the very best books on this subject. In addition to his writing, Joe maintains a fact-filled website at www.savingforcollege.com, where you can get lots of free information on the various college savings plans.

Keep in mind that the programs and tax laws are constantly changing, as are the income limits that apply in order for you to qualify for part or all of the tax-free benefits offered by some of these educational investment options. Some of the tax benefits that are in effect today are scheduled to be eliminated unless extended or made permanent by Congress. Therefore, this is an area where you will definitely need to stay abreast of all the latest tax changes.

Here are some of the investment options we'll discuss:

- Personal savings
- Custodial accounts (UGMA & UTMA)
- U.S. Savings Bonds

- Coverdell Educational Savings Accounts (Education IRAs)
- 529 Qualified Tuition Plans (QTP), including education savings accounts and prepaid tuition plans
- IRA withdrawals
- Some additional funding options available to you

Personal Savings in Parents' Names

This is, perhaps, one of the most flexible of all the savings options available to parents. It's funded with after-tax dollars. The investments remain the property of the parents, and are under their complete control. There are no income limits to worry about. The funds can be invested in any manner that the parents choose (stocks, bonds, mutual funds, CDs, etc.). Proceeds from the account can be used for any qualifying or non-qualifying educational expense, in any way the parents see fit, since there are no conditions on when, how, or even if the money has to be spent, or who it has to be spent on.

While this option doesn't offer tax-free growth, as do some of the other options available, when parents eventually do sell some of their investments to fund their children's college expenses, any equity holdings they sell would qualify for the more favorable long-term capital gains tax rate. Another advantage of personal savings is that the money doesn't have to be earmarked for any particular child, as it does with some other plans. Finally, should some or all of the funds not be needed for college expenses, the money remains the parent's property, and can be used for other purposes, such as retirement.

Custodial Accounts (UTMA and UGMA)

Custodial accounts created under either the Uniform Transfer to Minors Act (UTMA) or Uniform Gifts to Minors Act (UGMA) are one way that parents can earmark funds for their children's education. Often gifts of cash for a child's birthdays and other special occasions end up in this account, and it grows over time.

There can be tax benefits to a custodial account through the early accumulation years. The smaller amounts of earnings escape taxation entirely because the child does not have enough income to owe taxes. Later, when the earnings increase enough to require that taxes be paid for children under the age of 14, they're taxed at the child's low rate until such time as they exceed the child's unearned income limit. Once the earnings exceed the child's unearned income limit, all excess earnings are subject to the *kiddie tax,* which means those excess earnings will be taxed at the parents' tax rate. When the child reaches age 14, earnings are once again taxed at the child's own rate, which is typically lower than the parents' tax rate.

Custodial accounts have several potential problems associated with them. First, the child gains full control of the account at the age of majority, which is either 18 or 21, depending on the state of residence. At that point, they can spend the money any way they want. If son Bill wants to buy a new car, a motorcycle, or a big-screen TV for his room or apartment, he can do so, and you can't do a thing about it. Or if daughter Marilu wants to travel and see the world, then she's free to do so. Obviously, it's impossible to know ahead of time if Bill or Marilu will spend the money for its intended use (college), or spend it on some other thing that he or she considers to be more important.

The second disadvantage is that under current law, custodial accounts are considered to be an asset of the child. Therefore, when it comes time to apply for financial aid for college, the government formula expects up to 35 percent of the child's accounts to be used to fund college costs each year. That can lower the amount of financial aid offered. By contrast, the government financial aid formula only calls for up to 5.6 percent of assets held in the parents' names to be used to pay for college each year, which means more financial aid might be available to help with the costs of your child's education.

Once parents learn about the government formula that's used in determining financial aid, and learn that the child will have full control over the custodial account at majority, many parents realize that this may not be the best investment vehicle for funding their child's education. They feel that it would be more desirable to transfer the custodial account funds to some other educational plan. Although some educational investment options allow the rollover of custodial accounts into their plans, others do not. As far as the government is concerned, even when transferred to another plan, the former custodial assets remain the property of the minor, and will be considered as such when it comes time for financial aid. Therefore, for these reasons, many parents decide that these custodial accounts are probably not the best way to save for their children's college expenses.

U.S. Savings Bonds

We learned about U.S. Savings Bonds (both EE and I Bonds) earlier in our discussion on bonds. We'll now focus specifically on how the tax-free educational benefit portion of these U.S. Savings Bonds works.

It's very important that Savings Bonds be titled correctly in order for the bonds to qualify for the tax-free educational benefit. To qualify, bonds must be titled in one or both of the parents' names; they *cannot* be titled in the child's name. The child cannot be listed on the bond as either an owner or co-owner. However, if the child is listed on the bond as the beneficiary, the bond will still qualify for the tax-free educational benefit. If grandparents, friends, or other relatives plan to give your child Savings Bonds to be used for their college education, you need to let them know before they purchase the bonds that they *must* be titled in one or both of the parent's names. If they want to designate the bond as belonging to a particular child, they can always list them as the beneficiary, and that will be fine. It's sad, but so many well-meaning relatives and friends have given children Savings Bonds as gifts, intending them to be used later for the child's education, and incorrectly titled them in the child's name. Although these bonds can still be used to pay some of the child's nonqualifying college-related expenses, they won't be eligible for the tax-free benefit.

In addition to being titled properly, there are other requirements that you must meet in order to take advantage of the Savings Bonds' tax-free educational feature.

- You must have been 24 years or older when you purchased the bonds.
- If married, you must file a joint return.
- To get the full tax-free exemption, you must use the entire proceeds (both interest and principal) to pay for qualifying educational expenses for you, your spouse, or your dependents in the year that you redeem the bonds.
- You must meet the income requirements that are in effect at the time you use the bonds for qualifying education expenses (these figures are adjusted for inflation and change annually).

IRS Publication 970 (Tax Benefits for Education) gives full details on the Education Savings Bonds Program, including updated income requirements.

After you've purchased Savings Bonds with the intent of using them for your children's education, you may find that your career is advancing at a rapid pace, causing you to realize that your earnings might exceed the Savings Bonds' tax-free income limits by the time your children reach college age. If that ever becomes a concern for you, remember that as long as you meet the then-current income limits, you could always cash in your Savings Bonds at that time and transfer the proceeds into a 529 Plan, which we'll discuss shortly. By doing this, you'd avoid paying any taxes on the increase in value of your Savings Bonds, since transferring the proceeds from the redeemed Savings Bonds to the 529 Plan qualifies for the tax-free benefit.

And, since the bonds are in your name(s), if they're not needed to fund your child's college education (perhaps little Butch will get a scholarship), they can continue to grow, tax-deferred, for up to 30 years, acting as an emergency fund and possibly contributing later to your retirement assets.

Coverdell Education Savings Account (ESA)

The Coverdell Education Savings Account (ESA) was formerly known as the Education IRA. The annual contribution limit was increased from the previous unreasonably low $500 to the current limit of $2,000 per student. Although the contribution is made with money that has already been taxed (after-tax money), the growth in the account is tax-free as long as the proceeds are used to fund any qualifying educational expense. This ESA offers lots of flexibility, since its definition of qualifying educational expenses is much broader than most other plans. In addition to paying for college expenses, ESA proceeds can also be used to pay for the following:

- Elementary and secondary education (kindergarten thru grade 12) tuition and fees, including public, private, and religious schools.
- Books and supplies.
- Room and board.
- Computers and Internet access.
- Transportation.
- Tutoring.
- Contributions to a 529 Qualified Tuition Program (QTP).

Anyone who meets the current income requirements listed in IRS Publication 970 can open a Coverdell ESA and make contributions on behalf of a child, including persons who aren't related to the child. However, while there can be any number of these ESA accounts opened in the child's name in any given year, the total amount contributed to all of these accounts on behalf of a single beneficiary cannot exceed $2,000 per year.

Contributions cannot be made once the child turns 18, and the funds must be used by the time the beneficiary turns 30. If not, any remaining funds can be transferred to another family member who's under age 30.

The Coverdell ESA has many very attractive features going for it. Perhaps it would be the ideal educational funding mechanism for many investors if only the contribution limits were higher than the current $2,000 per year. However, despite this drawback, if you meet the income limits, it may still be the best choice for the first $2,000 of your education savings.

529 Qualified Tuition Plans (QTP)

There are two types of 529 plans: education savings plans and prepaid tuition plans. Some plans are sold by brokers, while others give you the option to buy direct and avoid the extra costs associated with brokers. It's hard for us to understand why anyone would pay a broker's commission for a 529 plan if they can buy direct from the state of their choice.

The 529 education savings plans are offered by every state, and each comes with its own set of rules. Even though you might have learned how one state's program works, you can't assume all states' programs are the same. Investing in these state-run 529 plans doesn't necessarily guarantee that your investment will cover all of your child's future college expenses, as prepaid plans do. Your investment choices are limited to those offered by the particular 529 state plan you choose. Many of the investment choices in these plans are age-based, and they automatically get more conservative as the child gets closer to college age.

The plan you decide to invest in doesn't have to be run by the state where you reside, or even where you expect your child to go to college. Although some state plans require you to be a resident at the time of enrollment, most don't. Therefore, you're free to shop around for the best available plan that offers solid investment choices and low costs. However, since some states do offer tax breaks to residents who invest in their plans, you'll have to factor that into your decision, if applicable. The proceeds from these plans can be used for any qualifying educational expense at an approved postsecondary school, regardless of which state it's located in.

The 529 plans allow substantial contributions. For instance, an individual can make a single contribution of five times the current gift tax limit and a couple can make a single contribution of 10 times the annual gift tax limit without exceeding the gift tax limit. The 529 programs allow these large contributions to be treated as five annual gifts per person. However, no additional gifts may be made to that beneficiary during that five-year period without triggering the gift tax. Contributing a large sum in a single payment to their grandchildren's 529 plans can be a great way for well-to-do grandparents to quickly reduce the size of their taxable estate while benefiting their children and grandchildren. In addition to the generous individual contribution limits, in some states, contributions from all sources are allowed to be made until the total balance in an account reaches as high as $300,000 per individual.

The earnings in the 529 plans grow tax-deferred, and withdrawals for qualifying education expenses are currently tax-free.

529 plans offer other attractive features as well. There are no income limits for those contributing to a 529 plan, as there are with other education investment options. You can invest in both a Coverdell ESA and a 529 plan at the same time. You're allowed to change the beneficiary to another family member. Finally, unlike an UGMA or UTMA Custodial account, you retain complete control of the assets.

The second type of 529 plan is a prepaid tuition plan that can be offered by either a state or an approved educational institution. If your state offers a 529 prepaid tuition plan, you can prepay some or all of the tuition for your child's future education at a state university at today's prices. The prepaid tuition can be paid in a lump sum or in installment payments. The amount you'll have to pay is determined by the age of the child when you pay for the tuition via the 529 prepaid tuition plan; the younger they are, the less you'll have to pay.

After you've prepaid your child's tuition at a state university, should your child decide to go to a private school, or attend college in another state, the state where you prepaid the child's tuition will allow you to use some or all of the value of your 529 plan to pay for your child's education at the other school. However, since the rate of return on the prepaid tuition plan is tied to the rate of tuition inflation at the state university, the rate of return you receive on your original investment may turn out to be much smaller than you might have gotten had you invested in a 529 education savings plan, rather than the 529 prepaid tuition plan.

Every state has a 529 plan of one type or another, and some offer both prepaid and savings plans. You can get the specifics on each state's 529 plan at www.savingforcollege.com/.

IRA Withdrawals

Even if you're under age 59½, you can legally make withdrawals from your IRA to fund qualifying educational expenses without incurring the 10 percent early withdrawal penalty. Some savvy investors might even use a Roth IRA as a college-funding vehicle. However, for most investors, we feel that unless you have more-than-adequate retirement assets, using your retirement funds for educational expenses is an option that's best left unused. Remember, you can always borrow for college, but you can't borrow for your retirement. It's also important to keep this thought in mind if somewhere along the line you experience financial difficulties and have to make the hard decision whether to fund your own retirement account or your children's education account. Hopefully, you'll find a way to do both.

Other Options Available

There are a number of other options available for funding higher education, including employer-paid tuition plans, scholarships, loans, Federal Pell grants, work-study programs, and saving on the part of the student. The IRS regulations allow certain deductions and credits (Hope Scholarship Credit and Lifetime Learning Credit) for higher education.

Attending a local community college for the first two years might be a lower-cost option. Many of these community colleges work hand in hand with local four-year colleges, and successful community-college graduates might be guaranteed admission into their four-year program.

SUMMARY OF COLLEGE SAVINGS PLANS

As we said in the beginning of this chapter, this is a very complex issue. No one plan is necessarily ideal for everyone. As with all things, an educated consumer is the best consumer, so we'd strongly advise that you take the time to read a good book or two that's devoted entirely to this subject. In addition, there's a wealth of free information available in IRS Publication 970 (Tax Benefits for Education). You can read or download a free copy of this publication at www.irs.gov/. If you don't have Internet access, you can order a copy of Publication 970 by phone. Remember, the tax laws are always changing, so you'll want to make sure you continue to review the latest copy of Publication 970. Each new edition will include all the latest information, and you certainly can't beat the price!

Before you know it, your children will be marching in their graduation parades, and, with a tear in your eye, you'll wonder where the time went. But at least you won't have to wonder where the money went!

CHAPTER FIFTEEN

How to Manage a Windfall Successfully

If only God would give me some sign ... a clear sign! Like making a large deposit in my name at a Swiss bank.

—Woody Allen

Imagine coming into a large sum of money in a very short period of time. That's the definition of a windfall. The amount might be more money than you've ever had in your life.

You may be thinking, "I wish! It should happen to me!" Well, believe it or not, over the course of a lifetime it probably will happen to you at least once.

Windfalls aren't limited to lottery winners, entertainers, and athletes who sign enormous contracts. Although those examples garner lots of media attention, millions of people come into sizable sums every year. Some common sources of windfalls follow:

- Inheritance
- A divorce settlement
- A lawsuit settlement
- Widowhood

- An insurance settlement
- A real estate sale
- Stock options
- A one-time, huge income bonus
- Sudden growth of a business
- Sale of a business
- A new job with a big increase in income
- Retirement

Successfully managing a windfall can be very challenging. A commonly heard statistic is that more than 75 percent of windfalls are squandered. We don't know if that's true, but most financial practitioners agree that well over 50 percent are lost in a relatively short period of time. *NBC News* reported that more than 70 percent of lottery winners exhaust their fortunes within three years.

The purpose of this chapter is to prepare you for the day when a windfall floats into your life, as one almost certainly will. By understanding what's going on and taking the right steps, a windfall can enrich your life rather than leaving you with regrets.

WINDFALLS ARE ABOUT A WHOLE LOT MORE THAN MONEY

Money buys a whole lot more than food, clothing, and shelter. It's the power symbol of society. Money buys freedom, possessions, status, access, opportunities, experiences, and more choices. How people spend their time is a good indication of what they value most. You may have noticed that most of us who are employed spend half or more of our waking hours pursuing the almighty dollar. To be sure, most of us work for more than just money. But how many of us would get up and go to work every day if we weren't paid?

Not surprisingly, when there's a sudden influx of money, it triggers emotions that can range from ecstasy to depression. One lottery winner feels euphoric, while another feels unworthy. A business owner who sells his or her business after years of working hard to build it may feel wonderful, unburdened, and relieved. Another owner who sells his business may feel lost. One person receiving a divorce settlement looks forward to the opportunity to build a new life, while another feels a bitter sense of loss. To one retiree, a lump-sum settlement represents the opportunity to pursue hobbies and travel. To another retiree, it represents a loss of identity and purpose. It's common for windfall recipients to feel inadequate, stressed, and paranoid. If you have never had to manage a large sum of money before, you may be thinking, "I'm not prepared to deal with this. Whom can I trust? What should I do?"

The following four steps will enable you to manage a windfall and keep most of it in the process. Most windfalls are needlessly squandered while experiencing the emotions that come with it. For that reason, the first step is critically important.

1. Deposit the money in a safe account for at least six months and leave it alone.
2. Get a realistic estimate of what the windfall can buy.
3. Make a wish list.
4. Get professional help.

Deposit the Money and Leave It for Six Months

The emotions that accompany a windfall are temporary and usually go away within six months. The most important secret to preserving a windfall is to not touch it until the emotions subside and you come up with a sound plan for putting the money to work.

There are some exceptions, of course. Taking a percent or two of the money to celebrate is fine. Go ahead and treat yourself and/or your family to something nice. Also, if you have any credit card or high-interest debts, use windfall proceeds to pay them off as soon as possible. Finally, if there are any taxes due on the proceeds, be sure and pay them, too.

Once you've paid off debts, paid the taxes, and had a nice celebration, take the rest of the money and deposit it in a bank savings account or money market fund and don't touch it for at least six months. Resist all temptations to do any of the following:

- Invest in "can't miss" investments or products pitched by brokers, insurance salespeople, and other financial types.
- Lend or give money to friends or relatives who want to treat you like a bank.
- Buy a luxury home to tell the world, "I've made it!"
- Buy an expensive, flashy car to impress your friends.
- Take a first-class, round-the-world luxury cruise.
- Go on a shopping spree to buy expensive clothing and jewelry.
- Make a large donation to a favorite charity or cause.
- Buy a boat, airplane, or other expensive toy.
- Quit your job.

Although you might be able to buy and do all of these things, this is not the time to do it. It's time to pause, chill out, and do some serious reflecting, information gathering, and planning. For the time being, just go on living the way you did prior to the windfall.

Know What You Can Buy

It's been said that whom the gods would destroy they first make mad. A large sum of cash can create illusions of endless wealth, especially if it's a new experience. Many people squander windfalls simply because they overestimate what the money is capable of buying. By the time they realize their mistake, the money is gone, and many are saddled with more debts than ever.

For example, let's assume that 40-year-old Joe Fortunate is the recipient of a $1 million windfall. Is Joe a millionaire? He probably won't be after the taxman gets through with him. If the windfall is taxed as ordinary income, he will be lucky to have $600,000 after taxes. Unless his previous net worth was at least $400,000, he isn't a millionaire.

A more important question is, "How much can Joe expect the remaining $600,000 to add to his yearly income if he invests it all?" It's generally agreed by financial planners that one can spend $5,000 per year for every $100,000 of capital invested in a well-diversified, balanced portfolio. That means Joe can expect his windfall to add $30,000 per year to his income before taxes. His net addition to income will depend on his particular federal and state income tax brackets. If he wants to make inflation-adjusted withdrawals, it's recommended that he begin by withdrawing only 4 percent of the portfolio, or $24,000, in the first year and increase the amount he withdraws each year by the rate of inflation. Joe may be delighted to have an additional $24,000 to $30,000 of annual income. However, if Joe believes that his million-dollar windfall is a ticket to lavish living and free spending, he's in for a rude surprise.

Of course, Joe has another option. He can go on living at the level he is accustomed to and invest the entire windfall for his children's college fund, an early retirement, and other long-term financial goals. A windfall left to compound can have an enormous, positive impact on one's life. Unfortunately, most people don't choose to do that. Joe's after-tax windfall of $600,000, invested at an annual return of 8 percent, grows to $1.2 million in 9 years and $2.4 million in 18 years.

Calculate the size of your windfall after taxes and debts are paid. If you want to use it to increase your annual income, you can withdraw 4 to 5 percent of it each year. Bear in mind that the money you withdraw will be subject to income taxes, too. You may also find it useful to calculate how much the windfall will be worth if left untouched for 5, 10, or 20 years, and left to compound at 8 percent per year. You can use Excel, your financial calculator, or the online calculator at the "Choose to Save" website listed in Appendix III to do these calculations.

While you have the calculator out, try to get an overall picture of your financial present and estimate how it will look in the future. Calculate your new net worth. Estimate the amount of any pensions or other sources of income that may be coming your way in the future and when you can expect them. Once you have that information, you are better equipped to decide how to get the most lifetime satisfaction from the windfall, which leads to our third step.

Make a Wish List

Once you have a realistic assessment of the windfall, the next step is to reconcile it with what you want out of life. Write down what you would like your life to be like if money wasn't a factor. Would you quit your job? Where would you live? How would you spend your days? What would you like to become? Where would you like to visit? Are there any particular causes you would like to become involved in? Envision how you want your life to be:

- Now
- In a year
- In 5 years
- In 10 years

Once you have a wish list, translate those dreams into written, specific goals with realistic deadlines for achieving them. Make three lists of goals on three separate sheets of paper:

1. Short-term goals: the ones you want to complete within a year
2. Intermediate goals to complete in the next 5 years
3. Long-term goals for all the rest

Once you have a list of short, intermediate, and long-term goals, rank the goals in each category in order of importance. You now have a checklist of goals and priorities for getting the most out of life.

The next step is to align your spending with your goals. If you want to quit work, can you afford to do it now? If not now, when will you be able to? If you want to start your own business, is now the time? Can you afford that second home or to move to a place where you've dreamed of living? If not, how long will the windfall have to compound to make that dream a reality? Is there a part of the world you want to visit? Can the windfall lighten the burden of future financial expenses, such as paying for the cost of college? Is there a hobby or activity that you've always wanted to pursue? Refer to your goals list when deciding what to do with your windfall. Instead of frittering the money away, you'll invest in making your dreams come true.

Get Professional Help

Unless you are well educated in matters of financial, estate, and tax planning, this is no time to go it alone. Acquiring a windfall can be wonderful, but it comes with its own set of problems. Enlisting the help of the right financial professionals is usually a very worthwhile investment that saves time, money, and headaches.

As you will learn in Chapter 16, the terms *financial professional* or *financial planner* are meaningless. Many so-called financial professionals are really financial salespeople. While you may need what they have to sell, this is not the time to ask them for financial advice. That's like hiring a fox to guard the henhouse. What you need is someone you can pay to provide you with objective advice that's in your best interests. Asking people who sell financial products for financial advice creates a potential conflict of interest. Although many will act in your best interest, many are more interested in selling you what makes the most money for them. It's a risk that you don't have to take. Get your advice and your investments/insurance from different sources.

A good place to begin seeking advice is from a Certified Public Accountant who does not sell investment products. A good CPA can do the following:

- Assess your overall financial well-being.
- Calculate any taxes due on the windfall.
- Recommend any additional types of insurance you may need or what types of insurance you currently carry that can be dropped.
- Help you decide if you need to enlist the services of an estate planning attorney.
- Calculate if it's better to take a lump-sum payment or monthly distributions on a windfall such as a retirement package.

- Give you a clearer picture of how the windfall can help you achieve your long-term financial goals.

The American Institute of Certified Public Accountants has a PFS designation for CPAs specializing in personal financial services. To locate one nearby, go to the AICPA website and do a search at http://apps.aicpa.org/credentialsrefweb/PFSCredentialSearchPage.aspx. Once again, we recommend asking a CPA at the outset if he or she sells financial products, or is in any way compensated by the people they recommend, and steering clear of those who do.

Other possible advisors you may wish to hire are an estate planning attorney and a financial planner. A CPA can likely recommend a number of competent attorneys to handle any requirements you may have. If you want to check out the credentials of an attorney, Martindale & Hubble (www.martindale.com) is the place to go. Some financial professionals are both attorneys and CPAs and can handle most of the work for you.

As for financial planners, we have a lot more to say about them in Chapter 16. If you feel you need one, you will want to look for a reputable planner who has experience in dealing with clients who suddenly find themselves in possession of a windfall.

In summary, successfully managing a windfall requires an understanding of both the psychological and financial realities that come with it. Like most bounties in life, it comes with its own set of problems. But all things considered, a windfall is a very nice problem to have.

CHAPTER SIXTEEN

Do You Need an Advisor?

I helped put two children through Harvard—my broker's children.

—Michael LeBoeuf

Michael's quote, made in jest, elicited a chuckle at our second annual Bogleheads get-together, which was held in Valley Forge, Pennsylvania, in June 2001. However, it isn't funny when you examine the reality of it. A number of years ago, a college friend of Mel Lindauer, who later became a broker, confided that they had a "cute" saying at the brokerage house where he worked: "When someone buys or sells an investment, the broker makes money, and the brokerage house makes money, and two out of three ain't bad." Basically, Mel's broker friend was saying that at his firm, at that time, the emphasis was on encouraging clients to buy and sell frequently (called *churning*) so they could earn commissions. Although we feel certain they didn't purposely set out to lose any of their client's money, nevertheless they knew that even if their investor clients didn't make money, both the broker and the brokerage company would. You need to keep that thought in mind when you decide whether you want to handle your own investments or turn them over to a broker, since their interests and yours aren't aligned.

Most Bogleheads are do-it-yourself investors (DIY investors). Some of us have used brokers in the past and at some point came to realize that they weren't looking out for our best interests when they sold us those high-cost, loaded mutual funds and other expensive investments, such as annuities, that earned them big fat commissions. Sometimes we learned (too late) that the investments they sold us weren't even appropriate, such as that annuity with a long surrender period for an already tax-deferred IRA. Some of us have had costly and sometimes unpleasant experiences when dealing with brokers, so we eventually decided we had to educate ourselves and take control of our own financial destiny. Other Bogleheads may have started with brokers and had pleasant experiences but simply reached a point where they felt they were now capable of handling their own financial affairs. And some of us simply never wanted to delegate this most important aspect of our lives—our own financial well-being and that of our children and grandchildren—to a stranger, so we've never used a broker or any other investment advisor.

No matter which route we took to becoming DIY investors, at some point along the way, we had to take the time to educate ourselves before we could feel comfortable about making our own investing decisions without the aid (and cost) of a broker or advisor. Armed with knowledge and confidence, and having discovered that we could buy good no-load, low-cost investments, such as those offered by Vanguard and other low-cost providers, directly from the company without paying any loads or commissions, the lightbulbs went off and it was goodbye to the brokers. I have no doubt that, upon learning that one of their clients was transferring her investments from them to Vanguard, some of the brokers and advisors probably sounded a whole lot like the guy in the Ditech commercials, with cries of, "Yikes. Lost another one to Vanguard!"

Financial education is the key. However, unless we majored in finance in college, or were fortunate enough to have parents who taught us about saving and investing, most of us have no formal training or background in this most important arena. So, whether we plan to become a DIY investor or hire a broker or financial advisor, we still need to become better educated. Otherwise, we'll be ill prepared and ripe for the picking when that slick "Give me your money and I can make all your dreams come true" sales pitch comes along.

In our opinion, it's a real tragedy that investing and financial basics aren't required subjects that are taught at every level of schooling. But since they aren't, we'll try to give you some background on what to look for, and what to look out for, should you decide that you simply don't want to be a DIY investor and opt, instead, to hire a broker or financial advisor.

THE ALPHABET SOUP OF FINANCIAL DESIGNATIONS

Pssst! Wanna be a financial advisor? Or would you rather be a financial analyst? How about becoming a financial consultant, a financial planner, or an investment consultant? Well, believe it or not, you can simply print up some business cards with any of those titles, hang out your shingle, and you're in business. It's really that easy.

Those five titles are all generic designations that require no special education, no experience, no testing, and no certification process. According to the U.S. Securities and Exchange Commission (SEC), *Anyone can use these terms without registering with securities regulators or meeting any educational and experience requirements.* Boglehead author Richard Ferri, a "reformed" former broker, who's now a fee-only investment advisor, warns that "at brokerage firms, everyone is a vice president. If they are not a VP, they are either very new or on their way out the door."

Lots of fancy titles are meant to impress us, but in reality, they signify nothing. Now that's pretty scary stuff, isn't it? Hopefully, you're beginning to see what you're up against if you decide to turn your financial affairs over to someone else.

In addition to those generic titles, if we include all the various insurance and employee benefits designations, the Financial Industry Regulatory Authority (FINRA) lists nearly 150 professional designations in its database. It's important to note that FINRA simply supplies the information and does not endorse any of these professional designations.

Unlike advisors who use the noncertified generic titles we just mentioned, which require no special training or skills, the advisors who've earned the various professional designations listed in the FINRA database had to meet some level of education, testing, or work experience to become certified. In addition, many of these professional designations require that the holder sign a code of ethics agreement and then continue to earn a certain number of approved continuing education units (CEUs) in order to be able to continue to use the designation.

However, the requirements for these various professional designations vary widely, and some designation-conferring organizations have much higher standards and requirements than others. As a result, advisors who've earned designations from institutions with these tougher standards are more highly regarded by most Bogleheads. Two of the professional designations that fall into this highly regarded category include the Chartered Financial Advisor (CFA) and the Certified Financial Planner (CFP).

Holders of the CFA designation must have met the following requirements:

- Have an undergraduate degree
- Must be working in the financial field
- Have either three years of professional experience involving investment decision making, or four years qualified work experience (full time, but not necessarily investment related)

In addition, the educational requirements are extensive. They include 750 hours of study (250 hours for each of three levels). Finally, they must pass a comprehensive exam for each of the three levels, and they can only take one level exam per year.

Some CFAs work as analysts and some as pension fund managers. Some manage hedge funds and still others manage mutual funds. However, some of these highly trained CFAs do choose to become financial advisors, and these advisors are considered by many Bogleheads to be among the most highly qualified in the field.

Like CFAs, CFPs are highly trained. They must master more than 100 financial planning topics. The topics cover major areas such as the following:

- General principles of financial planning
- Insurance planning
- Employee benefits planning
- Investment planning
- Income tax planning
- Retirement planning
- Estate planning

The approved courses that must be completed before one can sit for the CFP exam are taught at a number of colleges throughout the country. Although a college degree was not a requirement to earn the CFP designation in the past, beginning in 2007, an applicant for the CFP designation must have earned at least a bachelor's degree in any discipline from an accredited institution.

Completing the educational requirements is by no means a guarantee that an applicant will pass the comprehensive CFP practical examination.

In fact, a large number of applicants fail the exam on the first try, despite having satisfactorily completed the required course work. Knowing how challenging the exam can be, many applicants take additional courses specifically geared to prepare them for it. These courses are similar to prep courses for other professional exams, such as the CPA exam or the legal profession's bar exam. Passing this exam and earning the coveted CFP designation is certainly an achievement one can be proud of.

In addition to the CFA and CFP designations, there are a number of other financial professional designations you might come across when looking for a financial advisor. Let's take a look at the alphabet soup of designations in Table 16.1, and see what they stand for.

TABLE 16.1 PROFESSIONAL DESIGNATIONS AND THEIR ACRONYMS

INITIALS	PROFESSIONAL DESIGNATION
AAMS	Accredited Asset Management Specialist
AEP	Accredited Estate Planner
AFC	Accredited Financial Counselor
AIF	Accredited Investment Fiduciary
AIFA	Accredited Investment Fiduciary Auditor
BCA	Board Certified in Annuities
BCAA	Board Certified in Asset Allocation
BCE	Board Certified in Estate Planning
BCM	Board Certified in Mutual Funds
BCS	Board Certified in Securities
CAA	Certified Annuity Advisor
CAC	Certified Annuity Consultant
CAIA	Chartered Alternative Investment Analyst
CAM	Chartered Asset Manager
CAS	Certified Annuity Specialist
CCPS	Certified College Planning Specialist
CDP	Certified Divorce Planner
CDS	Certified Divorce Specialist
CEPP	Chartered Estate Planning Practitioner
CFA	Chartered Financial Analyst
CFG	Certified Financial Gerontologist
CFP	Certified Financial Planner
CFS	Certified Fund Specialist

(continued)

TABLE 16.1   (CONTINUED)

INITIALS	PROFESSIONAL DESIGNATION
ChFC	Chartered Financial Consultant
CIC	Chartered Investment Counselor
CIMA	Certified Investment Management Analyst
CIMC	Certified Investment Management Consultant
CMFC	Chartered Mutual Fund Counselor
CPM	Chartered Portfolio Manager
CRA	Certified Retirement Administrator
CRC	Certified Retirement Counselor
CRPC	Chartered Retirement Planning Counselor
CRPS	Chartered Retirement Plans Specialist
CSA	Certified Senior Advisor
CSC	Certified Senior Consultant
CSS	Certified Senior Specialist
CTEP	Chartered Trust and Estate Planner
CTFA	Certified Trust and Financial Advisor
CWM	Chartered Wealth Manager
FAD	Financial Analyst Designate
MFP	Master Financial Professional
PFS	Personal Financial Specialist
QFP	Qualified Financial Planner
RFA	Registered Financial Associate
RFC	Registered Financial Consultant
RFP	Registered Financial Planner
RFS	Registered Financial Specialist
WMS	Wealth Management Specialist

As you can see from the descriptions, some of these designations are geared toward specific situations or groups, such as divorce, seniors, estate planning, college funding, and retirement funding. The vast majority, though, are more general in nature and cover a much broader cross section of the financial and investing field.

You can learn more about each of these professional designations, including information on the issuing organization, the prerequisites and experience required for obtaining the designation, as well as the educational requirements (including the complete course outline in some cases) and the examination type, from the FINRA website at www.finra.org/index.html.

So, if you've decided to hire an advisor, how should you go about finding one who's right for you? First, because of the high standards and educational requirements for earning the CFA and CFP designations, we feel that an advisor with one of these designations should certainly be on your short list.

Second, since you'll definitely want an advisor whose interests are aligned with yours, you need to understand how advisors are paid so you can be sure there's no possible conflict of interest.

You need to understand that not all financial advisors are paid in the same manner. Some are paid on a commission basis, and thus might not have your best interest in mind when they try to sell you those high-commissioned products. These include full-service brokers, independent brokers, brokers who work in banks, and insurance agents posing as financial advisors, all selling high-cost mutual funds with front- or back-end loads, and insurance products, such as annuities. We suggest you just say "No, thanks" to this type of commissioned salesperson.

Fee-only advisors normally use the Assets Under Management (AUM) payment arrangement. This involves paying a set percentage of your total assets to the advisor on an annual basis. Depending on the advisor, the costs of AUM can vary widely, from 0.25 percent to more than 2 percent per year. This fee is often negotiable, especially for larger accounts. The AUM does not include trading costs, custodial charges, or any other miscellaneous expenses involved in managing the portfolio.

There are good and bad features with the AUM payment arrangement, depending on the advisor. On the plus side, since your annual fee is paying the advisor, the advisor is free to offer good, no-load mutual funds and other appropriate low-cost investments. On the downside, many good advisors often have higher minimum account requirements that may be out of reach for many investors. And, even if you can meet the advisor's minimum account requirements, paying up to 2 percent for a bond fund that's only yielding 4 percent is very costly. In fact, it can consume up to 50 percent of your return. And even with a return of 8 percent per year, a 2 percent fee still represents 25 percent of your total return. It's important to remember, too, that even in bad years, when your portfolio might suffer a loss, you'll still be paying the AUM fee. Obviously, then, you want to choose a good financial advisor whose fee is on the low end of the range, since every dollar you pay in fees reduces your total return by an equal amount.

You have to be careful to differentiate between fee-only advisors and brokers and insurance agents who call themselves *fee-based*. It's common for salespeople to use the term *fee-based,* which is a very ambiguous term. Many are actually selling commissioned products and yet are telling their clients that the commission they're getting is a fee paid by the insurance company or mutual fund company. This occurs most frequently when brokers and insurance agents sell B shares in mutual funds and variable annuities that don't have front-end loads, but nevertheless includes a hefty commission charge. Brokerage firms also sell *wrap accounts*. These wrap-fee setups include the AUM fee for management, commissions, and most other expenses in one bundled fee. That fee normally runs from 2 to 3 percent per year.

Although it might sound attractive to have all fees included and known in advance, the problem with the wrap account is that the amount these brokers charge for these programs is generally 1 to 2 percent higher than it should be, especially when compared to no-load mutual funds. In the worst-case scenario, a broker will sell a high-commissioned product and then charge the client an AUM to manage the account. The total cost of this could run to 4 percent per year. This is called a *wealth transfer*, since it transfers the money from your pocket into the broker's pocket. Now you understand why so many brokers and insurance agents tell people they're fee-based. Since there could also be a conflict of interest with this setup, again we suggest you just say "No, thanks" to this arrangement.

Two alternative payment options include a one-time fee or an hourly rate arrangement. Those payment methods are best suited for those investors who would like some help in creating a financial roadmap that they'll then follow as they implement the financial advisor's plan on their own. They might also pay for follow-up advice on a regular or irregular basis. Under this type of payment arrangement, since you're paying the entire bill, the advisor is working for you, which means that you're both sitting on the same side of the table. Unlike a broker who is steering you into high-commissioned products, the fixed or hourly fee advisor is free to recommend the most appropriate investment for you. And some mutual fund companies, such as Vanguard, also offer one-time financial planning services for a fixed fee. If you have enough assets invested with the fund company, the fee for this planning service might be reduced or even eliminated. This fee-only method of payment is probably the most popular arrangement used by those Bogleheads who do seek professional financial advice. Our friend and mentor, Jack Bogle, says this about cost: "Asset allocation is critically important; but cost is critically important, too. All other factors pale in significance."

The U.S. Securities and Exchange Commission (SEC) has published a list of helpful guidelines for investors thinking about hiring an investment professional. Here are some of the highlights.

- Think about your financial objectives and know what type of financial services you need. Knowing what you need will not only help you find the professional that's right for you, but it will also help prevent you from paying for services you don't want.
- Get the names of professionals from friends, neighbors, family, or business colleagues. Talk with several professionals. Ask each of them about their areas of specialization, professional designations, registrations or licenses, education, work history, investment experience, products and services, and disciplinary history.
- Understand how you will pay them for their services. Ask whether they receive any additional compensation or financial incentives based on the products they sell.
- Make sure that the investment professionals and their firms are properly registered with FINRA, the U.S. Securities and Exchange Commission, or a state insurance or securities regulator. Most investment professionals need to register as investment advisers, investment adviser representatives, or brokers (registered representatives). Registration simply involves completing paperwork and paying a fee; it's not an endorsement and does not imply any special level of training or expertise. Some investment professionals may only be licensed to sell insurance.
- If the investment professional will sell you investment products, ask if the firm the person works for is a member of the Securities Investor Protection Corporation (SIPC). SIPC provides limited customer protection if a firm becomes insolvent.
- Remember, part of making the right investment decision is finding the investment professional that best meets your financial needs. Do not rush. Do your background investigation. Resist investment professionals that urge you to immediately hire them.

The Certified Financial Planner Board of Standards also offers free online information on how to choose a planner. You can check out its website at www.cfp.net.

Armed with the information in this chapter, you should now understand that even if you're considering hiring a financial professional, you still need to do your homework first in order to become a better-educated consumer. When it comes to your financial future, remaining an uninformed consumer simply isn't an acceptable option. And, perhaps by the time you've finished reading this book (and a few others) and discover that investing isn't rocket science, you may just decide that you can handle the task, and that you, too, will become a DIY investor.

الصبح

PART II

---◆---

FOLLOW-THROUGH STRATEGIES TO KEEP YOU ON TARGET

CHAPTER SEVENTEEN

Track Your Progress and Rebalance When Necessary

Foolproof systems don't take into account the ingenuity of fools.
—Gene Brown

There is no foolproof "one-size-fits-all" system for rebalancing your portfolio. Each investor must choose a rebalancing method that's right for them. We want to make sure that whichever method we choose, it will be one that we'll stick with through thick and thin during all market conditions. However, before we can make an educated choice, we need to know what rebalancing is all about, and what some of our options are.

In this chapter, we'll discuss the reasons for rebalancing your portfolio, and cover a number of rebalancing options that you can choose from. We'll also touch on some of the things we want to consider when it comes time to rebalance.

PRINCIPLES OF REBALANCING

Rebalancing is simply the act of bringing our portfolio back to our target asset allocation after market forces or life events have changed the percentages of our various asset classes and segments of those classes.

Why Rebalance?

Rebalancing controls risk. It brings our portfolio back to the level of risk that we determined was appropriate for us and that we were comfortable with when we first established our asset allocation plan. As we learned earlier in Chapter 12, one of the primary reasons we hold a diversified portfolio is that asset classes don't always move in sync, and even when they do, they don't all have the same expected rate of return or risk level. And, at times, one asset class, or segment of an asset class, might greatly outperform the others, resulting in the outperforming asset class or segment becoming a much larger percentage of our portfolio than desired, while the other portions of our portfolio make up a smaller percentage than called for in our asset allocation plan.

Rebalancing forces us to sell high and buy low. We're selling the outperforming asset class or segment and buying the underperforming asset class or segment. That's exactly what smart investors want to do.

Although it might be hard for some investors to understand why they shouldn't simply let their winners run, by doing so, they'd be letting the market dictate the makeup of their portfolio, and thus their risk level. Those who followed this path during the late 1990s dot.com craze suffered huge losses when the tech wreck hit the market after the millennium. By choosing not to rebalance, and letting their tech winners run, many of these investors' portfolios suffered greatly when the NASDAQ lost 70 percent. By contrast, investors who rebalanced regularly into their underperforming bond funds minimized their losses when the tech market subsequently collapsed.

In "Rebalancing Diversified Portfolios of Various Risk Profiles," (Article 14 of the October 2001 issue of the *Journal of Financial Planning*), author Cindy Sin-Yi Tsai, CFA, looked at a number of rebalancing methods:

- Never rebalancing
- Monthly rebalancing
- Quarterly rebalancing
- Rebalance if more than 5 percent from target at month's end
- Rebalance if more than 5 percent from target at quarter's end

Often, investors who don't rebalance are simply letting their winners run in the belief that doing so would produce much higher returns. Contrary to what these investors might believe, the article reported that the increased returns were actually found to be small or even nonexistent when compared with the additional risk (as measured by the volatility) taken on by those investors who didn't rebalance.

In addition, the study showed that portfolios that were never rebalanced had the lowest Sharpe ratios of all the rebalancing methods studied. Since the Sharpe ratio measures the additional return an investor receives for taking on more risk, this lower ratio indicates that investors who didn't rebalance were not being compensated for the additional risk they were taking. This study's results came to the same conclusion as did Jack Bogle when he previously reported on the results from his 25-year rebalancing study in his classic 1993 book, *Bogle on Mutual Funds.*

Rebalancing may also improve your returns, since asset classes have had a tendency to revert to the mean (RTM) over time. By rebalancing, you're selling a portion of your winning asset classes before they revert to the mean (drop in price) and you're buying more of your underperforming asset classes when their prices are lower, before they revert to the mean (increase in value). So, you're selling high and buying low. If you believe in RTM, rebalancing could increase your returns. Jack Bogle believes in RTM, and we do, too.

Even if you don't believe that RTM will occur in the future, but rather, believe that the market is a random walk and that each market move is independent of previous moves, remember that you'll still benefit from rebalancing because you're controlling the level of risk in your portfolio. Experienced investors have learned that risk control helps to keep your emotions in check and that in turn keeps your portfolio in line with your long-term plan. So you're a winner either way when you rebalance.

How Do We Know If We Need to Rebalance?

We need to know several things in order to determine if our portfolio needs to be rebalanced. First, we need to know our desired asset allocation. This was determined when we first established our asset allocation plan, and possibly revised and refined it later as life cycles and events made changes to our plan necessary.

Our allocation plan includes, at a minimum, the basic breakdown between stocks, bonds, and cash. Our plan may also include desired percentages within each of those major asset groups. For instance, besides listing the percentage of our total portfolio that we want to maintain in equities, our target asset allocation may also include a breakdown of the desired percentages of suballocations we want to hold in segments of the equity market, such as large caps, small caps, and international. Additionally, our bond allocation may be further broken down into desired percentages in sub-allocations of the bond market such as intermediate-term investment grade bonds and inflation-protected securities. However, the thing that matters most in asset allocation is our stock/bond/cash mix, and we want to get that right, because it's the primary determinant of our portfolio's risk and return.

ASSESSING A PORTFOLIO

The second thing we need to know is where our portfolio currently stands in relation to our target asset allocation. We discussed how to go about establishing our asset allocation plan in Chapter 8. Now we'll discuss a number of ways to determine exactly where our portfolio stands in relation to our target asset allocation.

When Should I Check My Portfolio?

Since we need to track our portfolio for rebalancing purposes, this would be a good time to touch on the oft-asked question "How often should I check my portfolio?" Like so many other things that have to do with investing, there's no one right answer for everyone.

If you're an educated investor who understands and accepts market volatility and has the right asset allocation in your portfolio, and are confident that you won't panic and feel the need to take action every time the market hits a downdraft, there may be some benefits to checking your portfolio on a more frequent basis. Perhaps the greatest benefit is educational, since it will clearly demonstrate just how the different asset classes and segments of the market react and interact under various market conditions. Ideally, frequent checking of one's portfolio can help an investor see how a well-diversified portfolio works, thus helping the very patient long-term investor to understand the benefits of holding a portfolio that's made up of funds that zig while others zag. Investors who check their portfolios frequently will, we hope, also take note of the overall upward movement of their portfolio's value over time, including the recovery and growth in some of their funds that were down.

There are others who won't benefit at all from frequent monitoring. That would include "skittish" investors, as well as those who aren't confident that they have the correct asset allocation for their comfort level. Conventional wisdom says that these investors probably shouldn't look at their portfolios too often, since it may tend to scare them when they see their portfolio's market value decline. Once they see one or more of their funds decline in value, they're likely to shoot themselves in the foot, since they're apt to panic and sell funds that drop in value. That blows up a well-thought-out investment plan. Perhaps the best solution for those investors who can't stand the market's volatility would be to simply put their statements away unopened. Only open your December statement to see where your portfolio stands and whether you need to rebalance.

Since you probably already have a pretty good idea which of those two types of investor you are, and how you're likely to react to volatility in your portfolio, let that be your guide in determining how often you want to check your portfolio (daily, weekly, monthly, quarterly, or annually). Obviously, at a minimum, you have to check your portfolio as frequently as you've decided to rebalance.

How Do I Track My Portfolio?

There are a number of ways to track your portfolio's performance and asset allocation. Personal finance programs, such as Quicken, can handle that task for us. Many mutual fund companies also routinely offer a portfolio tracking service. For instance, if you're a client, Vanguard offers Portfolio Watch, a free online service that shows the percentages of the various asset classes in your portfolio each time you log on to your account. And since Vanguard allows you to include any non-Vanguard holdings in your online portfolio, Portfolio Watch can give you an accurate picture of your entire portfolio's asset allocation at any point in time. Finally, Portfolio Watch can also show any deviation from your target asset allocation, so it's an excellent rebalancing tool. Morningstar.com also offers a free online portfolio tracker. And, if you're a subscriber to its Premium Service, you can also use its enhanced Portfolio X-Ray feature that can provide a much deeper analysis of your portfolio. In addition to Vanguard and Morningstar, there are a number of other mutual fund companies and financial websites that offer free portfolio tracking, so chances are good that you'll be able to find one that's right for you.

If, after checking out some of these portfolio trackers, you find that none of them satisfies your needs, you can always create a custom portfolio tracker of your own using a spreadsheet program such as Excel or MS Works. However, with these do-it-yourself portfolio trackers, you may need to enter your data manually, and you must have a sufficient level of knowledge of how the spreadsheet of your choice functions.

For those of you who are not software savvy, some mutual fund companies routinely provide a portfolio's breakdown, showing the percentage held in each asset class, as part of the periodic statements they send to clients.

So, as we've seen, investors have lots of options when it comes to portfolio tracking. Simply choose the one that works best for you.

WHEN SHOULD I REBALANCE?

You're probably going to read and hear a number of opinions on when you should rebalance. Some people will recommend rebalancing on a strict time interval, such as each quarter, semiannually, or annually. Others suggest rebalancing based on percentage changes in your portfolio known as *expansion bands*. In either case, you need to consider two factors: costs and taxes. Costs would include any commissions and fees incurred by trading. Taxes would be a factor if the rebalancing takes place in a taxable account, because you may realize capital gains. Keep in mind that long-term capital gains are taxed at a lower tax rate than short-term capital gains.

The most common method of rebalancing is based on time. The typical time frame is either quarterly, semiannually, or annually. However, Morningstar found that investors who rebalanced their investments at 18-month intervals reaped many of the same benefits as those who rebalanced more often, but with less costs. Another advantage of the Morningstar method in a taxable account is that you're assured of having long-term capital gains, since you've held the fund for longer than 12 months.

A second method of rebalancing involves the creation of expansion bands. With this method of rebalancing, you create a window, such as plus or minus 5 percent from your desired allocation. You would rebalance whenever the asset class exceeds those bands. For example, if our desired equity allocation was 60 percent, we'd only need to rebalance whenever the equities in our portfolio fell below 55 percent or rose above 65 percent. However, if you plan to use the expansion band method and intend to rebalance as soon as your allocation touches either band, this would require more frequent monitoring of one's portfolio than the predetermined time-interval method, especially in a volatile market. In addition, if strict expansion band rebalancing were to be done in a taxable account, it could create short-term capital gains which are taxed at a higher rate than long-term capital gains. Therefore, you may want to consider delaying your rebalancing until you have held the asset for more than 12 months.

When it comes to rebalancing specific segments, or subclasses, of our equity or bond holdings between things like large and small caps, value and growth, or investment grade and high-yield, Morningstar found that rebalancing whenever any of these segments makes up 25 percent more or less than its original asset allocation can be an effective strategy. So, if your asset allocation plan calls for 60 percent of your equity portfolio to be in large caps, using this method you'd want to rebalance back to 60 percent anytime your large cap fund(s) rose or fell by 15 percent. In this example, the 15 percent figure represents 25 percent of the original 60 percent we want to hold in large caps (60 percent × 25 percent = 15 percent). Therefore, in this case, we'd rebalance our large caps whenever they rose to 75 percent of our equities or dropped to 45 percent of our equities. Although this is similar to the expansion band method, it's important to note that in this case we're working with a *percentage of the original asset allocation*, rather than a fixed number, such as we used in the 5 percent expansion band method.

No matter which method you choose (time interval or expansion bands, or a combination), you will want to rebalance your portfolio whenever it falls outside the desired asset allocation limits that you have set for yourself.

MARKET FORCES

Every day, market prices move. That means that the day after you've rebalanced your portfolio, it's already out of balance. Let's look at some examples of how market returns can change our asset allocation, and what action we might want to take as a result.

First, we'll look at an investment of $100,000 in a target asset allocation of 60 percent stocks, 35 percent bonds, and 5 percent cash. We have decided to rebalance on an annual basis. Let's look at what would happen if, at the end of the first year, the stock market returned +10 percent, the bond market returned +6 percent, and cash had a return of +3 percent (see Table 17.1).

TABLE 17.1   EFFECT OF MARKET FORCES ON RETURNS: STOCKS UP

ASSET CLASS	STARTING AMOUNT	MARKET RETURNS	ENDING AMOUNT	PERCENTAGE OF PORTFOLIO
Stocks	$ 60,000	+10%	$ 66,000	61%
Bonds	$ 35,000	+6%	$ 37,100	34%
Cash	$ 5,000	+3%	$ 5,150	5%
Total	$100,000		$108,250	100%

In this case, the ending percentages are still close to our target asset allocation of 60 percent equities, 35 percent bond, and 5 percent cash, so we might choose not to rebalance, especially if it were a taxable account or there were other costs involved.

Now let's look at another situation, where our desired asset allocation is still 60 percent equities, 35 percent bonds, and 5 percent cash, but we'll change the year's market returns to −20 percent for equities, +6 percent for bonds, and +3 percent for cash and see what that does to our portfolio.

In this situation, our portfolio's ending asset allocation has shifted more dramatically than in the first example. As you can see in Table 17.2, we now have 7 percent less in equities than our target, 6 percent more in bonds than we want, and 1 percent more in cash than our plan calls for. Since the ending percentages differ so much from our target allocation, we'd want to rebalance back to our target asset allocation of 60 percent equities, 35 percent bonds, and 5 percent cash. Using this second example, let's see what adjustments we'd have to make in order to get the portfolio back to our target asset allocation.

Looking at Table 17.3, we can see that we need to add to our equity holdings, reduce our bond holdings, and reduce our cash holdings to get back to our desired asset allocation. Now that we know which asset classes need to be adjusted and by how much, there are a number of ways we can accomplish this rebalancing. We will go over some of those options now.

TABLE 17.2   EFFECT OF MARKET FORCES ON RETURNS: STOCKS DOWN

ASSET CLASS	STARTING AMOUNT	MARKET RETURNS	ENDING AMOUNT	PERCENTAGE OF PORTFOLIO
Stocks	$ 60,000	−20%	$48,000	53%
Bonds	$ 35,000	+6%	$37,100	41%
Cash	$ 5,000	+3%	$ 5,150	6%
Total	$100,000		$90,250	100%

TABLE 17.3   CHANGES NEEDED TO REBALANCE PORTFOLIO

ASSET CLASS	STARTING AMOUNT	MARKET RETURNS	ENDING AMOUNT	PERCENTAGE OF PORTFOLIO	AJUSTMENT NEEDED TO REBALANCE
Stocks	$ 60,000	–20%	$48,000	53%	+$6,150.00
Bonds	$ 35,000	+6%	$37,100	41%	–$5,512.50
Cash	$ 5,000	+3%	$ 5,150	6%	–$ 637.50
Total	$100,000		$90,250	100%	

HOW TO REBALANCE

There are many different ways to get a portfolio back to its target asset allocation. Our first thought might be to simply sell the outperforming asset class(es) and buy more of the underperforming ones. Although this is certainly one way of handling our periodic rebalancing, there may be better options available to us.

- For those who need current income, rebalancing might also be accomplished by withdrawing funds from the asset class that's had the *hot hand* (selling high).
- Investors can also rebalance their portfolios by directing new money into funds that are below their target asset allocation.
- You have a number of options when it comes to mutual fund distributions. Rather than have the distributions reinvested in a fund that may already be overweighted, you can choose to have the distributions in your taxable account directed to your money market account, and then redirected to the fund that needs it for rebalancing.
- Finally, if you use a portfolio manager, such as Vanguard's Asset Management Service, or an even lower-cost advisor such as Portfolio Solutions of Troy, MI, you won't have to worry about doing the rebalancing because it's part of their service. However, as with all portfolio management services, there is a cost involved and a minimum investment required.

Now that we've covered the what, why, when, and how of rebalancing, let's look at some other things we want to consider when we're rebalancing:

- Rebalance your tax-deferred account first, whenever possible, since there are no tax consequences.
- Consider getting rid of any fund(s) that no longer fit into your overall plan.
- If you're in the withdrawal phase, use both voluntary and/or required distributions from your tax-deferred account to help rebalance your portfolio.
- Use tax-loss harvesting in your taxable account as part of your rebalancing strategy. If you have losers to sell, then sell them prior to December 31, so you can get the tax benefits on this year's tax return.
- If you have winners to sell in your taxable account, you might want to wait until after January 1 to sell in order to push the tax bill into the following year.
- The more frequently you rebalance your portfolio by selling profitable funds in your taxable account, the sooner you'll pay taxes on any profits.
- If you plan to rebalance on a timetable, pick a date that's easy for you to remember, such as each December, each January, or perhaps your birthday.
- A simple solution may be to consider owning a fund of funds that meets your desired asset allocation requirements, such as one of the LifeStrategy or Target Retirement series from Vanguard that automatically handles the rebalancing chore for you.
- Broad market index funds rebalance themselves automatically.

OTHER REBALANCING
CONSIDERATIONS

Life changes, such as an inheritance, can also cause us to rethink and possibly change our asset allocation, which means that we'd then need to rebalance our portfolio in accordance with our new asset allocation plan.

In addition, we tend to get more conservative as we get older and accumulate assets, so we should revisit our asset allocation plan to see if any changes are in order when it's time to rebalance. If you'd rather not have to worry about this, then consider owning one of the funds from

Vanguard's Target Retirement series or Fidelity's Freedom series, since they'll automatically rebalance and grow more conservative with time.

We now understand that rebalancing controls risk and might increase returns. We also understand the need to track our portfolio so that we know where we stand when it comes time to rebalance. All that's left to do now is to figure out when to get started. We'd suggest that now's the perfect time. Make a plan, pick a rebalance trigger, and stick with it; you'll be better off for it.

CHAPTER EIGHTEEN

Tune Out the "Noise"

It's Almost Always Wrong

A fake fortuneteller can be tolerated. But an authentic soothsayer should be shot on sight.

—Lazarus Long

Welcome to the age of the investor class. In 1980, very few Americans owned stocks and only 6 percent owned mutual funds. Today, over half of all U.S. households own marketable securities in one form or another. It has been the single greatest financial change in U.S. households in the past quarter century and has created an enormous new market for financial products and services.

As you might suspect, this new investor class has an enormous thirst for investment knowledge. As a result, the number of media outlets dedicated to investing and money management has mushroomed. We have 24-hour radio and television networks, newspapers, books, magazines, newsletters, and Internet websites, all churning out an endless stream of material—some of it useful, but much of it dangerous to easily influenced investors.

Whether it's newspapers, TV, radio, or the Internet, all media have one primary goal: to attract and hold an audience. That's the key to making money in a media business. The media make money either by charging the audience and/or by selling advertising. Assuming they attract a large enough audience, media outlets charge advertisers handsome fees for allowing them to promote their wares. If the advertising proves profitable for the advertisers, it's a win-win for both parties. However, when it comes to investing, it's not always a win for the audience.

The investment media perform an extremely valuable service when they provide the public with objective information to make better investment decisions. Unfortunately, that's more the exception than the rule. It's not that the investment media and Wall Street don't want you to be successful. They probably do. The problem is that both parties are more interested in maximizing the money in their pockets than in yours. As a result, the customer frequently gets taken to the cleaners through a combination of high fees and misinformation. Call us paranoid, but as the old saying goes, *Just because you're paranoid doesn't mean they aren't out to get you.* Let's look at how Wall Street and the media's best interests often directly conflict with yours.

THE GREAT WALL STREET MARKETING MACHINE

Most sales and advertising pitches from brokerage houses, actively managed funds, and money managers are variations of one single message: "Invest with us because we know how to beat the market." Far more often than not, this promise is fictitious at best and financially disastrous at worst.

There are only two ways to outperform the stock market: By choosing superior investments and/or through superior market timing. The research conclusively shows that the ability to do either with any degree of consistency is so rare that it might as well be chalked up to chance.

To be able to choose superior stocks means that there are inefficiencies in the market that the broker, fund manager, or money manager is aware of that he or she can exploit. We don't believe markets are 100 percent efficient. However, we do know that they are so highly efficient that the vast majority of stock pickers are not able to equal the market after the costs of transactions, management fees, and taxes take their toll. That's not opinion; it's fact.

To be sure, some investment pros do outperform the market for a given period of time. But the longer the time frame, the smaller are the odds that any given one will be able to do it. In fact, they have about an 80 percent chance of underperforming the market over the long haul. We don't like those odds. Think about this way: If you were a business owner, would you hire someone who has an 80 percent chance of decreasing your profits? Well, that's precisely what you are doing when you pay someone to actively manage your investments.

As you probably realize, these are facts that most in the investment industry don't want the public to know. If enough people knew, a lot of them would lose their high-paying jobs and be forced to make a living doing something else. It's in their best interest that the public believes they can beat the market. Consequently, they spend billions every year churning out investment propaganda. Brokerage houses and mutual fund companies frequently run ads boasting of market-beating returns over specific periods of time, which they happen to choose. The law requires they also put a disclaimer in the ads stating, "Past performance does not guarantee future results."

Perhaps they should be required to add a second disclaimer: "Dangerous if swallowed." As author and investment manager Rick Ferri so aptly put it, "Wall Street wants you to believe they are there to make money for you, but their true purpose is to make money from you." In a world where 80 percent of the investment pros fail to beat the market, they collectively spend enormous sums of money trying to convince you that they can.

WHAT THE INVESTMENT MEDIA DON'T WANT YOU TO KNOW

If you have read this far, you know that effective investing can be incredibly simple:

- Create a simple, diversified asset allocation plan.
- Invest a part of each paycheck in low-cost, no-load index funds according to your plan.
- Check your investments periodically, rebalance when necessary, then stay the course.

You can simplify it even more by buying a single fund of funds that will take care of the allocating and rebalancing for you. Do this for a lengthy period of time and you will outperform about 80 percent of investment professionals. Once the plan is set up, it takes minimal investment knowledge and practically no time to manage. All it takes is the self-discipline to stay with it. It isn't rocket science, and is about as difficult as fogging a mirror.

The simplicity of sound investing creates a real problem for the investment media. They're in the business of selling investment information and advertising. They have white space to fill on pages and time to fill on the air. How on earth can they attract and hold an audience or advertisers if effective investing is so simple? If they tell the public the truth, most will turn their attention to something more exciting, like the Breathing Channel.

You can't attract an audience by being boring, but sound investing is about as exciting as watching grass grow. According to Warren Buffett, "Inactivity strikes us as intelligent behavior." But that's what most of the investment media and the Wall Street marketing machine don't want you to know. If effective investing is that simple and that easy, you don't need what the vast majority of them sell. You only need investments and information that are worth more to you than the money you pay for them. Otherwise, they're wasting your time and money.

Consequently, in order to fill all the space and time, the investment media churn out massive amounts of what has become known as *investment pornography*. Unlike valuable information, investment pornography is designed to hold your attention, get you excited about beating the market, and get you to buy products or information with the hope of getting rich. When you stop and think about it, calling it *investment pornography* is actually somewhat flattering. Real pornographers deliver what they promise. Investment pornographers are more like the hooker who takes the customer's money, sits on the side of the bed telling him how good it's going to be, and then leaves. It may be exciting, but it's ultimately unfulfilling.

Most of us haven't learned the basics of effective investing for several reasons. First, the concepts of efficient markets and modern portfolio theory, while not new, have only been available to the general public in recent years. Second, most investors today are first-generation investors. They have no formal education about the subject and learned little or nothing about investing from parents, friends, or relatives. Finally, there's a lot of noise out there with hidden sales agendas disguising itself as sound financial information. Put those three things together, and you get a gullible public that's ripe for the picking. It may not be possible to fool all the people all the time. However, it's possible to fool many of the people enough of the time for many others to make a very comfortable living.

THE THREE BIGGEST LIES—WALL STREET VERSION

Many of us have heard the old joke about the three biggest lies in the world. There are many versions, but the first lie is always, "The check's in the mail." The other two lies vary. Some of the more popular ones are:

- "Of course, I'll love you in the morning."
- "If you're available, I'm rich."
- "I'm from the government, and I'm here to help you."
- "I'm the personal injury lawyer who advertises on the back of the phone book, and I'm your friend."

Well, here is the Wall Street version of the two other lies:

1. "It's a stock picker's market."
2. "The trend is your friend."

The first lie wants you to believe that the world of investing has changed radically. The pitch goes something like this: Although index funds have historically beaten most actively managed funds, from now on look for those with savvy stock-picking ability to beat the market.

It's true you can find short periods of time when active management prevails over indexing. However, the longer the time period chosen, the greater the odds favor indexing. Identifying those brief periods of superior active management is easy in hindsight and impossible in foresight. To quote University of Chicago professor Eugene Fama, one of the giants of modern portfolio theory: "I'd compare stock pickers to astrologers, but I don't want to badmouth astrologers."

The second lie does have a grain of truth to it. There is one trend that is your friend. We have more than 200 years of U.S. stock market history, and the only long-term trend was up. Here's what recent history tells us: If you bought a market portfolio of stocks and reinvested the dividends, your odds of losing money in any one particular year were 32 percent. Your odds of losing money over any 5-year period dropped to 13 percent, and for any 10-year period the odds of losing money fell to only 2 percent. There has never been a 15-year period when stocks lost money. That's all you need to know.

Although many claim to see historical patterns and trends that forecast future stock market conditions, they amount to little more than selective perception. People see what they want to see. Study after study has found that trying to forecast the direction of the economy or the stock market in the short-run is largely an exercise in futility.

Nevertheless, hope springs eternal. Because people want to believe there are gurus and experts who hold the Holy Grail to future returns, there are plenty of self-anointed investment/media gurus out there pushing investment pornography. At the same time, there are a number of excellent investment pros and people working in the investment media who level with the public and provide honest, objective, very valuable information.

SEPARATING SOOTHSAYERS FROM THE TRUTH SAYERS

The nineteenth-century humorist Artemus Ward wrote, "It ain't so much the things we don't know that get us in trouble. It's the things we know that ain't so." There's an abundance of investment noise out there trying to teach you things that "ain't so." If you care about your financial future, it's imperative that you know how to recognize and ignore it. With that thought in mind, here are three guidelines for tuning up your noise detector:

1. All forecasting is noise.
2. Listen to the helpers; ignore the hustlers.
3. Be a bona fide skeptic and do your homework.

   Let's look at these in detail.

All Forecasting Is Noise

Pretend with us for a moment. Let's assume you wake up one day with a one-year gift of stock market prophecy and are aware of your new powers. For the next 12 months, you will know which stocks are going to be winners and which will be losers. Better yet, you will know when to get in and out of the right stocks at the right time. Would you:

- Write, publish, and sell a stock market newsletter telling people what's going to happen?
- Call the investment magazines and tell them the names of the six hottest stocks everybody must own in the next six months, so they can publish a cover article about them in the next issue?
- Produce and air a TV infomercial selling a course that teaches people how to duplicate your gift of foresight?
- Send out a mailer inviting people to a free dinner or seminar and try to sell them an investment course, or talk them into letting you manage their money?
- Get a coast-to-coast radio or TV show telling the world how to invest?
- Keep your mouth shut, mortgage the farm, and make a fortune?

   Well, if you did any of these things except the last, you'd be leaving a boatload of money on the table. With a gift like that, the smart thing to do is keep quiet, borrow as much money as you can, and invest it in the right stocks at the right time. Buy low and sell high. Do that, and in well under a year you are the world's richest person. With just a one-year gift of stock market prophecy, you could make enough money to buy out Bill Gates, Warren Buffett, and a few wealthy Arab sheiks with pocket change.

Market forecasting is much like sports forecasting. We all have opinions about what's going to happen, and any one of us has about as much of a chance as the other of getting it right. But betting on sports or stock market forecasts is playing a loser's game. The winners are the forecasters, gambling houses, money managers, and brokerage houses because they get paid while the investor takes the risk.

If you're a sports fan, try this sometime: Buy and read one of the sports magazines that forecast the upcoming football or basketball season. You'll notice something very interesting. Almost all the teams predicted to do well this year, did well last year. Now, put the magazine away and make a note to look at it after the season is over and see how accurate the forecasts were. You'll be sure to see some real surprises that the prognosticators missed. Some teams predicted to finish at or near the top had disappointing seasons, while others not expected to do well had great seasons.

Well, stock market forecasters work in much the same manner. Predictions about the future direction of the market and which stocks are likely to be winners are usually based on recent performance. Our tendency to believe that what has happened recently will continue to happen in the immediate future is a behavioral trait called *recency bias*, which we discussed in Chapter 6.

For example, after the stock market's dismal performance in the 1970s, the August 13, 1979, issue of *Business Week* magazine published a cover article titled, "The Death of Equities." Less than three years after stocks were declared dead by *Business Week*, the greatest bull market in history arose from the ashes and lasted for nearly two decades.

By contrast, at the peak of the bull market in early 2000, very few voices were heard calling for caution. Most forecasters proclaimed something like, "The ten hot tech stocks you must own now!" In the late 1990s it was common to hear people say they were counting on stocks to earn 20 percent per year forever. Those are examples of recency bias. It causes us to believe things that aren't so.

There are three kinds of investment experts:

1. Those who don't know what the market will do and know they don't know
2. Those who don't know what the market will do but believe they know
3. Those who don't know what the market will do and get paid to pretend they know

When it comes to predicting what the stock market will do in the short run, all of us are equally blind. Your predictions have as good of a chance at being correct as Nobel Prize–winning economists, last year's top-performing mutual fund manager, *Peter Porn's Hot Stocks Newsletter*, and Joe Six-pack. Don't bet the farm on any of them, including yours. It's just noise.

Listen to the Helpers; Ignore the Hustlers

There are many excellent sources of advice available for people who want to learn about investing. They can be found in every conceivable media form: books, radio, television, newspapers, lectures, seminars and invest-ment courses, magazines, newsletters, audio and video courses, and the Internet. That's the good news.

The bad news is that there are many more bad sources of investment advice dedicated to selling than helping. Separating the two isn't easy, but it can be done. Here are some guidelines of what to look for in various media forms. Let's begin with the most likely sources of noise.

Radio and TV Infomercials

These programs are usually manned by slick sales people who make get-ting rich sound like child's play. Just order their books, audio and video programs, or investment course, and you, too, will learn the secrets to un-limited wealth. Of course, the way these guys hope to make their wealth is by selling bad information to a gullible public. It's a con that would make a carnival barker blush. Follow what many of them advocate and you'll likely end up broke, in trouble with the IRS, or in prison, the same way some of them did.

Investment Newsletters

There are a few good ones around, but most have the lifespan of a fruit fly and a track record of providing terrible advice. We discussed invest-ment newsletters in detail in Chapter 13. Suffice it to say that when it comes to investment newsletters, we feel that Malcolm Forbes said it best: "The only way to make money with a newsletter is by selling one."

Invitations to a Free Investment Seminar and Dinner

These are almost always sales pitches that run the gamut from legitimate financial planners to "Meet the Grifters." One retired Boglehead we know delights in accepting the dinner invitations, listening to the sales pitches, and then remaining invested in index funds. When Jack Bogle says "costs matter," this guy listens. We suggest you do the same.

Investment Call-In Shows on Radio and TV

All of the hosts/guests usually are selling investments, insurance, portfolio management, financial planning, or newsletters. However, that doesn't preclude many of them from dispensing excellent advice. The good ones hope you will see the value in their honesty and expertise and do business with them. The bad ones talk about which stocks/funds are hot, predict what the market is going to do, and brag about their market-beating abilities. You can learn a lot by listening to the good ones without spending a dime. That's what we recommend.

Noncredit Investment Courses

Offered by colleges and universities, investment courses can be excellent vehicles for learning the basics of financial planning and investing. However, just because it's an institution of higher learning offering the course doesn't mean it's automatically free from bias and veiled sales pitches. Brokers and financial planners often teach the courses for no charge as a way to attract new clients. There's always a conflict of interest when purchasing investment products and investment advice from the same source. Please keep that in mind if you decide to take one of these courses.

Audio/Video Investment and Wealth-Building Programs

These programs range from excellent to horrible. The good ones teach the basics of saving, principles of sound investing, and encourage you to get and stay out of debt. They tell you that achieving financial freedom takes a good plan, plus years of time, work, and sacrifice. The bad ones serve up investment porn by the bucket. If they promise to teach you a way to time the market, earn incredibly high returns, pick the right stocks, buy real estate with no money down, or flip properties, it's a hustle.

Investment Print Journalism

An article appeared in the April 1999 issue of *Fortune* titled "Confessions of a Mutual Funds Reporter." In it, the author, who signed his byline as "One Anonymous," writes:

> *Mutual funds reporters lead a secret investing life. By day we write "Six Funds to Buy NOW!" ... By night, however, we invest in sensible index funds.*

Some of the best advice on investing can be found in magazines, newspapers, and online blogs. Two of the best individuals to follow for financial advice are Jason Zweig and Jane Bryant Quinn. Jason Zweig offers excellent investing advice regularly in his column, "The Intelligent Investor" in the *Wall Street Journal.* Jane Bryant Quinn has been writing outstanding financial and investment advice for decades. Today you can read her thoughts at her blog, janebryantquinn.com. Both writers are also authors of excellent books.

Books
The public often perceives books as having instant credibility, especially when a major publisher publishes the book. Don't believe it for a minute. Publishers are far more interested in book selling than truth telling. Some of the biggest-selling investment books dispense some of the poorest investment advice. Many are just printed infomercials that aim to per-suade the reader to hire the author as a money manager, broker, or finan-cial planner, to subscribe to his/her newsletter, or to buy the author's expensive investment course.

Many publishers love investment porn authors because the authors spend a fortune promoting the book while the publishers sit back and col-lect huge profits. The publisher's attitude is, "Who cares about the truth? The book's on the bestseller list and the author is footing the advertis-ing/publicity bill." Fortunately or unfortunately, many of the authors who spend a fortune to get their books on bestseller lists end up declaring bank-ruptcy. However, since they are bestselling authors and are forever coming up with new angles to pitch their drivel, publishers eagerly embrace them.

Just because an investment book is a national bestseller doesn't mean it's a source of good information. It just means the book has been heavily promoted. Look at the author's credentials. See what the book is promis-ing. Charles J. Givens wrote several huge money bestsellers, including *Wealth Without Risk.* Shortly before dying, Givens declared bankruptcy. We can only assume that he saw the wealth but not the risk. Robert Allen's multimillion-copy bestseller, *Nothing Down,* teaches readers how to buy real estate with no money down. He, too, went bankrupt, and had the IRS on his back. If it's possible to get rich buying real estate with no money down, why did he go broke? Former taxi driver turned financial guru Wade Cook writes books promising readers annual returns in the hundreds of percent by following his stock market investment techniques. He has a lengthy history of being in financial hot water with creditors and the IRS. These and numerous other authors have the gall to tell readers what to do with their money while they go broke. What's wrong with this picture? Physician, heal thyself.

At the same time, bookstores and libraries are filled with lots of excel-lent books on investing. There is a list at the back of this book of some of our favorites that is by no means complete or exhaustive. If you're interested in reading excellent books about investing, the books on the list are a good place to start.

Internet Websites

This newest media drops endless sources of information on our computers, tablets, and smartphones at the speed of light. That's the good news. The bad news is that practically all of it is unregulated. Anybody with access to a server can put up a website making any kind of statement or claim. Worse yet, it may be posted by someone claiming to be a person or company other than the real poster, and can originate from anywhere in the world. When it comes to media, the World Wide Web is like the Wild, Wild West. It's a frontier with little or no control.

Nevertheless, the Internet can be an excellent place to learn the basics of sound investing and get many of your questions answered. At the same time, it's the easiest place for anyone to make unsubstantiated claims without being held accountable. It's a pretty sure bet that the three of us would have never met had it not been for the Internet. A list of our favorite financial and investing websites is provided at the end of this book.

Be a Bona Fide Skeptic and Do Your Homework

The best antidote to noise is knowledge based on empirical research done by competent, unbiased parties who don't have an interest in selling investment products and services. If you take the time to read books and articles written by leading finance professors and investment practitioners, you will find the results of their research to be very similar to each other and the information presented in this book. We strongly urge that you do so. It's your money, and having the knowledge to successfully invest it puts you in control. It's always possible that someone claiming to have incredible market-beating abilities will do so over the course of a career. However, the research makes it very clear that it's not the way to bet.

The ideas in this book are nearly all the result of extensive academic research. Many of our best suggestions are taken from the experience, writings, and speeches of our friend and mentor, Jack Bogle. These ideas also reflect the lessons we've learned from our combined investment experience (good and bad) totaling over 100 years. When it comes to investing, there's a world of difference between good, sound information and information that sounds good. Your financial future depends on knowing the difference.

CHAPTER NINETEEN

---◆---

Mastering Your Investments Means Mastering Your Emotions

You aim for the palace and get drowned in the sewer.
—Mark Twain

"*If we can dream it, we can do it.*" That's the traditional American attitude of unbridled optimism and confidence. It's rooted in a core belief that we live in a land of freedom, abundant wealth, and unlimited opportunity. Americans believe that if we want something badly enough and work hard to achieve it, we will ultimately succeed in getting it. We believe that holds true for individuals, families, teams, businesses, and the nation as a whole. In short, Americans aren't afraid to go for it. It's a wonderful attitude, and the motivational engine that drives the largest, most successful economy in world history.

Motivation can't be seen or measured, but we know it exists. It stirs emotions in us that cause us to behave in a particular manner. Behavior, the product of motivation, is what we can see and measure.

Emotions are extremely important because we all live at the feelings level. Better to be happy and poor than miserable and rich. It's our wants, our desires, and our feelings that cause us to make thousands of choices every day that ultimately determine who we become. We are the sum of our choices, and most choices are made emotionally. If you doubt that, look at the food we eat, the clothes we wear, the people we associate with, where we choose to live, who we marry, and the careers we choose. Emotions rule.

Relying on our emotions to make decisions often leads to a happier, better, more successful life. People who rise from rags to riches almost always attribute much of their success to a burning desire to succeed and a willingness to pay almost any price. Love, hope, anger, fear, frustration, and many other emotions, when properly channeled, propel us to do a better job of learning, earning, saving, giving, growing, and becoming better human beings.

However, when it's time to make investing decisions, *check your emotions at the door*. This is one area of life where acting on emotional impulses will likely lead you down a path of financial wreck and ruin. Playing your hunches, blindly following the crowd or an investment guru, trying too hard, acting on a hot tip, relying on supreme self-confidence, going for it to make a quick killing, playing it ultrasafe, and a multitude of other emotionally based investment decisions will almost always leave you poorer. The paradox of money is while most people are very emotional about acquiring it, behaving emotionally about money is a recipe for losing it.

WELCOME TO THE FIELD
OF BEHAVIORAL ECONOMICS

Classical economics assumes that human beings make conscious, rational choices about how to allocate their dollars to maximize their total satisfaction. Effective advertisers and good salespeople know that, in the short term, that assumption is about as realistic as the tooth fairy. From years of hands-on experience, they understand that people usually buy emotionally and justify with logic. Although the customers or investors may be able to give you a sound, logical reason why they buy or invest in a certain way, more often than not, it's not the real reason. Moreover, many times they aren't even aware of the real reason.

While many economists were busily assuming away the real world, a couple of psychologists working in Israel pioneered a field that became known as *behavioral economics*. In the late 1960s, Amos Tversky and Daniel Kahneman were at Hebrew University in Jerusalem performing psychological experiments to determine how people go about making economic choices.

It didn't take Tversky and Kahneman long to realize that people don't always make rational choices in their own best interest. From their experiments they began to organize and classify the rules of thumb people used to make quick, economic decisions and named them *judgmental heuristics*. As you might suspect, most are more emotional than rational.

Later, both men relocated to the United States, with Tversky finally settling at Stanford and Kahneman at Princeton. In 2002, Kahneman shared a Nobel Prize in Economics for his pioneering work, the first psychologist ever to do so. Unfortunately, Tversky died of cancer in 1996 at age 59.

Thanks to the pioneering work of Tversky, Kahneman, and a number of other researchers in this relatively new field, we now have a list of judgmental heuristics that people use to make economic decisions. In this chapter we look at the ones that get us in trouble when investing, and how you can avoid them. But before we do that, let's take a look at the two major emotions of Wall Street.

GREED AND FEAR

The two very primitive emotions of greed and fear drive many investors as individuals and the stock market in general. Nobody invests to lose money. We all invest our dollars in a very uncertain market with the ultimate goal of making profits while avoiding losses.

Prehistoric man depended heavily on greed and fear to stay alive. When meals were sparse and came along infrequently, only a fool didn't gorge himself and horde as much extra food as he could. And running in terror from the saber-toothed tiger meant the chance to live another day. Better yet, it gave man a chance to retreat to his cave and plan how to make the tiger his meal, instead of vice versa. In the world of the jungle, acting on the emotions of fear and greed is critical for survival.

But in the world of investing, fear and greed diminish and destroy returns. Consider the results of the Dalbar study discussed in Chapter 7 To refresh your memory, the study found that from 1993–2012, the average mutual fund investor underperformed the S&P 500 Index by an average of 3.96 percent per year. While part of the underperformance can be attributed to brokerage commissions, high fees, and taxes, most of it's caused by investor behavior. Thanks to greed, investors excitedly chase performance and buy when the market is up. Thanks to fear, they panic and sell when the market is down and lock in their losses. To quote the old comic strip character, Pogo, "We have met the enemy, and he is us." It's hard to make a profit when you buy high and sell low.

HOW SMART PEOPLE MAKE
BAD INVESTMENT DECISIONS

Although fear and greed cause a lot of poor investment decisions, they don't explain them all. Have you ever looked at your investment decisions in hindsight, slapped your forehead, and thought, "What on earth was I thinking?" Rest assured, most of us have. Chances are that you made a poor investment decision using one or more of the following judgmental heuristics that have been identified by researchers in behavioral economics.

When we blindly assume that today's happenings will be tomorrow's results we are practicing recency bias (see Chapter 18). If the market is down, we assume it's going down further and we sell. If the market is up, we assume it's going to continue going up and we buy more. The result is that we sell our stocks at bargain-basement prices, buy somebody else's stocks at high prices, and lose money in the process. Here are some other emotional traps that can cause us to feel like investment boneheads in hindsight.

Ego and Overconfidence

Overconfidence may be the biggest return killer of them all. Throw in a little greed for good measure and you have the bankruptcy Blue Light Special. Our American attitude of optimism and confidence left unchecked can lead us to make horrible investment decisions.

Despite the statistical impossibility, at least 70 percent of Americans believe they are above average. The vast majority of us think we are above average drivers, above average in intelligence, above average in appearance, and so on. Our need to believe in ourselves and feel in control of our future serves a very important and useful purpose. It gives us the courage to try and achieve successes in life that we might not otherwise attempt and achieve.

However, if you carry that attitude into your investment decisions, you're probably headed for hard times and big losses. Even if you are more brilliant and a better investor than you believe you are, overconfidence will betray you for one simple reason: In the short-run, stock market ups and downs are random happenings. When variations are unpredictable, intelligence, skill, and knowledge give you no edge. Believing that they do is hazardous to your wealth. Here are three examples that illustrate the point:

1. During the 1990s, 14 Illinois grandmothers who called themselves "The Beardstown Ladies" formed an investment club and claimed to have earned a 10-year average annual return of 23.4 percent while the

S&P 500 earned an average of 14.9 percent. After a string of best-selling books, a journalist checked their figures and learned that their true average return was only 9.1 percent. It should be noted that there was no intent on the part of the Beardstown Ladies to defraud the public. Rather, they simply did not know how to calculate their performance numbers correctly.

2. Mensa is an exclusive society whose membership is restricted to persons scoring in the top 2 percent on IQ tests. During a 15-year period when the S&P 500 had average annual returns of 15.3 percent, the Mensa Investment Club's performance averaged returns of only 2.5 percent.

3. In 1994, a hedge fund called Long-Term Capital Management (LTCM) was created with the help of two Nobel Prize–winning economists. They believed they had a statistical model that could eliminate risk from investing. The fund was extremely leveraged. They controlled positions totaling $1.25 trillion, an amount equal to the annual budget of the U.S. government. After some spectacular early successes, a financial panic swept across Asia. In 1998, LTCM hemorrhaged and faced bankruptcy. To prevent a world economic collapse, the New York Federal Reserve orchestrated a buyout by 14 banks that put up a total of $3.6 billion to buy out the fund. Billions were lost. It was a very expensive way to learn that genius doesn't guarantee success in investing.

If you think you can pick stocks, time the market, or know more about what's going to happen in the economy than other people do, you're a good candidate to fall into the overconfidence trap. Not surprisingly, this malady strikes more men than women. As a result, women tend to earn better returns than men because they trade less and take more prudent risks. Men, on the other hand, are taught that it's their role to take action and solve problems. The problem is that taking bold action to solve investment problems usually creates worse problems. We hope you believe in yourself and are far more brilliant than you believe you are. But when it comes to investing your hard-earned dollars, please keep this thought in mind: *The stock market is a very expensive place to learn that neither you nor anyone else is endowed with the gift of investment prophecy.*

Loss Aversion

Do you check your portfolio every day? Do you sell a stock or mutual fund when it earns a healthy return to lock in the profit? Do you sell stocks/mutual funds whenever you see them going down? Are you a young person who keeps most of your savings in bonds or safe, ultraconservative investments? If so, you may be hurting your potential returns through loss aversion.

Loss aversion is the flip side of overconfidence. Although overconfidence tends to make us overly bold, loss aversion makes us overly timid about investing. Experiments have determined that at the emotional level, we feel the pain of a $100 loss twice as much as we enjoy the benefit of a $100 gain. Consequently, many people once burned by a stock market loss vow to never invest in it again. As Mark Twain said, "A cat who sits on a hot stove will never sit on a hot stove again, but he will probably never sit on a cold one either."

Perhaps you have known people who lost a fortune in the stock market crash of 1929, the 1973–1974 bear market, the tech wreck of 2000, or the housing bubble and credit crisis of 2007–2009—who now keep all of their money in bank certificates of deposit. They may think their investments are risk-free. However, if you factor in the taxes due on the interest earned and inflation, many of them are actually losing purchasing power. What's perceived as safe isn't always as safe as those who are loss averse believe it to be.

Paralysis by Analysis

This investment trap is the first cousin to loss aversion. When it comes time to invest, we have literally thousands of funds to choose from and an abundance of noise telling us why we should invest in a certain way. The more choices people are given, the harder it becomes to choose one. As a result, some people don't make a choice and don't invest.

The problem is that by failing to invest they incur an opportunity loss. The money doesn't come out of their pockets, so they probably aren't aware of it. Nevertheless, it's money that won't be compounding in their accounts and building their net worth. Employees pass up billions every year in free money offered by their employer's matching retirement plans simply because they won't decide which investment course to take. If you have a hard time pulling the trigger on investment decisions, remember that investing is like basketball in this respect: You miss 100 percent of the shots you don't take.

The Endowment Effect

Many of us have a tendency to confuse the familiar with the safe and overrate the value of what we already own. That's the endowment effect. One common investment mistake caused by the endowment effect happens when employees invest the bulk of their money in their employer's stock. If you believe this is a prudent thing to do, ask former employees of Enron. The employee who does this is already investing half or more of her waking hours in the company. On top of that, she is now betting a large chunk of her monetary investments on the company too. To call her *undiversified* is an understatement.

Another common practice caused by the endowment effect is to buy only domestic funds in the belief that U.S. investments are safer. Historically, U.S. and international funds have similar returns over the long run, although they tend to peak at different times. Some make the case that international funds aren't necessary in a globally, interdependent world. The reasoning goes that since many U.S. corporations earn a good chunk of their revenue abroad, U.S. funds are globally diversified. However, that line of reasoning is very different than simply assuming U.S. funds are safer. As we said earlier, we feel that most investors will benefit by having approximately 20 percent of their equities invested in foreign stocks.

Following the Herd

Being human, we feel the need to conform and have an innate tendency to follow the crowd. Conformity serves us well in many business and social situations. Many of us were taught the old saying, "To get along, go along."

But if you follow the herd when investing, you might as well walk around with a sign on your back that reads, "Take my money, please!" Once again, consider the lessons from the Dalbar study about mutual fund investor performance. Following the herd will likely earn you negative real returns.

The sad truth is that when it comes to investing, you can follow the herd to the slaughterhouse. Herd investors have certain traits. They don't have a sound investment plan, they listen to the noise, buy and sell at the wrong times, and have no idea how badly they underperform the market. In fact, thanks to the endowment effect, most believe their investments are performing far better than they actually are. Call it *The Beardstown Ladies Effect.* Since most believe they're above average, they conclude that their returns are above average, too.

Mental Accounting

This emotional trap causes us to be poor savers, rather than poor investors. Nevertheless, since you can't invest what you don't save, it's a habit to be aware of. Mental accounting is the habit of treating money differently, based on where it comes from. Of course, all money is money regardless of how we obtain it. But not being totally rational, we tend not to treat it that way.

For example, when you get an income tax refund, do you think of it as found money and a nice windfall with which to reward yourself? If you do, you're practicing mental accounting. The truth is, you should kick yourself for giving the government an interest-free loan. Tell your employer to reduce the amount of income taxes withheld from your paycheck. That money should have been compounding in your account for the past year. If it had been, you would have more.

As another example of mental accounting, you buy a nonrefundable air ticket for a trip you are planning to take. Circumstances change and you don't want to take the trip but feel obligated to go because you don't want to waste the ticket. So, you go on the trip, spend more money on meals and lodging, and have a miserable time. The truth is that the airfare is a sunk cost that should be ignored when deciding whether to take the trip. To do otherwise is to risk pouring good money after bad.

Do you keep all of your retirement money in very safe investments but carry credit card balances? Do you spend more when you pay by credit card than when you pay with cash? Do you think of yourself as a good money manager but have trouble saving? All of these are symptoms of someone who practices mental accounting.

Anchoring

Do you stick with a money manager, broker, or financial planner without knowing if they earned you more or less than the market return? Do you hold on to an investment that has lost value, vowing only to sell it when it rises to a certain price? Do you cling to investment habits without making an effort to find the true facts? Those are all symptoms of anchoring—clinging to an old belief or comfortable opinion despite the fact that they may be harmful to your wealth.

The old saying, "My mind is made up, don't confuse me with the facts," best describes the attitude of anchoring. It's common for people to hold on to a house they want to sell until they get "their price." One couple we know has been holding out to get their price for more than 10 years, on an old house, in an old part of town, and getting older every year. They seem oblivious to the costs of taxes, insurance, maintenance, and subterranean termites dining in the neighborhood. Nevertheless, they continue to own and live in a house where they don't want to live, waiting for their house to be worth what they want to sell it for.

No doubt, there are still investors from the tech bubble, dearly holding on and patiently waiting for the return of NASDAQ 5000. Those kinds of anchors weigh down returns.

Financial Negligence

Finally, procrastination is the biggest detriment to financial success. Many people make poor investment decisions simply because they're preoccupied with other matters. They're too busy making or spending money to learn how to hold on to it and make it grow. For some people, it's too much effort to learn how to be a savvy investor. As a result, they delegate all financial tasks to their CPA, insurance agent, lawyer, broker, or financial advisor. They have no idea how much they're spending in commissions, professional fees, taxes, and management costs. They don't understand the economy, the financial markets, and the magic of compound interest or have any idea if the people they pay are doing a decent job for them.

One of us attended an investment seminar where the noted actor-economist Ben Stein was speaking. In his address, Stein told the story of a movie producer who gave him his big break in Hollywood. Like many people in Hollywood, this producer was a big spender and enjoyed taking frequent luxury cruises to Europe. Stein mentioned that the producer went broke and he (Stein) was currently helping the producer by paying the monthly payment on his home. The surest way to lose money is to pay no attention to it. Just as there are rags to riches stories, there are riches to rags stories, too. They just don't make the news as often.

KEEPING EMOTIONS IN CHECK

It's one thing to be aware of the emotional pitfalls of investing and another to take steps to keep them from ruining your investments. So, what do you do?

Begin by writing down your major financial goals on one sheet of paper with dates when you will need the money. Need money for college? How much and when? Need money for a new home? How much and when? Need money for retirement? How much and when? Good planning begins by setting financial goals and target dates.

Second, if you consistently practice the techniques recommended in this book, you will automatically side-step most of the emotional investment traps. Pay off your credit card and high-interest debts and stay out of debt. Formulate a simple, sound, asset allocation plan and stick to it.

Systematically save and invest a part of each paycheck in accordance with the asset allocation plan. The earlier you start, the richer you become. Invest most or all of your money in index funds. Keep your costs of investing and taxes low. Don't try to time the market. Tune out the noise, rebalance your portfolio when necessary, and stick with your plan. By doing those things, you will intelligently manage risk. You will buy low, sell high, and have the power of compounding working in your favor. You will slowly but systematically build wealth and a nest egg for a comfortable retirement. With a little luck, you will have more money than you dreamed you would ever have. These time-tested techniques have worked for millions of other people and they can work for you, too.

Third, forget the popular but misguided notion that investing is supposed to be fun and exciting. Investing is a process with the goal of building and preserving wealth. It's not Disney World, Las Vegas, the lottery, or the Super Bowl. If you seek excitement through investing, you're going to lose money. It's a short trip from the penthouse to the outhouse.

You want excitement? Get excited about your career. Get excited about your family, your community, place of worship, favorite causes, sports teams, hobbies, or anything else you want to feel passionate about. Get excited about earning and saving money, but be very dispassionate when it comes to investing. Once you have enough money, you can spend your time being excited and passionate about any blessed thing you want.

If you want to enjoy the thrills and spills of trying to pick winning investments or time the market, take a maximum of 5 percent of your portfolio and create a casino account. You're free to trade and try to time the market with this money as you see fit. However, there's one overriding rule: If you lose it all, it's gone forever. No more casino accounts. That way you can enjoy the excitement of chasing the action without jeopardizing your financial future.

Fourth, don't expect to be perfectly sane and rational all the time about investing. We are all emotional creatures, and sometimes our emotions get the best of us. If you make a poor, emotional investment decision, resolve to learn from it and not repeat it. That's all you can do. Author Elbert Hubbard wrote, "Everyone is a fool for at least five minutes a day. Wisdom consists of not exceeding the limit." During those few minutes a day, we highly recommend not making any investment decisions.

HOW TO ESCAPE THE EMOTIONAL TRAPS

Finally, for the common emotional traps mentioned earlier, we offer the following tools for escape:

- *Recency bias.* Never assume today's results predict tomorrow's. It's a changing world.
- *Overconfidence.* No one can consistently predict short-term movements in the market. This means you and/or the person investing your money.
- *Loss aversion.* Be a risk manager instead of a risk avoider. Believing you are avoiding risk can be a costly illusion.
- *Paralysis by analysis.* Every day you don't invest is a day less you'll have the power of compounding working for you. Put together an intelligent investment plan and get started. If you need help, seek out a good financial planner to assist you.
- *The endowment effect.* Just because you own it, or are a part of it, doesn't automatically mean it's worth more. Get an objective evaluation. Invest no more than 10 percent of your portfolio in your employer's stock.
- *Mental accounting.* Remember that all money spends the same, regardless of where it comes from. Money already spent is a sunk cost and should play no part in making future decisions.
- *Anchoring.* Holding out until you get your price to sell an investment is playing a fool's game. So is blindly assuming that your financial person is doing a great job without getting an objective reading of what's really going on. Get a second opinion.
- *Financial negligence.* Take the time to learn the basics of sound investing. It's really pretty simple stuff. Knowing it can make the difference between having a life of poverty or one of prosperity.

Investing is one area where acting on emotions is likely to lead you down the path to financial ruin. Playing your hunches, blindly following the crowd, acting on a hot tip, trying to make a big killing, or falling prey to any of the other emotionally based investment decisions described in this chapter will almost always leave you poorer. Understanding behavioral finance will better enable you to deal with your emotions and make better investment decisions.

CHAPTER TWENTY

Making Your Money Last Longer Than You Do

I've got all the money I'll ever need, if I die by four o'clock.
—Henny Youngman

"How much of my portfolio can I spend each year without running out of money?" That's the big question that all retirees and near retirees want answered in no uncertain terms. The thought of being unemployed and running out of money, with years of life ahead, conjures up all sorts of horrible images. We imagine spending our final years eking out a miserable existence, in an unheated flat eating cat food and crackers. We imagine our friends abandoning us, our families ignoring us, and, after dying alone, having very few people attend our minimal funeral.

If that question is plaguing you, you can answer it for yourself with 100 percent certainty. All you have to do is gather together the following information:

- Current value of your portfolio
- Your date of death

- Your portfolio returns every year leading up to your demise
- Your federal, state, and local tax rates each year until your demise
- Inflation rates
- Health care costs
- Amounts of your pension and any other income
- Future value of any real estate you may own
- All unanticipated changes in your pension and health care coverage

Once you have collected all that data, you can then run it through any number of online financial planning programs, and they will give you a spending figure that will allow you to run out of money on your last day on earth. You can even arrange for your check to the undertaker to bounce. For those wishing to leave assets, figure out how much you want to pass on to your heirs and the program will adjust your spending figures accordingly.

Are you starting to see the problems involved in answering the big question? Even if you have an ironclad date with Dr. Kevorkian, there are simply too many unknowns to provide a precise answer. But, oh, how we try. Inquiring minds want to know.

All we really have to work with are life expectancy tables and historical financial data. Armed with that information, investment scholars and researchers have come up with viable answers to the big question, "How much of my portfolio can I spend each year without running out of money?" While no two answers are exactly alike, they all prescribe withdrawal rates that tend to fall into a fairly narrow range.

Based on our research, we have a spending plan for you. We'll get to that later. But first, let's look at the dilemma that retirees face.

THE RETIREE'S SPENDING DILEMMA

Let's assume that after years of working and saving, retirement is at hand. Through choice or chance, you are facing life without employment. You must now establish a spending plan that will last you and your spouse (if any) as long as either of you is living. There are two basic ways you can go wrong when it comes to spending down your nest egg. First, you can live it up, overspend in the early years of retirement, and potentially run of out money later on. Spending too much too soon is a mistake you simply can't afford to make. Few, if any, of us want to spend our final years living as a ward of the state or a burden to others.

The second mistake is to underspend. This is usually driven by an irrational fear of running out of money—even when your portfolio and other sources of income are sufficient to sustain your desired standard of living. Underspenders deprive themselves and those closest to them of goods, services, and experiences that can make for a better, happier, and more fulfilling life. It's sowing the seed without reaping the harvest. Underspending can be a difficult problem for people in the habit of saving and investing to overcome.

The story of Jacob Leeder is a good example of underspending. He drove a 1984 Oldsmobile stationwagon and lived in a modest, one-story brick home. He had no children or pets. Since he didn't have cable TV, he spent up to eight hours a day at his girlfriend's house watching stock-market reports and using her phone to call his brokers. According to his girlfriend, Ann Holdorf, he was less than courteous to them.

Leeder and Holdorf rarely went out to eat, and when they did, it was to a cafeteria or a cheap restaurant. Most evenings, she cooked dinner for them at her home. For her birthday, Leeder would give her a $100 check. They never took vacations. When she brought up the subject, he would say, "Not now, the market is bad."

When Leeder died in 1997, he left an estate valued at approximately $36 million. The size of his estate came as a complete shock to many, including Ann Holdorf, his girlfriend of 24 years. Leeder did leave Holdorf the grand sum of $150,000 plus a $100,000 trust fund—a relatively small sum, considering the size of his estate and the number of years they spent together. Most of his fortune went to estate taxes, with the remainder earmarked for two nieces, animal rights groups, and veterinary schools.

As British clergyman and essayist John W. Foster remarked, "The pride of dying rich raises the loudest laugh in hell." The last suit we wear doesn't need any pockets.

THE TWO BEST WAYS TO INSURE INCOME FOR LIFE

What most of us want is a plan that ensures we do not outlive our money while enjoying it as much as possible. Choosing your yearly withdrawal rate is a good starting point for planning purposes, but realize that your withdrawal rate may have to be adjusted as the years go by. Stock market returns go through long periods of feast and famine. High inflation rates may come along and diminish purchasing power. Unexpected happenings in your life can raise or lower living expenses in ways you never anticipated. If the Boy Scout's motto is to "Be prepared," the retiree's motto is to "Be flexible."

Not surprisingly, there are two simple ways to remain financially flexible and reduce the odds of running out of money. First, keep your fixed living expenses as low as possible. Retirement is not the time to have an enormous mortgage, expensive car payments, credit card debts, or the like. Low overhead comes in very handy when the stock market goes in the tank and bears are growling on Wall Street. You need to have the flexibility of spending less during bear markets and more during bull markets. When the market has a great year, you can spend some of the profits. Take that round-the-world cruise or buy a new car. When the market is down, if your budget is tight, you put those purchases on hold for a year or two.

The second way to increase spending flexibility is to have a viable way to earn income if needed. We aren't suggesting going back to work full-time or becoming a Walmart greeter. Technology makes it possible to do many paid tasks from the comfort of our home, working as much or as little as we want. For example, Michael earned well over $1 million working from home without borrowing a penny or hiring a single employee. A publisher then paid him a very healthy sum to write *The Perfect Business*, a book that teaches others how to do it.

Surveys of baby boomers reveal that the majority of them plan to do some type of work after age 65. Although that may be due to choice or necessity, having a viable way to earn revenue can be extremely useful, especially during the early years of retirement when we are likely to be more active and spend more. Every extra dollar that comes in is one that doesn't have to be withdrawn from the portfolio. At the same time, the extra income can be used as a windfall to purchase goods, take trips, or contribute to a favorite charity. In addition to the pay, there's a psychological benefit. Working part-time keeps you productive, makes you feel like you are a contributing member of society, and keeps you mentally sharp.

Jack Bogle, the founder of Vanguard, is well into his eighties, yet he speaks frequently at conferences, writes books, appears on television, and acts as the conscience of an industry that badly needs one. Despite having a heart transplant in 1996, he's a bundle of positive energy and having the time of his life.

THREE MORE WAYS TO ENSURE INCOME FOR LIFE

Other ways to increase the odds of solvency are delaying retirement, waiting until full retirement age to draw Social Security, and purchasing an immediate annuity. Every year you delay retirement is one more year to add to your savings, one more year for your savings to compound, and one year less that you will be depending on your portfolio for income. Of course, you have to enjoy what you're doing, or the energy expended isn't worth the financial benefit.

As of this writing, the earliest retirement age when you can collect Social Security benefits is 62. Many people opt for Social Security as soon as they're eligible. However, delaying payments until full retirement age provides a larger, inflation-adjusted pension. For example, someone whose full retirement age is 66 will receive a pension that's 33 percent larger than he or she would receive at age 62.

If you are not earning very much income, it probably matters very little at which age you take Social Security. Over a 20-year period starting at age 62, the numbers tend to balance out about the same. However, if you earn more than $15,480 in 2014, you are penalized $1 in benefits for every $2 above the earnings limit. In the year you reach full retirement age, there is a higher earnings allowance before the penalty kicks in. Finally, once you enter the first full year after your retirement age, there is no earnings penalty. The amount of the earnings limit rises over time at the rate of inflation.

It's probably best to begin drawing Social Security at age 62 if you need the money, are not expecting to live a long time, and are not earning over $12,000 a year. If you're in excellent health, have great genes, and have earned income over $12,000 a year, waiting until full retirement age is likely a good decision. Waiting until age 70 will garner you a pension that is 8 percent per year higher for every year above your full retirement age. In cases where a couple are both eligible to draw Social Security, one wise strategy is to delay the retirement of the one having the higher benefit to age 70 while having the other begin drawing earlier.

A final way to ensure income for life is to use part of your savings to purchase an immediate annuity that guarantees a fixed monthly income (see Chapter 4 for details). Although an annuity can be a good option for those aged 75 or older, it has its drawbacks, especially for younger retirees. First, the younger you are, the lower the payout is. Second, the monthly income rate is based on current interest rates, and in recent years, interest rates have been low, making the payout relatively small. Third, most immediate annuities have no provision for inflation. With the possibility of retirement lasting 30 years or more, the purchasing power of an annuity will almost surely erode over time. An average inflation rate of 3 percent per year cuts purchasing power in half in 24 years. You can purchase inflation-adjusted annuities, but the initial payments will be lower than those of a regular immediate annuity. Finally, if you give the insurance company a hefty sum without choosing a term-certain payout option, and then die prematurely, it can be a very bad decision for your heirs. The money does not go back into your estate; rather, it's retained by the insurance company.

A PRUDENT PLAN FOR TAPPING YOUR PORTFOLIO

Incorrect assumptions about investment returns or spending can hurt your chances for a successful retirement. Here's an example of the kind of thinking that gets many retirees in trouble: "Let's see, now. Since the stock market has historically returned an average of a little over 10 percent per year, I can safely spend 10 percent of my portfolio each year and never run out of money, right?" WRONG! The problem with that kind of thinking is twofold. First, the performance of the market going forward is likely to be lower than it was in the past. Second, when stock market returns are above average, they are usually well over 10 percent per year. When they are less than average, they are usually negative and reduce the value of a portfolio. Worse yet, above- and below-average returns tend to run in consecutive years but without a predictable pattern. Believing you can withdraw 10 percent per year and not run out of money is akin to the idea that you can put your head in the oven, your feet in the freezer, and consider yourself comfortable on average. If you get lucky and retire at the beginning of a long-term bull market you can likely spend 10 percent and never have a care. But, if you retire at the onset of a long-term bear market, continued withdrawals can reduce your portfolio so much that it can no longer sustain the original withdrawal amount.

Most of the credible studies of 30-year portfolio survival rates conclude that you can withdraw from 4 to 6 percent of the portfolio value per year with a good chance of not exhausting the portfolio, depending on your portfolio's asset allocation. However, once spending rates rise over 6 percent, the odds of survival diminish rapidly. As you probably suspect, the lower the spending rate, the greater the odds of survival.

How long does your portfolio have to last? The answer is, "Longer than most of us think." For example, a 65-year-old man has a 20 percent chance of living to age 90. A 65-year-old woman has a 32 percent chance of living to the same age. If they are married, there is a 45 percent chance that one of them will live another 25 years to age 90. Remember, this is just average life expectancy. Half of all retirees live longer than their life expectancies.

In Chapter 8 we recommended portfolios for Vanguard and non-Vanguard investors in various stages of life. A major change in your personal life, such as retirement, is a call for a reevaluation of your asset allocation plan. You may have noticed that the primary change in our recommended portfolios as a person ages is the reduction in stocks and an increase in bonds to reduce the risk of loss when the bear market strikes—as it often does. When a retiree no longer has employment income, it's imperative to understand that keeping what we have is much more important than risking what we have in an attempt to gain even more. This is the reason our recommended portfolios for early and late retirees contain less stocks and more bonds as we age.

The portfolio allocations in Chapter 8 are not set in stone. Perhaps, on the one hand, you have substantial outside income in the form of a pension or Social Security income. Or maybe your portfolio is so large that you could suffer a substantial loss without reducing your standard of living. In situations like this, you could maintain, or even increase, your stock allocation in the hope of leaving more to your heirs and/or charity. On the other hand, you may be entirely dependent on income from dividends, capital gains, and return of capital from your portfolio. If that's the case, don't be tempted to take extra risk in the hope of a better return. It's far better to cut back on unnecessary spending or perhaps work part-time.

Finally, here's our answer to the big question about how much you can withdraw each year. If you want to make inflation-adjusted withdrawals, increasing the amount withdrawn each year in accordance with increases in the cost of living, begin by withdrawing no more than 4 percent of the portfolio's beginning value. If, by contrast, you want to simply withdraw a fixed percent of the current value of the portfolio, withdraw a maximum of 5 percent a year. Keep in mind that the value of the portfolio may go down in some years, so if you withdraw a fixed percentage, be prepared to take a pay cut or else plan to earn extra income. The good news is, the value of your portfolio will go up in some years, allowing you to withdraw a bit more. Also, as we age, it should be possible to increase our withdrawals because of the shorter time left to withdraw. Be aware that withdrawal rates are before taxes, so a chunk of the money withdrawn will go to the taxman.

No one can guarantee that any plan will keep you from outliving your money. However, based on historical performance, the odds are that these allocation and withdrawal strategies will enable you to live out your life without exhausting your portfolio. If you find yourself over age 75 and withdrawing only 4 percent due to the fear of going broke, either you have a profound faith in medical science or it's definitely time to loosen the purse strings.

In summary, the most important key to making your money last is to be financially flexible, particularly in the early years. Keep your fixed expenses low and have a viable way to earn extra income if needed. It may be reassuring to have an ironclad rule telling you to withdraw no more than a certain percentage of your portfolio each year. However, to dogmatically follow such a rule is to risk both over- and underspending. During our working years, we have to make financial decisions in the face of uncertainty, and this new stage of life is no different. Most important, don't let money concerns deprive you of enjoying the freedom to spend your time pursuing the activities—and enjoying the people—you treasure most.

CHAPTER TWENTY-ONE

Protect Your Assets by Being Well-Insured

Insurance is the business of protecting you against everything, except the insurance agent.

—Evan Esar

Bad stuff happens to everyone. That's just part of life. Sometimes that bad stuff can wreak havoc on your financial well being. One of the best ways to prevent it from wreaking financial havoc on you or your family is by carrying the proper types and amounts of insurance. Just one bad uninsured mishap can financially ruin you or your family forever. Carrying proper coverage is a must.

Specifically, you need to consider the following types of insurance:

- *Life insurance* for anyone in your family on whom others depend for financial support
- *Health care* coverage for everyone in your family
- *Disability* insurance on any breadwinner whose future income is vital
- *Property* insurance in case of fire, theft, or other disasters
- *Auto* insurance
- *Liability* protection against expensive lawsuits
- *Long-term care* for older family members to prevent nest-egg erosion

To be a successful investor requires being a good risk manager. Managing risk means having a plan to cover the downside. That's what insurance is all about—damage control to prevent the unforeseen from smashing your nest egg. The purpose of this chapter is to give you a broad overview of who should carry what types of insurance, how to decide how much coverage you may need, and how to find qualified people to help you make good insurance decisions.

COMMON INSURANCE MISTAKES

When it comes to buying insurance, just about all of us overinsure in some areas and underinsure in others. One reason is because we don't like to think about bad things happening and tend to ignore the possibility that they will. Consequently, most of us don't give much thought to a comprehensive insurance plan. Rather, we buy it in a piecemeal manner. As a result, we don't get the best insurance value for the money. Basically, people tend to make three types of insurance mistakes:

1. Insuring the unimportant while ignoring the critical
2. Insuring based on the odds of misfortune
3. Insuring against specific, narrow circumstances

Insuring the Unimportant While Ignoring the Critical

It's common for people to buy extended warranties on their cars, computers, or big-screen TVs but not buy a liability umbrella policy. A broken computer without a warranty is an expense, but a lawsuit without adequate liability coverage can be financially devastating. It's common to find people insuring packages at the post office who don't carry health care. Very often, people with no dependents carry unnecessary life insurance but fail to carry the disability coverage that they really need. Without a set of insurance priorities, we fall into the trap of insuring the relatively trivial while failing to cover the important areas of our life.

Insuring Based on the Odds of Misfortune

Here's a good rule of thumb to keep in mind: Never fail to buy insurance because the odds of something happening are small. For example, if you're moving to a desert city, you may think buying flood insurance is a waste of money. Not so. Floods can happen nearly anywhere, although the odds are much smaller in some places than in others. If the loss of your home and property in a flood would leave you financially devastated, you need flood insurance. If the odds of a flood are small, the price of insurance will be cheap.

Insuring against Specific, Narrow Occurrences

Are you one of those people who buys life insurance from an airport vending machine in case you die in a plane crash? Do you carry accidental death insurance? Do you carry a special health care policy for Alzheimer's disease? Those are examples of insuring too narrowly. Insuring against specific disasters is usually a waste of money. The insurance companies make large profits from selling special case types of insurance due to their emotional and impulse buying appeal. If you need life insurance, buy a policy that pays off no matter what the cause of death. Buy a comprehensive health care policy to cover all contingencies.

THREE KEY RULES FOR BEING PROPERLY INSURED

You can greatly reduce or eliminate common insurance mistakes by following three simple rules:

1. Only insure against the big catastrophes and disasters that you can't afford to pay for out of pocket. The cheapest insurance is self-insurance.
2. Carry the largest possible deductibles you can afford. The larger the deductible, the more you are self-insuring and the cheaper the premium will be.
3. Only buy coverage from the best-rated insurance companies. You need insurance companies you can depend on when you need to file a claim.

As Coach Lou Holtz remarked, "Sometimes the light at the end of the tunnel is a runaway train." There's no way of knowing beforehand when misfortune will strike, or what types of insurance you may need. You can only prepare for unexpected, worst-case scenarios and insure against them. With that thought in mind, let's look at some common types of insurance.

LIFE INSURANCE

The purpose of carrying life insurance is to provide financial support to dependents who would be deprived in the event of a breadwinner's death.

If you have no dependents or are financially independent, you don't need life insurance. If you have a substantial estate to leave to your dependents, you may not need life insurance.

If you need life insurance, buy term insurance. Term insurance is basic pay-as-you-go, no-frills insurance. It's the cheapest way to go and serves the purpose. When you tell an insurance salesperson that you want to purchase term insurance, get ready for lengthy sales pitch about how term insurance is insufficient, penny-wise, and pound-foolish. They will likely try to sell you more expensive policies that build cash value, such as whole life, universal life, and variable universal life. They may tell you that it's a good investment in addition to life insurance: "You don't have to die to win." Although cash-value policies *are* investment vehicles, the costs associated with them are typically too high to make them good investment options. We don't believe in mixing investing with insurance. Insurance is for protection and investing is for wealth building. Don't confuse or mix the two.

Insurance companies love to push cash-value policies because it's a high-profit item for the salesperson and the company. It's common for the salesperson to pocket between 50 to 100 percent of the first year's premium. Nevertheless, if you insist on buying only term insurance, an insurance agent will sell it to you. Insurance companies didn't amass enormous wealth by turning down a sale.

It's common for life insurance salespeople to descend like vultures on young people right out of college. The sales pitch to the new grad goes like this: "Buy your life insurance while you're young and in good health, and the rates are low. When you get older or need it, you might be disqualified due to poor health or unable to afford it." Young people shouldn't fall for it, since they normally don't have dependents who rely on them for support. Everyone should save and invest their money and not buy life insurance until the situation requires it.

How Much Do I Need?

Once you've decided that life insurance is a good idea, you will want to determine how much life insurance is necessary. The 10-step formula in Table 21.1 will help you come up with an estimate. Simply fill in the dollar amounts.

The net result (see line 10) is a rough estimate of the amount of life insurance needed. For a more complete analysis of your needs, you may want to consult a professional life insurance agent and/or financial planner.

TABLE 21.1   COMPUTING HOW MUCH LIFE INSURANCE YOU NEED

1. $_____ Annual income (in dollars) that will be needed by the survivor(s)
2. $_____ Annual income available (pension, Social Security, annuities, etc.)
3. $_____ Annual income shortfall (#1 minus #2)
4. $_____ Annual income shortfall multiplied by number of years income is needed
5. $_____ Emergency funds (3 to 6 months of living expenses)
6. $_____ Estimated funeral expenses (U.S. average is $5,000 to $10,000)
7. $_____ Other cash needs (taxes, college, bequests, etc.)
8. $_____ Total family needs (add lines 4 through 7)
9. $_____ Total assets available (savings, investments, existing life insurance)
10. $_____ Subtract line 9 from line 8

Term Insurance

Term insurance is purchased at a fixed rate for specified periods of time such as 5, 10, 15, or 20 years. The longer the period, the higher the rates will be. Buy the longest period that you can afford and need. Make sure the policy is guaranteed renewable, meaning that you will be able to purchase future coverage regardless of your health.

For the overwhelming majority of us, life insurance is sometimes a necessity and almost always a poor investment.

There are rare circumstances when low-load cash-value life insurance and term insurance policies can be good investments to persons in high tax brackets or to those facing high inheritance taxes. If your assets are such that you fall into this category, and you think this type of insurance may be appropriate for you, see an independent financial planner or estate-planning attorney for guidance.

HEALTH CARE

Most of us are painfully aware of the importance of carrying adequate health care insurance and the soaring cost that comes with it. Consider yourself very fortunate if you're covered by a relatively inexpensive plan offered by your current or former employer.

If you're not covered by a group plan and need to purchase your own health care insurance, the most important feature is major medical coverage. That's the part of the plan that covers the big bills such as hospitalization, X-rays, lab work, surgery, doctors' charges, and rehabilitation services. The lifetime benefit of the policy should be a minimum of $1 million and preferably $2 million.

You can reduce the cost of a health insurance policy by taking the highest deductible and co-payment percentage that you can afford. Co-payment is the dollar amount you are required to pay before coverage begins, such as $25 for doctor visits, $20 for prescription bills, or 20 percent of your hospital bill. Co-payments are usually capped at something like $1,000. So, with a 20 percent co-payment policy with a $1,000 cap, if you have a large bill, you'd pay 20 percent of the cost until you reached your maximum out-of-pocket expense of $1,000. The policy would cover the balance.

If you are under 65 and considering a high-deductible health care plan, you may want to consider establishing a health savings account (HSA). HSAs combine high-deductible health insurance with tax-favored savings. Here's how it works: You obtain coverage from a qualified health insurance plan with minimum deductibles of $1,000 for single persons and $2,000 for families. Each year, you are allowed to deposit an amount up to the amount of the deductible in a health savings account, subject to a maximum amount. The 2014 maximum is $3,300 for singles and $6,550 for families. Contributions to the HSA are tax deductible. The money in the savings account can be used to pay for the deductible or noncovered medical expenses such as dental or vision care. Any money taken out of the account to pay for health care is tax-free. Any money that remains in the account grows on a tax-deferred basis. It's a way to save, reduce health care insurance costs, and lower taxes at the same time.

Another option for lowering your health care costs is to join an HMO (health maintenance organization). While your premiums will be lower, your health care choices will likely be fewer. HMOs frequently limit your choice of doctors and some services. If freedom to select your choice of physician is important, you probably don't want an HMO policy.

Other features of a good health care plan include the following:

- The freedom to see the doctor of your choice, or specialists without referral or the need to obtain authorization from a primary-care physician
- No dollar limits on expenses such as hospital room rates, surgeries, procedures, and lab work
- An annual cap or limit on the amount of money you have to pay out of pocket

- International coverage, so if you are out of the country and need to obtain health care, it will be covered by your policy

Like most things in life, with health care coverage, you get what you pay for. You may not be able to afford or want all of those features, but by shopping at the larger and more established providers, you're likely to find a good health care plan that's right for you.

LONG-TERM DISABILITY COVERAGE

What's your most valuable financial asset? You may be thinking it's your home, your business, or your liquid assets. Well, unless you're financially independent or retired and drawing a secure pension, it's none of the above. Most people's greatest financial asset is their future earning power. Think about this: When you die, your living expenses are over. But let disability strike, and you can face real financial hardships. You still have to eat and pay for living expenses, but can't work to bring in income. And if that isn't bad enough, you're likely to be hit with enormous health care costs too. Most people need long-term disability coverage to insure their future earning power. Sadly, while 70 percent of us carry life insurance, only 40 percent of Americans carry insurance on their greatest financial asset.

A joint study conducted by the Harvard Medical and Law Schools of personal bankruptcies occurring in 2001 reveals that more than half of those bankruptcies were caused by illness and medical bills. Surprisingly, more than three quarters of those bankrupted had health insurance when misfortune struck. Moreover, 56 percent had attended college and owned a home. These people were not stereotypical deadbeats who tried to scam the legal system to avoid paying their debts. Most of them were just average Americans who happened to get sick or injured and were not adequately insured. Their misfortunes resulted in loss of income and job-based health care insurance, while piling up enormous medical bills. Health care coverage is vital but it isn't enough. Working folks also need disability coverage.

Here are some tips on buying disability coverage. First, buy as much disability coverage as you think you'll need. The maximum amount you can purchase is usually 60 percent of your income. Second, consider purchasing your own policy with after-tax dollars instead of buying one through your employer. Then, if you ever need to draw disability, the income from the personal policy would be tax-free. With the way jobs come and go in today's free-agent economy, you might not want to depend on your employer for disability coverage. If you lose the job and become disabled, you're in big trouble.

Here are some other features a good disability policy will have:

- It covers your inability to work in your own occupation.
- It requires a waiting period of no more than 90 days before coverage begins.
- It carries a cost-of-living adjustment.
- Benefits are provided for partial disability.
- It provides the longest benefit in your own occupation for as long as possible or at least until age 65.

If you're still thinking, "I don't need disability," please consider these statistics: There's a 20 percent chance that a 35-year-old will become disabled before age 65 and a one in seven chance that he or she will be disabled for at least five years. The odds of becoming disabled are far greater than the odds of dying prematurely. When you consider just the income lost, a year of total disability can erase 10 years of saving for someone who saves 10 percent of his or her income. Don't fail to insure your greatest financial asset.

PROTECTING YOUR PROPERTY

Life, disability, and health care insurance are all designed to protect you and your family from financial hardships in the event of death, disability, or illness. Let's now turn our attention to types of insurance that protect you from losing the dollar value of personal property and other assets that you already own.

First, you need a homeowner's or renter's policy to cover your residence and its contents in the event of a fire, flood, earthquake, robbery, or any major catastrophe. The two words you need to remember when buying this type of coverage are *replacement cost*. For example, maybe you purchased your home years ago for $100,000 but it would cost three or four times that amount to rebuild if it was destroyed. Be sure to insure your home and the contents in it based on the amount it would cost you to replace the assets insured. Don't assume that your policy covers all disasters such as floods and earthquakes, because it probably doesn't. You usually have to purchase a rider. Do it. Cover all potential disasters.

A homeowner's policy will generally insure personal property inside the home in an amount equal to 50 to 75 percent of the building's coverage, and this is usually sufficient. The land still has residual value. You will probably have to purchase a special rider to cover certain items such as expensive jewelry, electronics, silverware, or furs. Unless losing such items would constitute a financial catastrophe for you, it probably isn't worth buying.

Make a list of all personal possessions in your home or apartment, and store the list in a safety deposit box or somewhere off the premises. An even better and quicker way to document your possessions is to go through the house with a video camera and take pictures of everything you own. Update the video once a year and store it somewhere other than your domicile. It will be extremely useful if you ever have to make a claim.

The second most expensive asset most people own is their car. Although the law requires every licensed driver to carry bodily injury/property damage liability coverage, most auto policies cover a lot more. Some features are necessary and some are a waste of money if you have other policies or an older car. For example, if you drive an old car with a low book value, consider dropping the comprehensive and collision coverage. Once again, the only good purpose for carrying insurance is to protect yourself from the catastrophes you can't afford. Other add-ons such as rental car reimbursement and towing hardly qualify as disaster prevention and can be skipped. If you have a good health care plan you can skip coverage for medical payments too.

You can reduce the cost of homeowner's, renter's, and auto insurance by taking the largest possible deductible you can afford. You'll also probably be entitled to a discount if your home has a security system, smoke detectors, or fire sprinklers. Auto insurance discounts are often given when your car has a security system, antilock brakes, or certain types of air bags. Be sure and tell your agent if your car has them.

Third, you need to protect yourself against potential lawsuits that could wipe you out. In our litigious society, it's an absolute must. Purchase a personal liability umbrella policy of at least $1 million, or an amount to cover your total net worth. Umbrella policies are relatively cheap for the amount of protection and usually sold in $1 million increments.

Finally, if you own a business, make sure you have a sufficient business policy to cover contingencies, such as key-man insurance, or insurance to cover a buy-and-sell agreement. With home-based businesses on the rise, it's possible for a fire to destroy a home and a business simultaneously. Home-based businesses need an additional business policy to cover the loss of inventories, computers, office equipment, and the like. If you own a home-based business and want to protect its assets, ask your homeowner's insurance agent about a business policy.

LONG-TERM CARE

Sue Stevens, former director of financial planning for Morningstar, made a compelling case for carrying long-term care insurance this way:

> *Five out of 1,000 people will experience a house fire: average cost: $3,400. Seventy out of 1,000 people will have an auto accident: average cost: $3,000. Six hundred out of 1,000 people will require a nursing home stay: average cost: $50,000 per year, with an average stay of three to five years.*

Since Ms. Stevens wrote that article, nursing home costs have risen substantially. In some parts of the country, average nursing home costs are well over $100,000 per year and will surely continue to rise in the future.

Long-term care isn't for everyone. Two groups of people will never need it—those with very high net worth and those with little or no net worth. Those with multimillion-dollar portfolios can probably self-insure and pay for long-term care out of pocket. Those with little or no savings qualify for Medicaid, which means the government will pay for your nursing home care. Medicaid is the nursing-home equivalent of welfare, which means you won't likely get the best of care, but you won't be paying for it, either.

If you find yourself with liquid assets of between $200,000 and $2 million when you reach your mid- to late fifties, give serious consideration to buying long-term care policies for you and your spouse. With continuing advancements in health and medical care, more of us will be living longer. Add 76 million baby boomers who have retired or will be retiring to the mix, and it's a sure bet that many more people are going to require nursing home, assisted living, or home health care for extended periods of time.

In the early years of retirement, long-term care protects against the loss of earnings from investments in much the same way that long-term disability protects against lost income from the inability to work. If one spouse requires long-term care for an extended period of time, the cost won't consume the investments that provide retirement income. Similarly, for those with wealth who want to pass on their assets, owning a long-term care policy eliminates the need to retain a large portfolio in case long-term care were to be needed. This makes it much easier to give away (gift) assets while they're still alive, and it gives greater assurance that all of their remaining assets will be available for the heirs.

If you go shopping for long-term care, here are some of the features a good policy will contain:

- The daily benefit should equal the current daily cost of a nursing home in the area where you live. The higher the benefit, the higher your premium will be.

- Inflation protection of 5 percent per year, compounded to keep your daily benefit current with rising costs of care, should be built in to the policy.
- The benefit payment period should be at least three to five years. A lifetime benefit payment period is best.
- An elimination period should be affordable. The elimination period is like a deductible. The longer you can pay out of pocket before the benefits kick in, the cheaper your premium will be. Medicare will pay for the first 25 days. One hundred days is a good elimination period for most people.
- Coverage cannot be canceled for any reason other than for failure to pay premiums.
- The policy should cover both skilled and nonskilled care. Benefits should also cover home health and assisted living care without requiring a prior hospital stay.
- There should be no exclusions for particular illnesses such as Alzheimer's disease and dementia.
- Benefit triggers specify when coverage begins. The inability to dress or bathe are examples of benefit triggers. In the best and most expensive policies, proof of cognitive impairment such as Alzheimer's is a benefit trigger even if the person is able to dress and bathe himself.
- Waiver of premium, which allows you to stop making payments when coverage begins.
- Your annual premium cannot be raised unless it's raised for every policy holder living in your state.
- The policy is tax qualified. With a qualified policy the premium may be tax deductible and any benefits you receive will not be subject to federal taxes.

It's a good idea to purchase long-term care before age 60. If you wait until age 70, your premiums will be about 2.5 times higher than at age 60. Furthermore, the longer you wait the greater the risk you will contract a chronic illness and become uninsurable.

LOCATING GOOD INSURANCE COMPANIES AND AGENTS

Thanks to the Internet, you can get an education in insurance without leaving your home. You can shop for policies, get quotes, and compare benefits online. You can also check the financial strengths and quality ratings of an insurance company with the click of a mouse.

Here are some of the better insurance websites where you can learn more about insurance and shop for quotes:

- www.answerfinancial.com
- www.insure.com
- www.insurance.com
- www.insweb.com
- www.pivot.com
- www.quickquote.com
- www.reliaquote.com

For more than a century, the A. M. Best Company has rated insurance companies from A++ on down. We recommend buying insurance from a company with an A. M. Best rating of A or better. To check the financial strength and overall quality rating of an insurance company, go to www.ambest.com. Other companies that provide insurance ratings are Fitch Ratings (www.fitchratings.com), Moody's Investor Services (www.moodys.com), and Standard & Poor's (www.standardandpoors.com).

We also recommend finding a good insurance agent to help determine what types and amounts of coverage you may need. A competent, customer-oriented agent can save you both time and money.

Make it your goal to find an agent with a track record of high ethics, professionalism, and good service. As you probably know, all insurance agents aren't created equal. Some companies rigorously screen and train their agents in the interest of providing the kind of service that creates customer loyalty. Other companies hire whoever comes in off the street and have extremely high turnover.

A good place to start your search is by asking other people. Ask for recommendations from accountants, financial planners, lawyers, and successful businesspeople whose judgment you trust. If several people recommend the same agent, that's an excellent sign.

You can also screen by professional credentials:

- Chartered Property Casualty Underwriter (CPCU)
- Chartered Life Underwriter (CLU)
- Certified Insurance Counselor (CIC)

Such designations indicate that the person has dedicated many hours to study and has passed rigorous examinations in his or her respective field. That demonstrates a serious commitment to professionalism. You can search for a CPCU in your area online. Go to: www.cpcusociety.org

and click on the "Interest Groups" tab and then the link to "Agent &
Broker."

Some agents represent only one company. Other agents are
independent, which gives them more latitude to shop and find the policies that make the most sense for you. Once you locate a good agent, it's
a good idea to give the agent as much of your insurance business as you
can. By doing that, you become a more important customer and it's in
that agent's best interest to see that you are well covered and well served.
A good agent won't sell you insurance based on the cheapest price but,
rather, on what policy best fits your needs. Also, you won't be pressured
to buy what you don't need, and the agent will stay in touch with you regularly to see that your coverage is up to date and sufficient.

What we have covered in this chapter is just a broad overview of
the types and amounts of insurance you may need. It's by no means all-
inclusive. That's why we recommend that you seek the services of a good
insurance professional.

Although bad things happen to everyone, it's important to remember that you can reduce the odds of many of them happening to you
by following a few simple rules:

- Don't smoke.
- Exercise regularly.
- If you drink, limit yourself to two drinks a day if you are a man, or
  one drink per day if you are a woman.
- Wear seatbelts, and don't drive under the influence.
- Eat the right foods, and maintain your proper weight.
- Get enough rest.
- Get regular medical, dental, and vision check-ups.
- Keep a positive attitude, smile, and laugh a lot.

Following those rules doesn't mean you won't need insurance, but it's
an almost sure bet that you'll lead a better life.

CHAPTER TWENTY-TWO

Passing It On When You Pass On

Rich people plan for three generations. Poor people plan for Saturday night.

—Gloria Steinem

E ven though you may not feel rich, the tax collector may disagree with you. Remember, it's the tax regulations, not you, that determine who's rich. Therefore, the estate tax laws that are in effect at the time of your death will establish the level at which your estate will have to pay additional taxes on your accumulated assets for being *too rich*. The current tax exemption is $5,340,000. This figure is adjusted annually for inflation.

Although it's beyond the scope of this book to offer legal advice (that's what estate-planning attorneys are for), we will touch on a number of things you need to consider regarding estate planning and passing your assets on to those you want to have them. That is a better option than simply leaving those decisions up to the intestate law of your state, and perhaps leaving a major portion of your assets to the taxman.

We'd all like to think that we're special, that perhaps we're somehow even immortal. While we may, indeed, be special, we are all mortals and thus have to deal with the reality of our eventual demise. Therefore, there are two certainties in our lives—death and taxes.

The accumulation of assets is a lifelong endeavor, and it's almost always achieved with some level of personal and family sacrifice along the way. We want to make sure that the distribution of these assets after our death is not another long-term endeavor. Instead, we want to know that the fruits of our labor will go to those we choose, and that it will be accomplished in a timely and efficient manner, with the minimum expense possible.

DOCUMENTS WE'LL NEED

In some ways, it would be nice if we knew in advance when our time on this planet was up so that we could have everything in perfect order. But since we don't know the date of our demise, we need to plan now for any number of eventualities, including the distribution of our assets after our death.

It's important to know that getting our affairs in order involves so much more than just estate planning. There are a number of other legal issues that we'll have to deal with and documents that we'll want to have in place. These issues and documents are often handled by your attorney at the same time he or she is preparing your estate planning documents.

Let's take a look at some of the documents you might need and some things you'll need to consider about each of them.

A Will

You should have a will, even if you have a trust. If you have minor children, here's where you'd name the person you want to designate as the children's legal guardian in the event that both you and your spouse are deceased.

Your will also instructs your executor how you want your assets distributed. It takes care of the distribution of any assets individually owned by you that are not included in a trust or distributed by title, such as payable on death (POD) or transfer on death (TOD), or by beneficiary designation.

Except in some limited situations involving small estates, your will must go through probate. Depending on your state, probate can be both costly and time consuming. Some states have streamlined procedures for handling estates, which minimizes costs, while other states allow lawyers to run up your probate fees.

Remember that it takes time for your executor to be approved by the court before he or she can officially start to work. Courts often require the executor to be bonded. Once approved by the court, your executor must then get all of your affairs in order. The executor will determine what you owe and then pay your debts, have various assets appraised, transfer titles, perhaps sell some assets, and so on. Those tasks take time, and as a result, your estate might not be distributed to your heirs as quickly as you would have liked.

There are a number of ways to avoid probate, including placing your assets in a trust; distribution by title (joint accounts, POD or TOD, for example); and having a beneficiary and contingent beneficiaries listed on your tax-deferred accounts, such as an IRA or annuity. U.S. Savings Bonds allow you to list a beneficiary or a co-owner. Some mutual fund companies also allow you to designate a beneficiary for your taxable accounts, which means those accounts would also avoid probate. At Vanguard, this feature is known as the *Directed Beneficiary Plan*. You need to understand, though, that avoiding probate does not mean avoiding estate taxes.

Finally, you need to know that if you own assets individually and die without a will (intestate), the court would appoint both the executor and the legal guardian for any minor children. The intestate succession laws of your state of residence would determine who inherits your individually owned assets. Those laws may or may not be aligned with your desires.

Living Trust

The assets in a *living* or *revocable trust* avoid probate in your state of residence and also in other states where you might own property, if the out-of-state property is placed in the trust. After your death, the trust is similar to a will in some ways, in that the successor trustee will distribute the assets according to your wishes. However, since the trust assets don't go through probate, your affairs are kept private. With a trust, there is a much smoother transition after your death, and the disposition of assets can start immediately. However, trusts are more costly to create than wills, so you need to be sure a trust is warranted in your situation.

If you do decide to create a living trust, you'll need to retitle and transfer your assets into the trust. You can name yourself as the trustee while you're alive, which means that you'll still retain full control over the trust's assets, just as you did when you owned them outside the trust. If you want, you can also name your spouse as a cotrustee, in which case you'd both retain control over the trust's assets.

You'd also want to name a successor trustee. The person you select (spouse, child, good friend) should be someone you trust and who you have complete confidence in to carry out your expressed wishes in an honest and efficient manner in the role of successor trustee. The successor trustee would also manage the trust assets if you should become mentally incompetent.

A living trust doesn't eliminate the need for a will, since the will would handle the disposition of any of your individually owned assets that were not yet transferred into the trust's name or otherwise disposed of by title or beneficiary designation at the time of your death.

Finally, you should be aware that there are a number of different types of trusts that may be appropriate, depending on your particular situation. These include, but may not be limited to, bypass, irrevocable, special needs, QTIP, generation-skipping, grantor retained interest trusts, and charitable remainder trusts. Which, if any, of these trusts is appropriate for you is something that can be determined when you're working with your estate-planning lawyer.

Powers of Attorney

There are two primary types of powers of attorney. You can give someone a *limited power of attorney*, in which case they could only act on your behalf in very specific situations, as stated in the limited power of attorney document.

A *durable power of attorney for finances* allows someone you designate to manage your financial affairs and act on your behalf in financial matters if you should become incapacitated and unable to take care of them on your own.

A *durable power of attorney for health care* allows someone you designate to oversee your medical treatment and make medical decisions on your behalf when you're unable to do so. However, these decisions cannot be contrary to your *advance health care directive*, or *living will.*

Advance Health Care Directive

An advance health care directive conveys your specific wishes to medical personnel regarding certain medical treatments and life-prolonging efforts when you're unable to communicate your wishes to them. This document is also known as a *living will* or a *medical directive.*

The well-publicized Terry Schiavo case in Florida was debated numerous times through all levels of the Florida state courts and the U.S. court system, including the U.S. Supreme Court, from 1998 to 2005. Her case even ended up being legislated in the Congress of the United States. This was all a result of her failure to put her wishes in writing, even though court testimony showed she'd said on several occasions that she'd rather die than have her life maintained artificially by a machine if she were ever in a persistent vegetative state with no hope of recovery. Don't let this happen to you. Put your wishes in writing in the appropriate format in order to avoid bitter and heart-wrenching situations like this.

OTHER CONSIDERATIONS

The current estate tax laws allow your heirs to receive a stepped-up costs basis for certain inherited property, with the exception of tax-deferred accounts. The step-up in cost basis would include assets such as equity mutual funds, which may have large unrealized capital gains. Under the current tax code, this step-up in cost basis means that your heirs would pay no taxes on the gains you've accumulated over a lifetime, since their new cost basis would be the value of the inherited assets at the time of your death.

If you have more than adequate assets and plan to leave a legacy to your heirs, you may wish to consider going against conventional wisdom, which says to spend down your taxable accounts first and then your tax-deferred accounts last. By leaving these appreciated taxable assets to your heirs, you (and they) would avoid paying the capital gain taxes on these investments.

However, if you followed conventional wisdom and spent down your taxable assets first and then left your heirs part of your deductible IRA instead, you would have had to pay the long-term capital gain taxes on the appreciated taxable assets you sold for living expenses. Since IRAs don't get the step-up in cost basis, your heirs would owe taxes at their highest ordinary tax rates on all their withdrawals from the inherited IRA. So, for some investors, taking advantage of the stepped-up cost basis for taxable assets can be an effective estate-planning tool.

GIFTING

Gifting is a method you can use to reduce the size of your estate, perhaps to below the estate tax exemption level. Currently, an individual can give $14,000 per year to an unlimited number of people with no tax consequences. A couple can give double that amount if they share equally in the gift. This annual exclusion amount is indexed for inflation.

Although gifting can be an effective tool in reducing the amount of your estate, and thus the amount of taxes your estate would owe, it has other benefits as well. For instance, gifting can also give you the pleasure of seeing how your gift is being used and enjoyed by others while you're still alive.

Be aware that you might subject yourself to the gift tax if you exceed the annual exclusion limit to any one individual. There are, however, some exceptions to this annual gifting limit that you should be aware of:

- There is currently no limit on the amount you can gift to your spouse, as long as he or she is a U.S. citizen.
- There is currently no limit on the amount you can gift to pay for someone's school tuition or medical bills, *providing you pay them directly to the school or medical facility.* Be aware, though, that while you can pay for someone's college by paying their tuition bill directly to the college, you can't pay for their other college expenses, such as room and board, under this exemption.
- Gifts to charities and other tax-exempt organizations of up to 50 percent of income are also excluded from the annual gift limit.

Gifts to charities and other tax-exempt organizations are exempt from the annual gift tax-exclusion limit. However, even if we'd like to make a significant donation to our favorite cause, we may feel that we cannot afford to make this large gift while we're still alive, since it could possibly deprive us of the funds necessary to continue with our present lifestyle. Charitable trusts may be the answer to that dilemma.

With a *charitable trust,* you can make a donation, get a tax write-off, and receive annuity payments for the balance of your life. See Chapter 4 for various annuity payment options. Your gift can include appreciated assets, which allows you to avoid paying the capital gain taxes on the appreciation, and still get credit for the full value of the donation. The tax-exempt organization would be able to sell the appreciated assets without having to pay any taxes. Charitable trusts are a win-win situation for all concerned. You get the tax write-off and receive annuity payments for the balance of your days and your favorite charity or cause gets the donation.

LETTER OF INSTRUCTION

One final document that you should prepare is a letter that contains your desires and instructions regarding your funeral arrangements or cremation and possible organ donations, that gives the location of any important papers, and perhaps contains final messages for those you've left behind. Once you've prepared this document, be sure to give it to the person you want to carry out these instructions.

DISCLAIMER

As we stated at the outset of this chapter, nothing we've touched on here should be construed as legal advice. We're not lawyers, and we're not qualified to give legal advice. Rather, we've attempted to touch on a number of areas that you'll want to explore in greater detail and perhaps discuss with your family members before you meet with your attorney. Knowing a bit more about these important issues should help you prepare for your estate planning session with your attorney.

Mark Twain may well have had estate taxes in mind when he remarked, "The only difference between a taxman and a taxidermist is that the taxidermist leaves the skin."

CHAPTER TWENTY-THREE

— ◆ —

You Can Do It

The Bogleheads Will Help

Though no one can go back and make a brand new start, any-one can start from now and make a brand new ending.

—Carl Bard

A re you a relatively new investor who's just getting started? If you are, there's no need to be embarrassed, because that's actually good news. It means you haven't yet had a chance to make all the stupid and costly investing mistakes that we, the authors, have made in the past. You've got a clean slate to work with, and we're hoping that, with the knowledge you've gained from this book, you'll be able to avoid most, if not all, of the pitfalls that we have experienced. You're probably much further ahead in the knowledge department than we were at this stage. As a result, you don't have to learn about investing as we did, via the school of hard knocks. You're now equipped to start your investing career off on the right foot by simply applying the information we've provided in this book.

Maybe you've had some limited investing experience, but have always felt a bit uneasy or unsure when it comes to making those investment decisions. In this book, we've tried to give you solid information that you can both understand and use when you're planning your financial future and structuring your portfolio so that it's headed down the path to success. It's our hope that with what you've learned in this book, you'll feel much more confident when making your future investing decisions.

Perhaps you're a veteran investor who's made all the usual mistakes along the way but is now looking to right your financial ship. We've been there and done that. We hope that the information in this book will help guide your financial ship through calm seas and into safe harbors. You're now armed with a financial life preserver; just be sure to use it!

No matter how much or how little experience you've had, or which type of investor you are, each of you is the captain of your own financial ship, and you need to make sure that it's on the right course. Promise yourself that you'll start right now to create that "brand new ending" for both you and your loved ones. What's happened in the past is history and can't be undone. However, you can start now to use the tools and strategies we've outlined in this book as a beacon to help guide your way. So promise us you won't put it off any longer; getting your investments and financial affairs in order should be right up there at the top of your to-do list. Remember, procrastination is the biggest detriment to financial success!

Now let's summarize and review some of the important things we've covered.

WHAT WE'VE LEARNED

- Choose and live a sound financial lifestyle. We need to pay off our credit card debt, establish an emergency fund, get our spending under control, and most importantly, learn how to live below our means, since that's really the key to financial freedom.
- Start to save early and invest regularly. The earlier we start, the longer we'll enjoy the powerful benefits of compounding.
- Know more about the various investment choices available to us, such as stocks, bonds, and mutual funds. For most investors, mutual funds offer great diversity in a single investment. Don't invest in things you don't understand.
- Figure out approximately how much you might need for your retirement, so you'll know if you're on track. You can't reach your goal if you don't have a target!
- Indexing via low-cost mutual funds is a strategy that will, over time, most likely outperform the vast majority of strategies. If you decide

to own actively managed mutual funds, choose managed funds with low expenses and place them in tax-advantaged accounts.

- An asset allocation plan is based on your personal circumstances, goals, time horizon, and need and willingness to take risks. Risk and higher expected returns go hand in hand. There's no free lunch. Make your investment plan as simple as possible.
- Costs matter. We can't control market returns, but we can control the cost of our investments. Commissions, fees, and mutual fund expense ratios can rob you of much of your investment returns. Keep costs as low as possible.
- Taxes can be your biggest expense. Invest in the most tax-efficient way possible. Put tax-inefficient funds in your tax-deferred accounts, and select tax-efficient investments for your taxable account. Remember the importance of diversification. You want some investments that zig while others zag.
- Rebalancing is important. Rebalancing controls risk and may reward you with higher returns. Stick with your chosen rebalancing strategy.
- Market timing and performance chasing are poor investment strategies. They can cause investors to underperform the market and jeopardize financial goals.
- Invest for your children's education. There are several tax-deferred and tax-free options available.
- Know how to handle a windfall, if you receive an inheritance or get lucky and hit the lottery.
- Answer the question of whether you do or don't need a financial advisor, and some of the reasons for and against.
- Understand the importance of protecting the future buying power of your assets by investing in such things as inflation-protected securities. Remember, inflation is a silent thief that robs you of future buying power.
- Tune out the noise and do not get distracted by daily news events. Avoid hot investment fads and following the herd as it stampedes toward the cliff's edge. Believing that "It's different this time" can cause severe financial damage to your portfolio.
- Protect your assets with the proper types and amounts of insurance. Insurance is for protection. It's not an investment. Don't confuse the two.
- We need to master our emotions if we want to be successful investors. Letting your emotions dictate your investment decisions can be hazardous to your wealth.

- Make your money last at least as long as you do. Overly optimistic withdrawal rates may cause you to run out of money before you run out of breath.
- Proper estate planning ensures that assets pass to heirs in a reasonable time and with minimum taxes.

HELP FROM THE BOGLEHEADS

You now have the tools to set the course for a secure financial future. We know you can do it, but you don't have to be totally on your own. The Bogleheads are around if you need additional help. We hang out online at www.bogleheads.org.

You can find lots of useful information about the Bogleheads there. Some of the things you'll find include:

- Tips for posting on the Bogleheads Forum
- A recommended reading list
- A great search engine
- Links to the current ongoing conversations on the Bogleheads Forum
- Links to other financial sites

The Bogleheads.org website was donated, set up, and is maintained by two very technically gifted, generous, and dedicated Bogleheads, Alex Frakt and Larry Auton.

So, if you have additional questions, or need something in this book clarified, all you have to do is post your questions for us on the Bogleheads Forum, and we'll try to respond as best we can.

Realize that the three of us are not the only ones who respond to investors' questions on the Bogleheads Forum. There are lots of very bright and helpful Bogleheads who are ready, willing, and able to give you a helping hand when you have a financial question.

We have lawyers, doctors, educators, financial professionals (CFAs, CFPs, CPAs), and a host of other varied and really interesting folks who post on our forum, including financial authors such as William Bernstein, Rick Ferri, Bill Schultheis, and Larry Swedroe. And we're geographically diversified, with Bogleheads in just about every nook and cranny in the United States. We also have many foreign Bogleheads, including some from Canada, Australia, Hong Kong, India, Japan, and a number of other countries throughout Europe, Asia, and the Far East.

You'll find varied opinions on investment matters on the Bogleheads Forum. Bogleheads don't believe that one size fits all or that investing is my way or the highway. Taylor is fond of saying that *there are many roads to Dublin.*

There are often spirited debates on the forum on the subject of actively managed funds versus index funds, and a number of other hot topics. You don't have to post to learn. If you'd like, you can simply lurk in the background, as many do, and learn by reading the numerous questions asked and answered, as well as the exchanges and debates on various investment topics. There's also a lot to be learned from many of the useful links posted by other Bogleheads.

The Bogleheads continue to expand and evolve each year. A number of Bogleheads local chapters exist throughout the United States, and there are several foreign chapters as well. There are chapters in Dallas/Ft. Worth, Wisconsin, Southern California, Arizona (Michael belongs to that one), Central California, Oregon, Washington, DC, Seattle, San Francisco Bay Area, Central Florida, Hampton Roads, Virginia, Western New England, The Big Apple (NYC), Minnesota, Central Texas, the Sonoran Desert, San Diego, Cincinnati, Syracuse, Houston, Michigan, Nashville, Central Alabama, Research Triangle Park, Charlotte, Richmond, Castle Rock, Colorado, Eastern Iowa, Kansas City, Europe (Paris), Southern Nevada, South of Boston, Tulsa, South Carolina Low Country/Savannah, Gainesville/Ocala, Denver, St. Louis, Phoenix, Boston, Tucson, New Jersey, Orlando, South Florida, New Hampshire/Maine, Detroit, Northeast Ohio, Pittsburgh, Taiwan, New Orleans, Des Moines, Greenville Metro and Madison WI. At these local chapter get-togethers, Bogleheads meet to socialize and discuss various investment topics of mutual interest. If you're interested in getting together with other Bogleheads, you can learn more about the local chapters on the Bogleheads Forum Wiki at www .bogleheads.org/wiki/Boglehead%C2%AE_Local_Chapters. There's no fee to join a group; everyone pays his or her own way.

In addition to the local chapter meetings, there is an annual meeting with Jack Bogle. These events have been held at various locations throughout the country. The dates and location of these events are announced on the Bogleheads Forum, usually in the beginning of March of each year.

IN CLOSING

We can't stress enough how important it is to establish your own personal financial plan, and then carefully follow that plan. Select low-cost mutual funds, preferably index funds, as the core of your investment portfolio. We feel there's beauty in simplicity. Be forewarned that there will undoubtedly be numerous distractions along the way that will cause you to think about straying from your chosen course. However, if you are aware of that fact in advance and are prepared to handle the distractions, it will be much easier for you to resist the temptation to abandon your plan when the occasion arises.

Between this book and our online forum, you have all the necessary tools you need to become a successful investor. Perhaps you will visit the Bogleheads Forum at www.bogleheads.org, and possibly even attend one of the Bogleheads get-togethers. Who knows? Before long, you may even start calling yourself a Boglehead and help to spread the word. Until then, establish your plan and STAY THE COURSE!

APPENDICES

APPENDIX I

Glossary of Financial Terms

Active management: An investment strategy that seeks to outperform the returns of the financial markets or a particular benchmark.

Annualize: To make a period of less than a year apply to a full year. For example, a six-month return of 5 percent would be *annualized* at 10 percent.

Annuity: A tax-deferred insurance product that provides payments for specified intervals, including a lifetime. Annuity products and payments can differ, depending on which insurance company you select.

Automatic reinvestment: An arrangement whereby mutual fund distributions (dividends and capital gains) are used to buy additional shares.

Benchmark index: An index used by a mutual fund manager to compare against his or her fund's performance.

Beta: A measure of a fund's sensitivity to market movements.

Bond: A certificate of debt issued by a government or corporation.

2

74 APPENDIX I

Bond credit risk: The possibility that a bond issuer will not repay interest and/or principal in a timely manner.

Bond duration: Provides an estimate of a bond fund's volatility. For example, a bond fund with a three-year duration will decrease in value approximately 3 percent if interest rates rise 1 percent, while a bond fund with a five-year duration will decrease in value by approximately 5 percent if interest rates were to rise by the same 1 percent.

Bond fund maturity: The average length of time the bonds in a fund mature.

Capital gain: The difference between the purchase price and the sale price.

Capital gain distribution: Payments to mutual fund shareholders of gains on the net sale of securities in the fund.

Cash: A term used to describe safe, liquid assets such as CDs, money market funds, savings accounts, and sometimes very-short-term, high-quality bonds.

Chartist: Someone who attempts to use charts and graphs to forecast future prices.

Closed-end fund: A mutual fund that has a fixed number of shares, usually listed on a major stock exchange.

Commodities: Unprocessed goods such as grains, metals, oil, and other products that ultimately make it to the consumer. Although the markets operate somewhat differently, commodities can be traded like stocks through such markets as the Chicago Board of Trade.

Consumer Price Index (CPI): A measure of the change in the cost of a basket of goods and services over time. Its primary use is to measure inflation. Many payments, such as pensions and Social Security, are adjusted based on this number.

Correlation: A relationship between two variables.

Cost basis: A term used to describe the original cost of an investment with adjustments allowed by tax law.

Country risk: The risk in international funds such as war, political unrest, currency exchange rates, government default, poor accounting, and so on.

Credit rating: An evaluation by credit agencies of the financial strength of securities. Moody's, Standard & Poor's, and Dun and Bradstreet are among the largest.

Custodian: A person or entity responsible for the activities of another.

Defined benefit plan: A retirement plan that pays employees a lifetime annuity when they retire. The employee does not manage or control the investments in this plan.

Depreciation: A decrease in the value of an asset or investment.

Dollar-cost-averaging (DCA): Buying shares on a regular basis.

Efficient markets: A theory that stock and bond prices are so competitive, and information so readily available, that current prices reflect *true* value.

Efficient portfolio: A portfolio diversified in such a manner that for a given level of risk no other portfolio will provide a superior return.

Equities: Stocks.

Escrow: Placement of security with a third party until specified conditions are met.

Exchange-traded fund (ETF): An index fund that trades on the stock market. ETFs are purchased and sold through a broker.

Ex-dividend date: The date when a distribution is deducted from a mutual fund's assets. On this date the funds share price (NAV) drops by the amount of the distribution.

Expected return: The estimated future return on a particular investment or asset class.

Expense ratio: The percentage of a fund's net assets used to pay a portion of its annual expenses.

Fee-only advisor: A financial advisor who charges an hourly rate or charges a fee based on the percentage of assets managed.

Global fund: A mutual fund that invests in both U.S. and foreign securities.

Hedge fund: A fund used by wealthy individuals and institutions that is allowed to use risky strategies that are not available to mutual funds.

High-yield bonds: See *junk bonds*.

International fund: A mutual fund that invests in non-U.S. securities.

Junk bonds (also known as high-yield bonds): Bonds with a credit rating of BB or lower, which indicates that the bonds are considered to be below investment grade. Companies that issue *junk bonds* promise to pay higher yields in order to attract buyers who otherwise might purchase safer bonds.

Load fund: A mutual fund that levies a sales charge.

Long-term capital gain: Profit on the sale of a security held at least one year that generally results in lower tax.

Market timing: Attempting to forecast market direction and then investing based on the forecasts.

Money market fund: A mutual fund that invests in very short-term securities. Money market funds attempt to maintain a constant $1 net asset value (NAV).

Mortgage-backed securities: Bond-type securities representing an interest in a pool of mortgages.

Municipal bond fund: A mutual fund that invests in tax-exempt bonds. These funds are best suited for higher-income taxpayers in taxable accounts.

Nominal return: The return on an investment before adjustment for inflation.

Open-end fund: A conventional mutual fund that has the ability to issue or redeem (sell) shares based on the actual value of securities in the fund's portfolio.

Price/earnings ratio (P/E): A stock's current price divided by its earnings.

Prospectus: A legal document that gives investors the most reliable information about an investment.

Real estate investment trust (REIT): A company that manages a group of real estate investments.

Real return: Inflation-adjusted return (nominal return less inflation).

Risk: The possibility of loss or the possibility of not meeting a goal.

Risk premium: The reward for holding a riskier investment rather than a risk-free investment.

Risk tolerance: The investor's ability to endure declines in the value of investments without selling and without worry. Often called your *sleep factor*.

Rollover: A tax-free transfer of assets from one retirement plan to another.

Roth IRA: A tax-favored retirement plan. Contributions are not deductible, but earnings are tax-free during accumulation and also when withdrawn.

***R*-squared:** A figure from 0 to 100 that reflects the percentage of a fund's movements explained by movements in its benchmark index. The higher the number, the closer the correlation.

Sector/specialty fund: A mutual fund that invests in a narrow segment of the market, such as health, technology, utilities, or real estate.

Sharpe ratio: A measure of risk-adjusted performance developed by Nobel Laureate William Sharpe.

Spousal IRA: An IRA established for a nonworking spouse.

Standard deviation: A statistical measure of volatility.

Taxable account: An account in which the securities are subject to annual federal taxes.

Tax-deferred account: An account in which federal income taxes are deferred until withdrawn.

Total return: The most complete measure of a fund's gain or loss. Includes both capital gains and dividends.

Traditional IRA: A tax-favored retirement plan. Contributions are deductible and the tax on both the contributions and earnings are deferred during accumulation. Withdrawals are taxed at one's ordinary income tax rates. Penalties apply if withdrawals are made prior to age 59½ except in limited situations.

Trust: A legal plan used to put controls on property before and/or after death.

Turnover rate: An indication of the manager's trading activity during the past year.

Unrealized capital gain/loss: A gain or loss that would be realized if the fund's securities were sold.

Wash sale: An IRS rule that disallows the loss from the sale of a fund if the investor invests in a "substantially identical" fund within 31 days.

Yield: Income received from an investment expressed as a percentage of its current price.

Yield curve: A line on a graph that depicts the yields of bonds of varying maturities.

APPENDIX II

Books We Recommend

BOOKS FOR NOVICE INVESTORS

The Coffeehouse Investor by Bill Shultheis (Kirkland, WA: Palouse Press, 2005). A little book with a big message: How to invest simply and successfully.

The Informed Investor by Frank Armstrong III (New York: American Management Association, 2003). An easy-to-understand explanation of how the market works.

The Little Book of Common Sense Investing by John C. Bogle (Hoboken, NJ: Wiley, 2007). This is a short, delightful-to-read, small-size book. The legendary founder of retail index funds explains the many reasons he recommends broad market index funds for most investors.

The Millionaire in You by Michael LeBoeuf (New York: Crown Business, 2002). A primer on how to invest money and time intelligently to achieve financial freedom. An audio version of the book is published by Nightingale-Conant under the title *Beat the Time/Money Trap*.

Protecting Your Wealth in Good Times and Bad by Richard A. Ferri, CFA (New York: McGraw-Hill, 2003). A former Marine fighter pilot, stockbroker, and author of four financial books, Mr. Ferri has written this easy-to-read guidebook for a sound investment strategy.

Straight Talk on Investing by Jack Brennan, Vanguard's former CEO (New York: Wiley, 2002). Elegantly simple, eminently sensible, and delightfully readable.

You've Lost It, Now What? by Jonathan Clements (New York: Portfolio, 2003). An award-winning *Wall Street Journal* columnist gives straightforward advice people need in order to invest successfully.

BOOKS FOR INTERMEDIATE INVESTORS

Bogle on Mutual Funds: New Perspectives for the Intelligent Investor by Vanguard founder John Bogle (New York: McGraw-Hill, 1993). Jack Bogle wanted to make this first book on mutual fund investing equal to Benjamin Graham's classic, *The Intelligent Investor.* Not only did he succeed, but *Bogle on Mutual Funds* may be the best book about mutual fund investing ever written.

Common Sense on Mutual Funds by Vanguard's founder, John Bogle (New York: Wiley, 1999). Warren Buffett called this book "A must read for every investor." We agree.

The Four Pillars of Investing by Bill Bernstein (New York: McGraw-Hill, 2002). A brilliant, small-town doctor became fascinated with investing. The result is one of the best books on the subject.

The Only Guide to a Winning Investment Strategy You'll Ever Need by Larry Swedroe (New York: St. Martin's Press, 2005). An excellent insight into how to avoid Wall Street's "Loser's Game."

A Random Walk Down Wall Street by Burton G. Malkiel (New York: Norton, 2003). An investor classic—regularly updated. Malkiel is a professor at Princeton and a former member of the Vanguard board of directors.

BOOKS FOR THOSE WHO WANT TO LEARN MORE

Asset Allocation by Roger C. Gibson (New York: McGraw-Hill, 2000). One of the best books on the subject.

Capital Ideas by Peter L. Bernstein (Hoboken, NJ: Wiley, 2005). The founder of the *Journal of Portfolio Management* gives a fascinating history of the financial revolution of the past 30 years.

The Intelligent Investor by Benjamin Graham, with Jason Zweig commentary (New York: HarperCollins, 2003). A beautifully written book with updated commentary by one of the most respected financial writers in America.

The Only Guide to a Winning Bond Strategy by Larry Swedroe. Boglehead Larry Swedroe makes the complex world of bonds easy to understand as he guides us to their proper use in our portfolio.

Financial Websites We Recommend

(In Alphabetical Order)

www.altruistfa.com/readingroom.htm. The Reading Room of Boglehead contributor Eric Haas is a great place to learn about investing.

crr.bc.edu. The Center for Retirement Research at Boston College is an excellent source of research and articles about retirement issues.

www.bloomberg.com. Financial news and information, including current bond prices and yields, can be found at Bloomberg.

www.bogleheads.org. Volunteers Alex Frakt and Larry Auton have made their website the gateway to the finest investment forum on the Internet—the Bogleheads forum. It's our homepage. You might want to make it yours.

www.bylo.org. Boglehead Bylo Selhi operates a Canadian website filled with insightful mutual fund information useful to everyone.

www.choosetosave.org. Have trouble saving? Need a financial calculator? This is the place to go.

www.coffeehouseinvestor.com. Hosted by Boglehead author Bill Schultheis, this is a good resource for solid information.

www.efficientfrontier.com. Boglehead author Bill Bernstein runs this great website. Be sure to browse back issues of *Efficient Frontier*.

www.thefinanceprofessor.com. Jim Mahaer, assistant professor of finance at St. Bonaventure University, created this site to blend the academic world of finance with the real world.

www.financialpage.blogspot.com. This is the website of Boglehead Barry Barnitz, who maintains this outstanding source for current research articles useful to Boglehead investors, including articles and studies on indexing, Vanguard funds, asset allocation, and similar subjects. Extensive archive.

www.firecalc.com. A detailed online calculator for determining satisfactory portfolio withdrawal rates in retirement.

www.investorsolutions.com/?submit=Go&s=Books. Boglehead Frank Armstrong has an excellent online book, *Investment Strategies for the 21st Century*.

www.jasonzweig.com. One of the best financial columnists and authors in the business, Jason Zweig has created a site for investors who want to learn to think for themselves.

www.jonathanclements.com. Jonathan Clements is considered by many to be the best financial newspaper columnist in the business. This fine website, which opened in 2007, contains easy-to-understand and practical information for investors.

www.moneychimp.com. Everything about money; articles, calculators, and much more.

www.morningstar.com. Without question, the best source of general information about mutual funds. Also the home of the Bogleheads Unite Forum, where the Bogleheads hang out.

www.norstad.org/finance. This is the repository of Boglehead John Norstad's many articles. Mel Lindauer and Taylor Larimore contributed to his article, "Investing in Total Markets," which explains the sophisticated theory of Total Market Index funds.

www.portfoliosolutions.com. This is the homepage of Boglehead author Richard Ferri, CFA. Use the "Research" tab to read Rick's papers and published articles. The "Books" tab will bring you to his excellent (free) Internet book, *Serious Money*.

www.research-finance.com. John P. Scordo maintains this website to bring together a collection of the best academic and financial articles to be found on the Internet.

www.retireearlyhomepage.com. If you dream about retiring early and want to know how to do it, this is the site. The host, John P. Greaney, retired at age 38 and hasn't looked back.

www.rickferri.com. This is the homepage of Boglehead author and forum contributor, Richard Ferri, CFA. You'll find lots of good information here.

www.vanguard.com/bogle_site/bogle_home.html. For a great learning experience, browse the archives, where you'll find Mr. Bogle's many speeches.

Vanguard Asset Allocation Questionnaire and Pie Charts

Investor Questionnaire

1 I plan to begin taking withdrawals from this portfolio in . . .

	Points
Less than 1 year	0
1 to 2 years	1
3 to 5 years	4
6 to 10 years	7
11 to 15 years	12
More than 15 years	17

2 I plan to spend the money in this portfolio over a period of . . .

	Points
2 years or less	0
3 to 5 years	1
6 to 10 years	3
11 to 15 years	5
More than 15 years	8

3 When making a long-term investment, I plan to hold the investment for . . .

	Points
1 to 2 years	0
3 to 4 years	1
5 to 6 years	3
7 to 8 years	5
9 or more years	7

4 From August 31, 2000, through March 31, 2001, stocks lost more than 25%. If I owned a stock investment that fell more than 25% in seven months, I would . . . [If you owned stocks during this period, select the answer that corresponds to your actual behavior.]

	Points
Sell all of the remaining investment	1
Sell a portion of the remaining investment	3
Hold the investment and sell nothing	5
Buy more of the investment	6

5 Generally, I prefer investments with little or no fluctuation in value, and I am willing to accept the lower return associated with these investments.

	Points
I strongly agree	0
I agree	1
I somewhat agree	3
I disagree	5
I strongly disagree	6

6 During market declines, I tend to sell portions of my riskier assets and invest the money in safer assets.

	Points
I strongly agree	1
I agree	2
I somewhat agree	3
I disagree	4
I strongly disagree	5

7 I would invest in a mutual fund based solely on a brief conversation with a friend, coworker, or relative.

	Points
I strongly agree	1
I agree	2
I somewhat agree	3
I disagree	4
I strongly disagree	5

⑧ From January 31, 1999, through December 31, 1999, some bonds lost almost 9%. If I owned a bond investment that lost 9% in 11 months, I would . . . [If you owned bonds during this period, select the answer that corresponds to your actual behavior.]

	Points
Sell all of the remaining investment	1
Sell a portion of the remaining investment	3
Hold the investment and sell nothing	5
Buy more of the investment	6

⑨ The chart below shows the greatest one-year loss and the highest one-year gain on three different hypothetical investments of $10,000.* Given the potential gain or loss in any one year, I would invest my money in . . .

	Points
Fund A	1
Fund B	3
Fund C	5

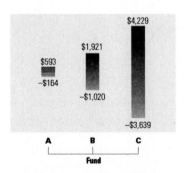

*The maximum gain or loss on an investment is impossible to predict. The ranges shown in this chart are hypothetical and are designed solely to gauge an investor's risk tolerance.

⑩ My current and future income sources (such as salary, Social Security, pension) are . . .

	Points
Very unstable	1
Unstable	2
Somewhat stable	3
Stable	4
Very stable	5

⑪ When it comes to investing in stock or bond mutual funds (or individual stocks or bonds), I would describe myself as a/an . . .

	Points
Very inexperienced investor	1
Somewhat inexperienced investor	2
Somewhat experienced investor	3
Experienced investor	4
Very experienced investor	5

Asset allocation **strategy for your goals**

Based on your total point score for each goal, select a suggested mix of asset classes from the table on page 291. The asset allocation indicated by each total point score is only a suggestion, and you still might reasonably select a different mix, one with slightly higher or lower risk. Record your choices in the spaces below, since you'll need to refer to them when you select specific funds.

Goal	Total Point Score	Asset Mix
1. _____ _____ _____	_____	_____% stocks _____% bonds _____% cash investments
2. _____ _____ _____	_____	_____% stocks _____% bonds _____% cash investments
3. _____ _____ _____	_____	_____% stocks _____% bonds _____% cash investments

Types of funds **to include in your portfolio**

Stock funds. Actively managed growth or value funds, or index funds that track the total stock market or segments of it.

Bond funds. Actively managed short-, intermediate-, or long-term corporate, government, or tax-exempt funds, or index funds that track the total bond market or segments of it.

Money market funds. Actively managed taxable or tax-exempt funds that invest in cash investments issued by governments, corporations, banks, or other financial institutions.

Balanced funds. Actively managed or index funds that hold a mix of stocks, bonds, and (sometimes) cash investments. This type of "all in one" fund can automatically maintain your target asset allocation through a single investment.

Choose **an asset allocation according to your score**

Stocks Bonds

Your Total Point Score	Suggested Asset Allocation	Average Annual Return (1960–2004)	Worst Annual Loss (1960–2004)	Number of Years With a Loss (1960–2004)
69–75 points	100%	10.6%	−28.4%	12 of 45
62–68 points	20% / 80%	10.1%	−22.7%	12 of 45
55–61 points	30% / 70%	9.8%	−19.8%	12 of 45
49–54 points	40% / 60%	9.5%	−17.0%	11 of 45
42–48 points	50% / 50%	9.2%	−14.1%	8 of 45
36–41 points	40% / 60%	8.9%	−11.3%	6 of 45
29–35 points	30% / 70%	8.5%	−8.4%	5 of 45
23–28 points	20% / 80%	8.1%	−8.2%	5 of 45
7–22 points	100%	7.2%	−8.1%	5 of 45

Source: The Vanguard Group.

These are sample portfolio allocations only. Depending on your tolerance for risk or your individual circumstances, you may wish to choose an allocation that is more conservative or more aggressive than the model suggested by your score. Keep in mind that these allocations are for longer-term financial goals. You may very well hold cash investments for shorter-term goals and emergencies. For stock market returns, we use the Dow Jones Wilshire 5000 Composite Index from 1971 to 2004 and the S&P 500 Index from 1960 to 1970. For bond market returns, we use the Lehman Brothers U.S. Government/Credit Bond Index from 1973 to 2004, the Citigroup High Grade Index from 1969 to 1972, and the S&P High Grade Corporate Index from 1960 to 1968.

This Investor Questionnaire is designed to help you decide how to allocate your investments among different asset classes (stocks, bonds, and cash investments), but does not provide comprehensive investment or financial advice. There is no guarantee that any particular asset allocation will meet your investment objectives. All investments involve risks, and fluctuations in the financial markets and other factors may cause declines in the value of your account. As your financial circumstances or goals change, it may be helpful to retake the Investor Questionnaire to see if your suggested asset allocation has changed.

The returns shown include the reinvestment of income, dividend, and capital gains distributions; they do not reflect the effects of investment expenses and taxes. Past performance is not a guarantee of future results.

About the Authors

Mel Lindauer, CFS, WMS (Daytona Beach Shores, FL) was dubbed "The Prince of the Bogleheads" by Jack Bogle. A Forbes.com columnist, he's one of the leaders of the Bogleheads community. He and Taylor have combined to contribute an incredible 84,000 forum posts, helping investors learn the Boglehead way to invest. A former Marine, he started investing in the late 1960s and has first-hand experience with both bull and bear markets. Together with Taylor, he initiated and continues to organize the grassroots Bogleheads' annual meetings. He's been quoted in a number of newspapers and national magazines and has appeared on CNNfn. Retired since 1997, he was founder and former CEO of a successful graphics arts company in the Philadelphia area for 30 years. Since retirement, he has earned credentials as a Certified Fund Specialist from the Institute of Business and Finance and as a Wealth Management Specialist from Kaplan College. He also holds commercial pilot and flight instructor licenses, and was commissioned a Kentucky Colonel by the governor of his former home state of Kentucky. In March of 2012, Mel was recognized by *Money* magazine as one of its "Everyday Heroes" for his work in investor education.

Taylor Larimore, CCL (Miami, FL) was dubbed by *Money* magazine as "the Dean of the Vanguard Diehards." Jack Bogle calls Taylor "King of the Bogleheads." Taylor is remarkably well informed after having spent most of his 90 years in the real world of finance and investments. A graduate of the University of Miami's School of Business Administration, Taylor served as a World War II paratrooper in the 101st Airborne Division during the Battle of the Bulge, earning five combat decorations. An avid sailing enthusiast, Taylor was named the American Sailing Association's "Instructor of the Year." Throughout his career, Taylor worked as a life insurance underwriter, revenue officer for the Internal Revenue Service, chief of the financial division of the Small Business Administration in South Florida, and director of the Dade County Housing Finance Authority. In 1986 Taylor became inspired when reading about the life and teachings of Jack Bogle. Combining his financial experience with Mr. Bogle's research and advice, Taylor and his wife, Pat, saw their portfolio improve dramatically. In March of 2012, Taylor was recognized by *Money* magazine as one of its "Everyday Heroes" for his work in investor education. Taylor now spends his time sailing and helping others discover the Boglehead way on the Bogleheads Forum.

Michael LeBoeuf, PhD (Paradise Valley, AZ) is an internationally published author and professional speaker. His eight books have sold almost 2 million copies, been translated into more than a dozen languages, and adapted to produce 17 audio and video programs. He has been interviewed on hundreds of radio and television talk shows including *The CBS Evening News*, *Oprah*, and *Good Morning America*. For 20 years, Michael was a professor of management at the University of New Orleans, retiring as professor emeritus at age 47 in 1989. His books include: *How to Win Customers and Keep Them for Life*, *The Millionaire in You*, *Working Smart*, *The Perfect Business*, and *The Greatest Management Principle in the World*.

Index

Index